650
.142
E566

P9-CDS-214

Best Resumes

for People Without a Four-Year Degree

Wendy S. Enelow, CPRW, JCTC, CCM

IMPACT PUBLICATIONS

Manassas Park, Virginia

NOV -- 2005

Sherwood Forest Library
7117 W. Seven Mile Rd.
Detroit, MI 48221

BEST RESUMES FOR PEOPLE WITHOUT A FOUR-YEAR DEGREE

Copyright © 2004 by Wendy S. Enelow. All rights reserved. Printed in the United States of America. No part of this book may be used or reproduced in any manner whatsoever without written permission of the publisher: IMPACT PUBLICATIONS, 9104 Manassas Drive, Suite N, Manassas Park, VA 20111, Tel. 703-361-7300 or Fax 703-335-9486.

Warning/Liability/Warranty: The author and publisher have made every attempt to provide the reader with accurate, timely, and useful information. The information presented here is for reference purposes only. The author and publisher make no claims that using this information will guarantee the reader success. The author and publisher shall not be liable for any losses for damages incurred in the process of following the advice in this book.

ISBN: 1-57023-204-0

Library of Congress: 2003100522

Publisher: For information on Impact Publications, including current and forthcoming publications, authors, press kits, online bookstore, and submission requirements, visit our website: www.impactpublications.com

Sales/Distribution: All bookstore sales are handled through Impact's trade distributor: National Book Network, 15200 NBN Way, Blue Ridge Summit, PA 17214, Tel. 1-800-462-6420. All other sales and distribution inquiries should be directed to the publisher: Sales Department, IMPACT PUBLICATIONS, 9104 Manassas Drive, Suite N, Manassas Park, VA 20111-5211, Tel. 703-361-7300, Fax 703-335-9486, or email: info@impactpublications.com.

The Author: Wendy S. Enelow is a recognized leader in the executive job search, career coaching, and resume writing industries, and author of 15 job search books. In private practice for 20 years, she has assisted thousands of job search candidates through successful career transitions. She is the Founder and President of the Career Masters Institute, an exclusive training and development association for career professionals worldwide. A graduate of the University of Maryland, Wendy has earned several distinguished professional credentials – Certified Professional Resume Writer (CPRW), Job and Career Transition Coach (JCTC), and Credentialed Career Master (CCM). Wendy can be contacted at wendyenelow@cminstitute.com.

Contents

Appendices

Preface

If you're one of the tens of thousands of professionals currently in the workforce who do not have a four-year degree, then this book is exactly what you need in order to create your own "best" resume. Unlike other job seekers who can focus their resumes on the strength of their educational credentials, you must focus your resume on the strength of your expertise, skills, qualifications, and achievements.

First things first. Before you even begin to write your resume, you have to "let yourself off the hook" and accept the fact that a four-year degree is NOT a mandatory requirement for career success. In fact, as you'll read in Chapter 1, there are many well-recognized professionals who have reached extraordinary levels of success without a degree! Although you may consider your lack of a college degree to be an obstacle to overcome and, in fact, in certain employment arenas that may be the case, you have to release any negative thoughts you have and move forward positively in your job search. Fortunately, there are countless positions for which a college degree is not required or may be overlooked due to the strength of your employment background, skills, and qualifications.

When I wrote this book, I wrote it for individuals like yourself who are the BEST or aspire to be the BEST – in their professions, their careers, and their lives. This book was NOT written for the faint of heart nor the faint of career. It was written for those who strive to move forward and upward in their careers, who push themselves to reach new heights, and who are energized, not intimidated, by challenge.

This book was written for all levels of job seekers, from the utility worker to the chief executive officer, from the administrative assistant to the technology director of a major corporation...and everyone else who has launched and continues to proactively manage their career despite the fact that they never earned a college degree.

In summary, this book was written for YOU – today's talented job seeker who aspires to greater professional challenges, achievements, and results.

Dedication

This book is dedicated to the 15 Professional Resume Writers who contributed their expertise to this publication (see pages 182-183). Each of these individuals has earned the prestigious designation of Credentialed Career Master (CCM) for their knowledge, expertise, and success in the writing and design of top-flight resumes that open doors and help land great new opportunities. It is these individuals to whom I give thanks for the outstanding samples you are about to see as you use this book to guide your own resume writing efforts and create you next "best" resume!

Thank you to:

Diane Burns, CCMC, CCM, CPRW, CEIP
George Dutch, PhD, JCTC, CCM
Joyce Fortier, MBA, CPRW, JCTC, CCM, CCMC
Susan Guarneri, MS, CCM, NCC, LPC, CCMC, CPRW, CEIP, IJCTC
Gayle Howard, CPRW, CRW, CCM
Myriam-Rose Kohn, CPRW, JCTC, CCM, CEIP, CCMC
Cindy Kraft, CCMC, CCM, CPRW, JCTC
Louise Kursmark, CPRW, JCTC, CCM, CEIP, MRW
Rolande LaPointe, CPC, CIPC, CPRW, IJCTC, CCM, CSS, CRW
Ric Lanham, MDiv, MA, MRE, CCM, CECC
Meg Montford, CCC, CCM, CPRW
Don Orlando, MBA, CPRW, JCTC, CCM, CCMC
John O'Connor, MFA, CRW, CPRW, CCM, CECC
Jennifer Rydell, CPRW, CCM, NCRW
Deborah Wile Dib, CCM, NCRW, CPRW, CEIP, JCTC, CCMC

1

Writing Your Best Resume

Don't Let It Bring You Down . . . It's Only a Degree

DID YOU KNOW THAT BILL GATES, the founder and chairman of Microsoft, doesn't have a four-year college degree? Neither does Michael Dell, the founder and CEO of Dell Computer. In fact, 52 of the top 800 company presidents and chief executive officers in the U.S. never earned their four-year degree. The list of talented and successful individuals who never attended or never graduated from college is remarkable. If you're one of those individuals, feel confident that you can include yourself in good company!

What these people did, and what you need to do, is move your career forward and not let the lack of a four-year degree impact your progression. Accept the reality – **you do not have a degree** – and move on. That's it. Don't focus on the negative, but, rather, focus your energies on what it is that you have achieved in your career, the knowledge and skills you have acquired, and the accomplishments you have delivered. It is this information that is most important in communicating your value to a new organization, and your resume is the tool that will allow you to do just that.

Resume writing (in particular) and job search (in general) are all about communicating your success and achievement – what you have accomplished thus far in your career and how that indicates what you might accomplish in the future. In today's difficult economic market, it is critical that each new hire bring value to an organization – value that can be measured in increased revenues, improved profits, cost savings, productivity improvements, efficiency gains, and much more.

Your challenge, therefore, is to write a resume that showcases your unique talents and qualifications and how they will benefit the hiring company. It's the same challenge as every other job seeker faces. However, as a non-degreed candidate, you have an additional challenge – **highlighting what you have accomplished while shifting the focus away from your educational credentials**.

Read that statement again, for it should be the strategy and underlying foundation for each and every word that you write on your resume, the format that you select, and the presentation style that you use. You want to create a document that demonstrates success in the workplace – yesterday, today, and tomorrow.

Showcase Your Talents & Qualifications

Over the past two decades, the employment market has become increasingly competitive. As companies downsize, reorganize, and, in some instances, close their doors, the entire resume writing and job search process has become more complex and more sophisticated. Today, resume writing is a competition among often well-qualified candidates vying for a limited number of opportunities. For that reason alone, resume writing has evolved into an art where, you, as the artist, must transition a blank canvas into a work of art that displays your talents, knowledge, expertise, and success.

A resume is the foundation for any successful search campaign and, in fact, it is virtually impossible to manage a job search without a resume. It is your calling card, your brochure, your marketing document. People look at it and are impressed with you and what you have accomplished. You mail it, you email it, you fax it, you hand-carry it, and you leave it behind after an interview so people have something to remember you by. Your resume is crucial in building your market visibility and, ultimately, facilitating your job search success and a great new career opportunity.

To understand the value of your resume to your job search process, it is best to start with a clear definition of what a resume is. It can be best defined as the following:

- *"Sales and marketing"* document written to sell you - the job seeker - into your next position.
- *"Distinctive"* communication that presents a clear and concise picture of "who" you are and the value you bring to an organization.
- *"Dynamic"* document that clearly communicates your professional skills, qualifications, knowledge, success, and industry expertise.
- *"Hard-hitting"* tool designed to sell the high points of your career – your successes and achievements.
- *"Visually attractive"* presentation that communicates a professional image.

A resume is not:

- A biography of your entire career, every job you have ever held, every internship you have ever completed, and every course you have ever attended.
- A document containing lengthy job descriptions and long lists of duties and responsibilities.
- A passive, low-energy, and narrative summary of your work history.

As a job seeker without a four-year degree, you must devote extra time and energy to developing your own winning resume. It is even more important that you be able to focus your resume on what you have accomplished so that prospective employers are so impressed with that quality of your work performance that you can overcome the missing degree.

To accomplish that, the writing, tone, style, and presentation of your resume must be superb. The wording must be sharp and the presentation top-of-the-line. The impression it leaves with the reader must be that of an accomplished and successful professional who has delivered strong results and met unique challenges. The resume must communicate "I bring value to you and to your organization." If you are ever going to "toot your own horn," **this is the time to do it!**

Translate Your Qualifications Into Hard-Hitting Resume Content

Etch these words into your head, your heart, and your soul...**resume writing is sales!!!** Say that phrase over and over until it becomes a part of you, for it is this mindset that will propel you to write a top-notch resume.

Your resume is a document that should be written specifically to market and merchandise **your** specific talents, skills, career highlights, and career successes. Critical to that concept is the *"sell it to me, don't tell it to me"* strategy. Think about that. When writing your resume you do not simply want to **tell** what you have done. Rather, you want to **sell** what you have accomplished and the results you have delivered.

So, how do you do that? You do that by writing powerful sentences, highlighting your achievements and qualifications, using action verbs, and creating a resume that communicates success.

To better understand the concept of selling your qualifications, here are a few examples:

Poor Example:
Managed 12 sales regions and 82 sales associates throughout the U.S.

Good Example:
Independently planned and directed a team of 82 sales associates marketing sophisticated networking and E-commerce products throughout the Northeastern U.S. Closed 2002 at 175% of revenue quota and 187% of profit goal.

Poor Example:
Managed accounting, financial reporting, budgeting, and MIS functions.

Good Example:
Chief Financial Officer with full responsibility for the corporate finance organization for a $270 million industrial plastics manufacturer. Directed fi-

nancial planning, accounting, tax, treasury, budgeting, and MIS functions. Managed a direct reporting staff of 12.

Poor Example:
Hired to reorganize the entire administrative function of the company.

Good Example:
Recruited by Chief Administrative Officer to plan and direct the complete redesign and reorganization of all administrative and support functions for Dell's 2,000-employee customer support network. Reduced operating costs 15% in the first six months through a diversity of efficiency improvement initiatives.

"Sell it to me, don't tell it to me" ... see what a difference it makes in the words, the tone, the style, and the impact? Remember that each and every word, phrase, and sentence in your resume should be written to communicate success, achievement, and results. If you can accomplish that, you will have created your own winning resume that is bound to open doors, generate interviews, and help you land your next position.

Use the "Right" Words

The words that you select create the tone and energy of your resume. If you use words such as "responsible for" and "duties included," your resume becomes passive, boring, and repetitive. But when you use words such as directed, designed, created, achieved, delivered, increased, improved, launched, revitalized, and other action verbs, your resume comes to life and communicates energy, drive, and achievement.

There are four key strategies to follow that will help you determine your appropriate choice of words. All except #3 are critical to every individual writing a resume. Strategy #3 is important only if your job search is focused within a particular industry or related group of industries.

Strategy #1: Always write in the active first-person (dropping the "I's"), never the third-person. What does this mean? Here's an example:

> **First-Person:**   Reduced annual purchasing costs by 12%.
>
> **Third-Person:**   Mr. Smith reduced annual purchasing costs by 12%.

Can you see the difference? The first example communicates "I did this." The second example communicates "Mr. Smith, the other guy, did that," and it moves ownership away from you. Your resume must be a part of who you are and not a distant third-party voice.

Strategy #2: Use KeyWords specific to your current professional goals. If you're looking for a job in sales, use sales, marketing, and customer service words. If you're looking for a position in manufacturing, use words related to production, product management, inventory, and workforce management. These KeyWords are essential if you want to communicate you have the "right" set of skills and experience for the type of position you are seeking. What's more, KeyWords are an essential component in the resume scanning process (when companies and recruiters use scanners to determine if you have the appropriate skills and qualifications for a particular opportunity). The computer, not a person, "reads" your resume. Therefore, word choice is critical.

Strategy #3: Use KeyWords specific to the industry and profession in which you are seeking a position. Strategy #3 is applicable only if your job search is industry-specific. If you are looking for a position in the technology industry, use the appropriate technology words, phrases, and acronyms, such as network administration, web page design, and systems migration. If you're looking for a position in the retail industry, write about buying, merchandising, and loss prevention. If the insurance industry is your objective, use words such as indemnity, E&O, and risk assessment. These KeyWords are essential if you want to communicate you have the "right" set of skills and experience for the industry in which you are currently seeking opportunities.

Here are a few sample KeyWords for 30 different professions and industries. Use this list to get you thinking about the KeyWords that are specific to your profession (Strategy #2) and your industry (Strategy #3).

Accounting	Payables, Receivables, General Ledger, Financial Analysis, Reporting, Auditing, Budgeting, Month-End Closings
Administration	Executive Liaison Affairs, Board of Directors, Minutes, Recordkeeping, Scheduling, Project Administration
Association Management	Fundraising, Corporate Sponsorships, Member Services, Outreach, Advocacy, Regulatory Compliance
Banking	De Novo Banking, Commercial, Retail, Back Office, Lending, Cross-Border Transactions, Regulatory Compliance
Construction	Commercial, Industrial & Residential, Project Planning, Scheduling, Contracts, Environmental Assessment
Corporate Finance	Tax, Treasury, Mergers, Acquisitions, Budgeting, Cost Avoidance, Investment Management, Forecasting, Analysis
Customer Service	Order Processing & Fulfillment, Customer Relationship Management, Customer Retention, Problem Resolution, Customer Satisfaction
Education	Curriculum Development, Instructional Systems Design, Program Administration, Testing & Placement, Training
Engineering	Prototype Development, Project Management, Failure Analysis, Reliability, Experimental Design, Product Functionality

Government	Regulatory Compliance & Reporting, Public/ Private Sector, Competitive Bidding, Fixed Price Contracts, VIP Relations
Health Care	Patient Management, Treatment Planning, Emergency Intervention, Invasive Therapies, Utilization Review
Hospitality	Food & Beverage, Guest Relations, Facilities Management, Meetings & Events, Amenities, Labor & Food Cost Controls
Human Resources	Staffing, Training & Development, Compensation, Benefits Administration, Employee Assistance, HRIS Technology
Human Services	Diagnostic Assessment, Case Management, Inter-Agency Relations, Crisis Intervention, Treatment Planning
Information Technology	Client/Server, Web-Enabling, Internet/Intranet, Integration, Migration, Configuration, Platform, Hardware, Software
Insurance	Claims Administration, Risk Management, Liability, P&C, E&O, LLC, Portfolio Management, Client Retention
Investment Finance	Mergers, Acquisitions, Joint Ventures, Venture Funding, ROI, ROA, ROE, Portfolio Management, NASD, Cross-Border Transactions
Law/Legal	Legal Research & Writing, Case Management, Judicial Proceedings, Investigations, Client Representation
Logistics	Purchasing, Supply Chain Management, Inventory Planning, Warehousing, Distribution, Transportation, Resource & Asset Management

Manufacturing	Productivity & Yield Improvement, Cost Reduction, MRP, JIT, Manufacturing Cell, Quality, Materials, Scheduling, Control
Marketing	Multimedia Communications & Presentations, New Market Development, Product Launch, Advertising, Branding, Competitive Intelligence
Media	New Media, Production, Direction, Broadcasting, On-Air Talent, Studio Engineering, E-Commerce
Purchasing	Supply Chain Management, Vendor Sourcing, Contract Negotiations, Fixed Price, Inventory Planing, Costing
Quality	Engineering, Reliability, ISO, TQM, Quality Assurance, Failure Analysis & Reporting, Product Performance, Quality Audits
Real Estate	Residential, Commercial & Industrial Properties, Buy/Sell Negotiations, Contracts, Regulatory Compliance, Marketing
Retail	Multi-Site Operations, Merchandising, Loss Prevention, Sales, Customer Service, Training, Facilities, Buying, In-Store Events
Sales	Customer Presentations, Negotiations, Sales Closings, New Product Launch, Contracts, Competitive Positioning, Customer Relationship Management
Security	Corporate Security, VIP Protection, Risk Assessment, Perimeter & Facilities Control, Emergency Preparedness
Telecommunications	Infrastructure, Technology, Networking, Internet/Intranet, Cellular, Base Station, Voice & Date, Secure Transmissions
Transportation	Multi-Modal Transportation Systems, Warehousing, Distribution, Routing, Safety Training, Hub Operations

Strategy #4: Write for the level of position you are pursuing - entry-level, mid-level, professional, managerial, or executive. Use hard-hitting words and phrases that communicate the level of expertise that you bring to an organization. Do not talk about "controlling revenues"; talk about "P&L management." Do not talk about "supervising staff"; talk about "building and leading a 20-person team." Use words and phrases such as:

Accelerating Revenue Growth

Aggressive Turnaround Leadership

Best-in-Class Operations

Capturing Cost Reductions

Competitively Positioning Products, Services, & Technologies

Continuous Improvement

Cost Savings & Avoidance

Cross-Cultural Communications

Cross-Cultural Sensitivity

Cross-Functional Team Leadership

Decision Making & Action

Distinguished Performance

Double-Digit Revenue & Profit Growth

Driving Product Development & Innovation

E-Commerce & E-Business

Emerging Ventures

Entrepreneurial Drive & Vision

Executive Presentations & Negotiations

Fast-Track Promotion

Global Business Development

High-Performance

Independent Thought & Action

International Business Expansion

Matrix Management

Mergers & Acquisitions

Multinational Organizations

Negotiating Strategic Alliances

New Media

New Ventures

Organization(al) Leadership

Outperforming Global Competition

Outsourcing

Partnerships & Joint Ventures
Performance Revitalization
Pioneering Technologies
Proactive Change Agent
Problem Solving & Resolution
Process Redesign & Optimization
Profit & Loss Management
Start-Up, Turnaround, & High-Growth Organizations
Strong & Sustainable Revenue Gains
Technologically Sophisticated Organizations
Visionary Leadership

If you can follow these four critical strategies to effective resume writing, you will have created a document that is powerful and clearly positions you for the type and level of position you are seeking. Despite what we are constantly hearing from the media about layoffs, downsizings, corporate reorganizations, and more, opportunities still abound. Your challenge is to write a document that positions you, your career, and your qualifications as a "cut above" the crowd, giving you a distinct advantage in today's competitive employment market. The words that you choose to use in your resume are what will give you that competitive edge!

2

Creating a Powerful Resume

Make the Best Choices

Before you can even begin to write your resume, you must decide the resume style and presentation style that are right for you. This chapter will help you make those decisions before you proceed to Chapter 3 - Building Your Best Resume.

The resume style you select will be dictated by your specific work history and your current career objectives. If you want to focus on your strong track record of employment experience, you'll most likely want to use a Chronological Resume. If, on the other hand, you want a heavy focus on your skills, qualifications, and achievements (more than on your work history), the Functional Resume will be your best choice. However, if you want to combine your strong work history with a great deal of emphasis on your skills and qualifications, you may consider using a Combination Resume. The latter offers the "best of both worlds," as you will note from many of the samples in this book.

The presentation style you select will be determined by the manner in which you are planning to use your resume. If you are going to be printing and mailing copies, you'll want to use a Printed Resume. If you plan to send your resumes via email, an Electronic Resume will be right for you. And, if you want to combine the aesthetic qualities of the Printed Resume with the ease in transmission of the Electronic Resume, you may consider a Web Resume.

The following sections explore each type of resume style and presentation style. After reading these sections you should be able to quickly determine which style is right for you based on your current career situation and objectives.

The Three Types of Resume Styles

For as long as resumes have existed (particularly in their current state over the past 20 years), there has been an ongoing controversy about the use and effectiveness of a chronological resume versus a functional resume versus the more recent combination-style resume. To better understand the difference between each of them and to help you determine which is right for you, let's explore the pluses and minuses of all three.

The Chronological Resume

Chronological resumes provide a step-by-step path through your career. Starting with your current or most recent position, chronological resumes are written backwards, allowing you to put the emphasis on your current and most recent experiences. As you progress further back in your career, job descriptions are shorter, with an emphasis on achievements and notable projects.

Chronological resumes are the resume style preferred by the vast majority of employers and recruiters. They are easy to read and understand, clearly communicating where you have worked and what you have done. Unless your particular situation is unusual, a chronological resume is generally your best career marketing tool.

The Functional Resume

Functional resumes focus on the skills and qualifications you offer to a prospective employer. It is this type of information that is brought to the forefront and highlighted, while your employment experience is briefly mentioned at the end. Individuals who might consider a functional resume are career changers, professionals returning to work after an extended absence, individuals who have been in the job market for a lengthy period of time, or candidates who are 55+ years of age. If you fall into one of these categories or any other related category, you will want to focus your resume on your specific expertise, qualifications, and competencies, and not the specific chronology of your employment experience.

Functional resumes are much less frequently used. Many corporate human resource professionals and recruiters look at these resumes with less interest, believing that the candidate is hiding something or attempting to "change reality." Be extremely careful if you decide this is the right style for you (which it might very well be), and be sure to include your complete job history at the end of your resume.

The Combination Resume

The most recent trend in resume writing is to combine the structure of the chronological resume with the skills focus of the functional resume. By starting your resume with a Career Summary, you can begin with a heavy focus on the qualifications and value you offer (functional approach), and then substantiate it with solid, well-written, and accomplishment-oriented position descriptions (chronological approach). Many of the resumes in this book reflect this new combination resume which is well received by both recruiters and corporate human resource professionals.

Combination resumes give you the "best of both worlds" - an intense focus on your qualifications combined with the strength of a solid employment history. They are a powerful marketing tool.

The Three Types of Presentation Styles

No resume discussion is complete these days without a dual focus on both printed resumes and electronic resumes. Chances are you will be sending just as many resumes via email as you will on paper, if not more. Therefore, it is critical to understand the similarities and the differences in the visual presentation of the two. What's more, over the past several years, the Web

Resume has appeared, a Web-based resume presentation that offers tremendous flexibility. You'll read about it later in this section.

The Traditional Printed Resume

The single most important thing to remember when you are preparing a printed resume is that you are writing a sales document. You have a product to sell – yourself – and it must be attractively packaged and presented. To compete against hundreds, if not thousands, of other qualified candidates, your resume must be sharp, distinctive, and dynamic in both its wording and its visual presentation.

Your resume should have an up-to-date style that is bold and attracts attention. This doesn't mean using an italic typeface, cute logos, or an outrageous paper color. Instead, be conservatively distinctive. Choose a sharp-looking typeface such as Bookman, Soutane, Krone, Garamond, or Fritz, or if your font selection is limited, the more common Times Roman, CG Omega, or Arial typefaces. The samples in this book will further demonstrate how to create documents that are sharp and upscale while still remaining conservative and "to the point."

Paper color should be clean and conservative, preferably white, ivory, or light gray. You can even consider a bordered paper (e.g., light gray paper with small white border around the perimeter.) It is only for "creative" professions (e.g., graphic arts, theater, media) where colored papers can be appropriate and are an important part of the packaging. In these situations, your additional challenge is to visually demonstrate your creative talents.

If possible, adhere to these formatting guidelines when preparing your printed resume:

- Do not expect readers to struggle through 10- to 15-line paragraphs. Substitute 2-3 shorter paragraphs or use bullets to offset new sentences and sections.

- Do not overdo bold and italics type. Excessive use of either defeats the purpose of these enhancements. If half of the type on the page is bold, nothing will stand out.

- Use nothing smaller than 10-point type. If you want employers to read your resume, make sure they don't need a magnifying glass!

- Don't clutter your resume. Everything you have heard about "white space" is true. Let your document "breathe" so readers do not have to struggle through it.

- Use an excellent printer. Smudged, faint, heavy, or otherwise poor quality print will discourage red-eyed readers.

The Electronic Resume

When discussing electronic resumes, take everything that is really important about preparing a visually pleasing printed resume and forget it! Electronic resumes are an entirely different creature with their own set of rules. They are "plain-Jane" resumes stripped to the bone to allow for ease in file transfer, email, and other technical applications. Professional resume writers, who work so hard to make each resume look distinctive and attractive, "freak out," while engineers love how neat and clean these resumes are!

If possible, adhere to these formatting guidelines when preparing your electronic resume:

- Avoid bold print, underlining, italics, and other type enhancements. If you want to draw attention to a specific word, heading, or title, use CAPITALIZATION to make it stand out.

- Type all information starting on the left-hand side of the page. Do not center or justify any of the text, for it generally does not translate well electronically.

- Leave lots of white space just as you would with a printed resume. Ease in readability is a key factor in any type of communication.

- Length is not as critical a consideration with electronic resumes as it is with printed resumes. Therefore, instead of typing all your technical skills in a paragraph form, type them in a long list. Instead of putting your KeyWords in a double-column format, type them in a single-column list. It is a much easier read for the human eye!

NOTE: Your electronic resume will automatically be presented in Courier typestyle. You have no control over this, for it is the automatic default.

The Emerging Web Resume

As one would expect, a new phenomenon is emerging that allows you to merge the visual distinction of the printed resume with the ease of the electronic resume. The new Web resume is hosted on your own website where you can refer recruiters, colleagues, potential employers, and others. Rather than pasting your plain-looking electronic resume into an email message, include a link to your URL. With just one click, your printed resume instantly appears. It is easy and efficient, the visual presentation is sharp and classy, and resume writers around the world are breathing much easier!

With a Web resume, you also have the opportunity to include more information than you would with the traditional printed resume that you mail. You can have separate sections (separate Web pages) for achievements, project highlights, management competencies, technology skills, and more. Everything is just a click away.

For those of you in technology industries, you can even go one step further and create a multimedia presentation of your Web-based resume. Never before have you been able to create a resume that actually demonstrates your technical expertise. Just think of the competitive advantage a Web resume can give your job search.

One final note about presentation style ... it is quite likely that you will have at least two versions of your resume - the printed version and the electronic version. In today's employment market, chances are that you will need both, allowing you to send your resume in the manner that is preferred by a particular company or recruiter. With that said, it is recommended that you prepare both versions immediately so you will have them available as necessary.

Web resumes are not yet the norm so you may not need one today. However, they are increasing in their acceptance and use, so don't be surprised if the opportunity for you to use a Web-based resume appears over the next year or two.

Top 20 Resume Writing Mistakes to Avoid

Many resumes are literally "dead upon arrival" because the job seeker made serious writing errors, most of which center on issues of focus, organization, trustworthiness, and intelligence. Reading between the lines, employers often draw conclusions about an individual's personality and competence based on the quality of the resume. If you make any of these errors, chances are your credibility will be questioned, so be sure your resume does not commit any of these writing errors:

1. Fails to include critical contact information - phone, email, or address.
2. Includes information unrelated to the position.
3. States a strange, unclear, or vague objective.
4. Has misspellings and poor grammar; is wordy and/or redundant.
5. Has punctuation errors.
6. Contains lengthy phrases, long sentences, and awkward paragraphs.
7. Is slick or gimmicky, and appears over-produced.
8. Is boastful, egocentric, and overly aggressive.
9. Repeatedly refers to "I" and appears self-centered.
10. Appears to contain dishonest, untrustworthy, or suspicious information.
11. Is difficult to interpret because of poor organization and layout.
12. Has unexplained time gaps between jobs.
13. Includes too many jobs in a short period of time.
14. Has no evidence of past accomplishments or a pattern of performance to predict future performance.
15. Lacks credibility and content; lots of fluff and "canned" resume language.
16. Contains distracting personal information that adds no professional value.
17. Uses abbreviations, acronyms, or KeyWords unfamiliar to the reader.
18. Appears under-qualified or over-qualified for the position.
19. Includes salary requirements that are too high or too low.
20. Includes "red flag" information (e.g., terminations, lawsuits, claims, health or performance problems).

Top 20 Resume Production, Distribution, & Follow-Up Mistakes to Avoid

Assuming that you have written an outstanding resume, your next challenge is to make sure you do not make any errors during the production, distribution, and follow-up stages. Here are some of the most common errors to avoid:

1. Unattractive with a poorly designed format, small typestyle, and crowded copy.
2. Extends onto an additional page with only 2-3 lines on that extra page.
3. Contains typographical errors.
4. Is poorly typed, poorly reproduced, and difficult to read.
5. Is produced on odd-sized paper.
6. Is printed on poor quality paper or on extremely thick or thin paper.
7. Is sent to the wrong person or department.
8. Misspells the hiring contact's name.
9. Folded too many times and inserted into a tiny envelope.
10. Envelope is double-sealed with tape and is virtually indestructible.
11. Back of envelope includes handwritten note with information that is missing from the resume or needs to be updated.
12. Arrives without proper postage and the company or recruiter has to pay.
13. Accompanied by enclosures (e.g., letters of recommendation, transcripts, samples of work) which were not requested.
14. Arrives without a cover letter.
15. Cover letter repeats the same information that is on the resume, and does not command attention or move the reader to action.
16. Follow-up calls are made too soon, before the resume and letter arrive.
17. Follow-up calls are too personal; refer to hiring manager by first name.
18. Follow-up calls are too aggressive or the candidate appears too hungry or needy.
19. Thank-you note not sent immediately after interview.
20. Failed to ask for the position.

Expert Resources

In order to give yourself a competitive job search advantage and be sure you avoid all 40 of the mistakes outlined previously, it is often wise to consult a resume, career, or job search expert. These individuals can provide you with insights and expert guidance as you plan and manage your search campaign. You have your choice of working with a professional resume writer, executive career coach, career counselor, outplacement consultant, recruiter, or others who deliver job search services and support to candidates like yourself.

What's more, there are companies that will post your resume online, other companies that post position announcements online, and others that produce targeted email and print campaigns to prospective employers that you select. There are reference checking companies, coaches who specialize in interview training, and publications galore on professional job search and career marketing.

The list of potential resources is virtually endless, from the resume writer down the street to the global outplacement consulting firm with offices on six out of seven continents. The emergence of all these firms has created a wealth of resources for job seekers, but it has also made the process much more difficult with so many choices. How do you determine exactly what help you need and from whom? And how do you find the right person?

We've made that easy for you! The 15 career professionals who have contributed to this book are all expert resume writers who work with job seekers worldwide to help them plan and manage successful search campaigns. In addition, many offer other career services such as coaching, counseling, Internet resume postings, direct mail campaigns, and more. You'll find complete contact information for each of these 15 individuals in Appendix A. Feel free to contact any or all of them for detailed information about their services, pricing, and specific experience.

3

Building Your Best Resume

Step-by-Step Process for Writing Your Best Resume

Writing the best resume would be an easy task if I could only give you a standard outline or template. All you would need to do is answer the questions, fill in the blanks, and your resume would be ready. Not much time, not much serious thought, and no tremendous effort.

Unfortunately, as you already know, this is not the case. Each resume must be custom-written to sell each candidate's individual talents, skills, qualifications, experience, educational credentials, professional activities, technical proficiency, and more. Resumes are NOT standardized, they are NOT prescribed, and there is NO specific formula. In fact, there are virtually no rules for resume writing. On the one hand, this gives you tremendous flexibility in what you choose to include and how you include it. In addition, it allows you to be creative in the visual presentation of your resume, designing a document that is unique to you.

On the other hand, the fact that there are no rules for resume writing is what makes it such a difficult task. There is no single roadmap to follow nor a "one size fits all" strategy. Each resume is unique to each individual.

Further complicating the resume writing process is the fact that you have to change your mindset and realize that what you are really writing is a SALES document. It is critical that you understand that your resume is designed to SELL you into your next position, not to simply list where you have worked, what you did, and when. Rather, your strategy must be to integrate all of your past experiences into a resume that clearly states "this is who I am" and "this is the value I bring to your organization."

You must also realize that writing your resume is not a two- to three-hour task. Most likely, it will take days and days of thought, writing, editing, and hard work to create your "best" resume. Invest the time that is necessary and you will see a remarkable increase in the number of responses and interviews you receive. The stronger your resume, the stronger your performance in the job market!

Now that we have clearly established that resumes are individualized documents that can vary dramatically in their structure, format, tone, and presentation, it is also important to note that resumes do share certain common features:

Most resumes will include Experience and Education sections, even if your education only includes some college and/or career-related training.

In addition, there are many other categories that you may include if they are relevant to your career, background, and current objectives:

- Objective
- Career Summary
- Honors & Awards
- Public Speaking
- Publications
- Personal Information
- Technology Skills & Qualifications
- Professional Affiliations
- Civic Affiliations
- Teaching Experience
- International Experience

Some of these categories will be appropriate for your resume; others will not. To help you better understand the structure and function of each resume section, a short but comprehensive discussion of each follows. Use the information below to help you determine (1) if you need to include a particular section in your resume, and (2) what style and format to use for that particular section.

Before you begin writing, refer to Appendix B for resume preparation materials that will help you outline and prepare the information you will want to include in your resume.

Objective

One of the greatest controversies in resume writing focuses on the use or omission of an Objective. There are three questions to ask yourself that will help you decide whether or not you need an Objective on your resume:

1. **Do you have a specific objective in mind?** A specific position? A specific industry? If so, you can include a focused objective statement such as: "Seeking a management position in the pharmaceutical R&D industry" or "Customer Service Supervisor with a nationwide call-center operation." As you can see, each of these objective statements clearly indicates the type of position the candidate is seeking along with his industry preference. If you are this focused in your job search, do include an Objective.

2. **Is your Objective constant?** Will your Objective stay the same for virtually all positions you apply for and all the resumes you submit? If so, include a focused Objective such as that outlined in #1 above. If not, do not include it. You do not want to have to edit your resume each and every time you send it, adjusting your Objective to fit the position. It's a time-consuming process and stalls the flow of resumes out your door. Only include an Objective on your resume, if your career goals are focused and constant.

3. **Is your Objective unclear?** Are you considering a number of opportunities? Are you pursuing a number of different positions? Are you interested in opportunities in many different industries? If your answer is yes, do not include an Objective statement, for it will be unfocused and vague. Consider an Objective such as: "Seeking a professional position where I can help a company achieve revenues and profits." Doesn't everyone want to help a company make money? These are useless words and add no value to your resume. They do not tell your reader "who" you are or "what" you are pursuing. If you are unclear about your Objective, do not include it on your resume.

Remember, every time you forward a resume you will also be sending a cover letter. If you do not include an Objective on your resume, let your cover letter be the tool that communicates your Objective in that specific situation to that specific employer or recruiter.

Here are a few sample formats if you choose to include an Objective:

PROFESSIONAL OBJECTIVE:

Challenging Sales Position in the Hospitality Industry.

CAREER OBJECTIVE:

Senior-Level Management position where I can apply my 15 years' experience in Information Systems and Technologies.

CAREER GOAL: PURCHASING MANAGEMENT - PLASTICS INDUSTRY

Career Summary / Career Profile

Consider this. When you write an Objective, you are telling your reader what you want FROM them. When you start your resume with a Career Summary or Career Profile, you are telling your reader what you can do FOR them, what value you bring to their organization, what expertise you have, and how well you have performed. In both, you are writing about the same concepts, the same professions, and/or the same industries. However, the Career Profile is a more upscale, more professional, and more hard-hitting strategy for catching your reader's attention and making an immediate connection. And isn't that the point of your resume? Your goal is to intrigue a prospective employer to (1) read your resume, (2) invite you for an interview, and (3) offer you a position.

To simplify this concept, compare the two examples below:

Example #1:

PROFESSIONAL OBJECTIVE: Management Position in Corporate Finance.

Example #2:

CAREER PROFILE:

Ten-year corporate finance career with Dow Chemical, American Express, and Microsoft. Experience in mergers, acquisitions, joint ventures, and international corporate development. Transacted $200 million in new enterprises, slashed $14 million from bottom-line operating costs, and contributed to a 33% increase in corporate earnings. Skilled planner and negotiator. PC and Internet proficient.

In both of these examples, is it clear that the individual is seeking a financial management position? Yes! They are both communicating the same overall message - that the candidate is a qualified finance executive.

Now, ask yourself which is a stronger presentation and which better sells the candidate's qualifications. Obviously, the Career Profile is a more powerful presentation. It is more dynamic, more substantial, and clearly communicates the value and success of the candidate.

Finally, ask yourself the following question: If you started your resume with a Career Profile as presented above, would you need an Objective that stated your goals? Probably not. The Career Profile paints a clear and concise picture of "who" you are. It is not necessary to include an Objective above a Career Profile that states, "I want a job as a such-and-such" when you have already indicated "who" you are.

In addition, there may be instances when you are not 100% focused on one specific objective and want to be open to a number of different opportunities in different industries. This is precisely the reason why you would not include an Objective and why a Career Profile would work so well. The Profile allows you to present a number of different, but generally related, qualifications; in turn, you can position yourself for a number of different opportunities. Be advised, however, that a well-targeted cover letter is essential in this situation. Your letter must highlight your specific qualifications as they relate to that specific position.

Consider the following example for a successful business manager who has a great deal of experience in both manufacturing and sales, and is looking at positions in both professions. The example below demonstrates how the Career Profile can be used to position a candidate for a vast array of opportunities.

MANAGEMENT QUALIFICATIONS

Manufacturing Manager / Sales & Marketing Manager
Graduate - Sales Leadership Training - Kellogg Academy

Fifteen-year management career with start-up ventures, turnaround companies, and high-growth corporations worldwide. Cross-functional, cross-industry experience in:

Manufacturing Management	Sales & Marketing Management
Multi-Site Operations Management	New Business Development
Technology & Process Automation	Key Account Development
Supply Chain Management	Client Relationship Management
Cost Reduction & Avoidance	New Product Design & Introduction

Note in the above example that the Career Profile was renamed Management Qualifications. Other headings you might consider include:

- Career Summary
- Qualifications Profile
- Summary of Qualifications
- Management Summary
- Professional Credentials
- Career Achievements
- Professional Profile
- Career Highlights & Achievements

Each of these headings communicates the same message, so select the one that you prefer.

When writing your Career Profile, consider these two strategies used by professional resume writers worldwide. I guarantee they will make writing your Career Profile faster and easier.

1. Resume writing is a condensation process. When you write your resume, you are, in essence, taking your career and consolidating it onto one or two pages. Then, to write your Career Profile, take those one or two pages and consolidate them into one or two inches at the top of your resume. You will then have your Profile.

2. The Career Profile is the LAST section you should write on a resume. How can you write the Profile if you have not yet written the text and determined what information you want to include in your Profile, how,

and where? You can't! Write the rest of your resume and save the Profile for last. You will find that the words will come much more easily.

Professional Experience

This is the single most important section on anyone's resume, but particularly for non-degreed candidates like yourself. It is your opportunity to highlight your professional experience, qualifications, and achievements as they relate to your current career objectives. It is your chance to "toot your own horn." It is the time to highlight everything that has contributed to your success and your professional excellence. Give careful thought and consideration to what you include under each position. **EVERY WORD COUNTS!**

When writing your Professional Experience, your challenge is to briefly, yet completely, describe your employment history with emphasis on four important topics as they are appropriate to your career track:

1. **The company.** Is it a manufacturer, distributor, worldwide technology leader, or multi-site service organization? What are the company's annual revenues? How many locations? How many employees? Give a brief summary of the company and its operations, customers, products, markets, or technologies as they relate to your current objectives and ONLY as they relate. If your current employer is a technology company and you are looking to remain in the technology industry, briefly highlight who the company is because it is relevant to your current career objectives. If, however, you currently work for a plastics manufacturer and your goal is a position with a technology manufacturer, do not mention what your current employer does. Rather, refer to them as a $29-million production operation. In essence, "leave" the industry behind if it is not related to your current objectives.

2. **The challenge.** Is this a start-up venture, turnaround, or high-growth company? Were you hired to lead a new initiative? Were the company's costs out of control? Were there organizational weaknesses? If there were any particular challenges associated with the company and/or your position, be sure to clearly state them. As an example, a great introduction under a job description for a sales representative would be, "Recruited by Northeast Regional Sales Director to launch the company's introduction into the Baltimore/Washington federal marketplace."

3. **Your accountability.** Include your major areas of responsibility (e.g., functions, departments, organizations, personnel, budgets, revenue and profit objectives, facilities, operations). In just a few sentences you want to communicate the depth and range of your overall responsibilities.

4. **Your achievements.** Herein lies the heart and soul of your resume. Not only do you want to "tell" your reader what you were responsible for, you want to "sell" how well you performed and the value you delivered to each company. Did you reduce costs? Design new products? Implement new technologies? Better train staff? Improve efficiency and productivity? Reduce liability and risk exposure? Penetrate new markets? Streamline operations? Eliminate redundant operations? Negotiate big deals? Raise money? The list of potential achievements goes on and on.

To begin writing your position descriptions, start with a brief introductory paragraph highlighting information about the company, your challenges, and your overall responsibilities. Then follow with a bulleted listing of your achievements, contributions, and project highlights. In essence, you are telling your reader, "This is what I did and this is how well I did it." The concept is simple; the impact, significant.

Here's an example of a sample position description for a Logistics Manager:

Logistics Manager   **1998 to Present**
SIMMONS MANUFACTURING, Dayton, Ohio

Directed the planning, staffing, budgeting, and operations of a 6-site logistics, warehousing, and distribution operation for $200-million automotive products manufacturer. Scope of responsibility was diverse and included purchasing, vendor management, materials handling, inventory control, distribution planning, and delivery operations. Led a team of 55 employees through six direct supervisors. Managed a $25-million annual operating budget and $5 million per year in capital improvements.

- Introduced continuous improvement and quality management programs throughout the organization and at all 12 operating locations. Results included a 35% increase in daily production yields, 22% reduction in waste, and 52% improvement in customer satisfaction/retention.
- Spearheaded cost reduction initiatives that reduced labor expense 18% and overtime 34%.
- Renegotiated vendor contracts and saved $4.5 million in first year.

- Sourced and implemented $2.2 million in IT improvements to improve workflow.

Prospective employers who read that description can sense the scope (range, size, and diversity) of the individual's experience as well as get a clear understanding of his specific accomplishments and successes.

Follow the same format all the way through your resume for each and every job description you write, becoming briefer and briefer as you get further back in time. Do not focus on the day-to-day responsibilities of your older positions, unless they were particularly unusual. Rather, emphasize your achievements, notable companies you have worked for or done business with, new products and technologies you have helped design or launch, international experience, or any other distinguishing characteristics of your career.

Here are some sample achievement statements to get you started in developing your own list of accomplishments and value-adds.

- Achieved/surpassed all performance objectives. Increased sales revenues 28%, market share 14%, and bottom-line profits 18%.
- Increased sales by 48% across six major customer segments within an intensely competitive market.
- Led development and market introduction of emerging client/server technologies and created new market that now generates $20+ million in annual sales.
- Drove market share from 10% to 22% within first six months by transitioning to customer-focused sales teams.
- Reengineered critical production planning, scheduling, and manufacturing processes for a 12% reduction in annual operating costs.
- Realigned field sales organization and reduced staffing expense 27%.
- Sourced new vendors throughout Southeast Asia, negotiated joint ventures, and saved 25% in annual purchasing costs.
- Spearheaded implementation of advanced robotics technologies to automate manufacturing operations, virtually eliminated major competition, and won a 5-year, $15 million contract.
- Revitalized customer service organization, recruited qualified management team, and improved customer satisfaction ratings from 76% to 98%.
- Structured and negotiated four mergers and acquisitions as part of the corporation's aggressive growth and corporate expansion effort.

- Wrote, produced, and directed award-winning corporate training film.
- Orchestrated the company's successful and profitable expansion throughout emerging international markets (e.g., Africa, Middle East, former Soviet Union).
- Personally negotiated $2 million in capital financing transactions to support product R&D.
- Restructured all administrative affairs for the organization and significantly improved productivity, efficiency, and quality of all business operations.
- Achieved and maintained a 98% customer satisfaction rating.
- Established a comprehensive, in-house maintenance program for the facility and reduced outside labor fees by more than $200,000 annually.
- Introduced a youth crisis intervention program that won statewide acclaim and recognition.
- Resolved long-standing regulatory compliance issues and achieved a 100% rating from local health department officials.
- Created new classroom curriculum, wrote all supporting instructional materials, and presented program at the 2002 National Education Association conference.

Education

For job search candidates without a four-year degree, the Education section can be particularly challenging to write. There are many questions you will need to ask yourself to determine what information to include in this section and, in some instances, whether to include an Education section.

To begin, ask yourself the following questions:

1. Do you have a two-year degree? If yes, include an Education section.
2. Did you attend college, even if you did not graduate? If yes, include an Education section.
3. Have you completed any professional training and development certificate programs? If yes, include an Education section.
4. Have you completed any professional training and development courses? If yes, include an Education section.
5. Do you have any technical certificates or licenses? If yes, include an Education & Credentials section.
6. Are you a high school graduate and is high school the appropriate education level to have attained for the type of position you are seeking? If yes, include an Education section.

The only situations in which you would NOT include an Education section are if you have no educational credentials at all or if your highest level of education is as a high school graduate which is "expected" for the type and level of position you are seeking. In fact, if you've reached a mid- to high-level professional, supervisory, or management position, including an Education section that only includes high school graduation can be a disadvantage, drawing attention to the fact that you do not have a four-year degree. In such a situation, it is better to omit the Education section altogether and focus the resume on your career progression and success.

Here's an example of an Education section for a well-qualified management candidate who did not have a four-year degree:

EDUCATION:

Executive Leadership Training, YALE UNIVERSITY, 2002
Finance & Business Administration, YALE UNIVERSITY, 1996 to 1998

Highlights of Continuing Professional Education:

- Center for Creative Leadership, 2000
- Strategic Planning & Leadership, Dow Jones & Company, 1998
- Management By Objectives, Xerox Learning Corporation, 1997
- Management Communications, Xerox Learning Corporation, 1994

Although you may not have attended Yale, the above example demonstrates how it is possible to create a strong Education section without a four-year degree. Carefully review your educational qualifications and select a format that will best "sell" them and you to a prospective employer.

Professional & Community Affiliations

Include a listing of professional and community organizations to which you belong and any specific leadership roles, committee memberships, or related accomplishments. You may also include volunteer experience if relevant to your current career objectives. However, do use some discretion. If you hold three leadership positions with notable professional associations and nonprofit organizations, it is not necessary to include the fact that you are on the board of directors of your local condo association! Here's an example of a well-presented Professional Affiliations section:

PROFESSIONAL AFFILIATIONS:

- Independent Manufacturers Representative Association (District President)
- American Marketing Association (Professional Member & Training Committee Chair)
- Sales Consultants of America (Professional Member)
- Junior Achievement (Volunteer Lecturer)

Technology Qualifications

Fifteen years ago, Technology Qualifications were virtually never seen on a resume, except for people working directly in the technology industry as programmers, database administrators, and the like. Today, that has totally changed. Technology is a part of every professional's life and must be addressed on your resume. You may include just a brief mention of your PC qualifications in your Career Profile, or you may have an entire section devoted to the topic, particularly if you're a programmer, hardware engineer, telecommunications engineer, technology project manager, network administrator, or CIO. You will have to determine the specific technology information and skills to include, based on your current objectives. Here are two examples:

If you are NOT a professional in the technology industry, include a brief statement in your Career Profile such as:

Proficient with Microsoft Word, Access, Excel, email, and the Internet.

If you ARE a technology industry professional, include a separate section in your resume as follows:

TECHNOLOGY QUALIFICATIONS:

Applications:	Microsoft Office 97-2002; MS Project
Databases:	MS Access
Platforms:	Windows 2000/NT/95/98/ME
Multimedia:	Media Player; Quick Time; Real Player
Networks:	Cisco VPN Altiga, Cisco Wireless Aironet; Net Store; TTIL 5.0
Email:	Lotus Notes; Outlook 97-2002; Eudora; Netscape Mail

Honors & Awards

Include your honors, awards, commendations, and other professional recognition. This information can be integrated directly into your job descriptions, included under Education (if related), or compiled into a separate category at the beginning or the end of your resume (depends on its impact and relevancy). If any of your honors or awards are significant and recognizable, you might integrate them directly into your Career Profile so that they will be "extra" visible. Here are a few examples of how and where to include your honors and awards:

In your Career Profile:

- Winner, 2000 Honors Club Award For Outstanding Sales Performance
- Winner, 1998 Presidential Award For Exemplary Service
- Winner, 1996 SuperMAX Award For New Business Development

In your job descriptions:

Honored for outstanding revenue and profit performance with five consecutive "Salesman of the Year" awards.

In a separate section titled Honors & Awards:

HONORS & AWARDS:

- Winner, 2003 Addy Award For Creative Design & Excellence
- Winner, 2001 Clio Award For Television Set Design
- Winner, 2001 Malcolm Award For Ad Campaign Design

Publications

Publications validate your expertise, establish your credibility, and impress your reader. Be sure to include your book and article publications, either in a separate category at the end of your resume or in your Career Profile if particularly noteworthy or relevant to your current career objectives. Include the title of the publication, name of publisher, and year of publication. Here are a few examples of how and where to include your publications:

In your Career Profile:

- Author, "Sales Leadership 2000," Forbes, 2002
- Author, "Team Building & Leadership," IMAX Magazine, July 2000
- Author, "Winning In The Technology Wars," Business Week, April 1997

In your job descriptions:

- Authored IBM's award-winning "Close To The Customer" book and accompanying multimedia presentation.

In a separate section titled Publications:

PUBLICATIONS:

- Author, "International Business Leadership 2002," Entrepreneurial News, May 2002
- Author, "Global Business & Economic Concerns," AMA Journal, Fall 2001
- Author, "Winning In The Global Marketplace," Time, November 12, 2000

Public Speaking

Public speaking is another way to boost your credibility in the eyes of a prospective employer. Be sure to list your public speaking engagements, including title of presentation, audience, location, and date. If the list is extensive, include only the highlights that are most notable and/or most related to your current search objectives. Here are a few examples of how and where to include your public speaking experience:

In your Career Profile:

- Keynote Presenter, "Automated Manufacturing Process & Technologies," American Manufacturing Association National Conference, Summer 2000
- Speaker, "Building A Top-Performing Manufacturing Management Team," Wharton Leadership Symposium, 2000
- Panel Member, "Supply Chain Management For The Technology Venture," Logistics 2000 Presentation, American Quality Council Convention, 1998

In your job descriptions:

- Presented "Community Outreach & Corporate Citizenship Strategies" at the 1999 Leadership Symposium sponsored by the Cleveland Chamber of Commerce in cooperation with the Fortune 500 business community.

In a separate section titled Public Speaking:

PUBLIC SPEAKING:

- Keynote Presenter, "Nursing Trends in Osteopathic Care," American Nursing Association Annual Conference, April 2002
- Speaker, "Chronic Patient Care & Rehabilitation," American Institute of Health Care Annual Conference, May 2000
- Panel Member, "Global Forum in Health Care," American Nursing Association Annual Conference, April 1998

Teaching & Training

If you are an educator, a corporate trainer, or otherwise employed in the fields of Teaching, Training, or Education, this section will be your Professional Experience section. However, if you are a business professional who has relevant teaching experience, be sure to include this information. Just like publications, it immediately validates your credentials and qualifications. List the names of the courses that you taught, the school or organization, and the dates. Here are a few examples of how and where to include your teaching and training experience:

In your Career Profile:

- Instructor, Management Philosophies, Wharton School of Business, Spring 2003
- Instructor, Statistics & Demographics, University of Pennsylvania, Fall 2002
- Corporate Trainer, IBM - International Sales Division, 1998 - 2002

In your job descriptions:

- Selected by corporate HR Director to design and deliver a corporate-wide training program on production scheduling and resource management for 2,000+ employees.

In a separate section titled Teaching Experience (or Training Experience):

TEACHING EXPERIENCE:

- Corporate Trainer, Customer Care Communications, Dell Business School, 2002
- Instructor, Customer Relationship Management, Dell Business School, 2001
- Adjunct Instructor, English Composition, Delgard Community College, 1996-2000

International Experience

Today, each of us is part of a global workforce with a global economy. And the more international experience and exposure you have, the better. Be sure to include your foreign language skills and travel experience either in your Career Profile or as a separate section if the information is directly relevant to your current career objectives. Here are a few examples of how and where to include your international experience:

In your Career Profile:

- Fluent in English, Spanish, French, and Portuguese.
- Lived and worked in Belgium, Portugal, France, and the UK.
- Graduate, Oxford University's Executive Leadership Course.

In your job descriptions:

- Traveled throughout Europe, Asia, and the Middle East to develop new supplier relationships and monitor supplier production controls.

In a separate section titled International Experience:

INTERNATIONAL EXPERIENCE:

- Fluent in English, French, and Mandarin Chinese.
- Lived and worked in U.S., Canada, and China.
- Member, Beijing University's Global Business Task Force.

Personal Information

Now on to the great controversy of Personal Information and whether or not that information should be included in your resume. Here are my recommendations. DO NOT include personal information such as birth date, marital status, health, number of children, and the like. DO NOT include the fact that you enjoy golfing, camping with your family, and reading. None of that is relevant to your job search, particularly early on when you are simply trying to get your foot in the door for an interview.

There are certain times, however, when it is appropriate to include personal information:

- Required by the employer.
- Important to clarify your citizenship or residency status.
- Important to clarify your age.
- Unique information. I've worked with executives who were past Olympians, ascended mountains on seven continents, raced as competitive triathletes, and trekked through obscure regions worldwide. This type of information attracts others to you and can be the single reason someone calls you for an interview. My motto is "Use what you have to get in the door."

If a Personal Information section is appropriate in your situation, consider the following format:

PERSONAL PROFILE:

- US Citizen since 1988 (native of Switzerland)
- Fluent in English, French, German, and Dutch
- Competitive Triathlete and Skier

Consolidate the "Extras"

A great strategy for consolidating all of the "extra" categories at the end of your resume (e.g., Affiliations, Publications, Public Speaking, Foreign Languages, Personal Information) is to integrate them into one consolidated section called Professional Profile. You will want to consider this if you have little bits of information to include in many different categories and/or you are having trouble comfortably fitting your resume onto one or two pages. Here's an example:

PROFESSIONAL PROFILE:

Affiliations:	Chairman, National Industries Association
	Chairman, Industry Oversight National Association
Publications:	"Business Management," Business World, May 1992
	"Emerging Technologies," Digital Design, January 1991
	"Strategic Marketing," Fortune, April 1987
Languages:	Fluent in Spanish, French, and German.
PC Software:	Microsoft Word, Access, Excel, Lotus, PageMaker,
	WordPerfect

Frequently Asked Questions About Resume Writing

How long should a resume be?

The recommended length of a resume is one to two pages, realizing that in many instances, a professional or management resume will be two pages long. It is virtually impossible to fit everything onto one page and have room for any substance or achievements.

There are, however, situations when a resume will be longer than two pages.

- If you are seeking a very senior-level (CEO, President, Chairman, Board Director) position. Consider this example: You are the CEO of a Fortune 50 company applying for a position as CEO of another Fortune 50. Although your professional work experience is critical, so are your professional affiliations, civic affiliations, non-profit affiliations, public speaking engagements, university teaching experience, and other professional activities. In a circumstance such as this, where the candidates are the top in the country, the search is quite selective, and the stakes are high, a longer resume can be a more appropriate tool. The company is not just hiring the professional. Rather, the company is hiring the person, his network of contacts, and his reputation. Longer resumes are quite acceptable in this situation.

- When you are writing a curriculum vitae (CV) and not a resume. If you are not familiar with CVs, these are career documents most frequently used in academia, research, medicine, science, and related fields. CVs are comprehensive documents that include ALL of an individual's experience, internships, externships, publications, affiliations, teaching experience, and more. Sections are not "highlighted" or summarized as in a resume. Rather, they are very detailed. It is not unusual to look at a CV that is 8, 10, or even 20 pages long. It has an entirely different "look and feel" than a resume.

Should you include dates of employment and education on a resume?

Ninety-five percent of the time the answer is a resounding YES. Dates give your readers a point of reference to understand how your career has progressed. Without dates, a reader cannot determine if you have been with your current employer 11 months or 11 years, and it makes the entire resume confusing.

It is also important to date your education, even if you do not have a four-year degree. Again, it is a good point of reference for your reader and clearly indicates the "beginning" of your career.

The exception to this rule is for over-50 job seekers. If you are in this category of job seekers, refer to the section below which focuses on the specifics of resume writing for over-50 candidates.

Should you include months of employment?

The answer to this question is generally NO. Most readers will not care if you started your current position in May 2000 or November 2000. Furthermore, at some point in the hiring process, you will most likely complete an application where you can share that specific information. The only time that months are recommended on resumes is for younger candidates with much less experience.

Are salary history and salary requirements the same thing?

NO. Salary history is what you have earned in past positions. Salary requirements, on the other hand, are your current compensation goals.

Should you include your salary history or requirements on a resume?

The resume is NOT the appropriate forum for a salary discussion. If, and only if, a prospective employer or recruiter asks for salary information should you provide it, and then, it is most appropriately addressed in your cover letter. In fact, it has been proven in study after study that, even if salary information is requested, you do not need to provide it. If a prospective employer is interested in you, they will contact you regardless of whether or not you supplied that information.

Must you always mail a cover letter with your resume?

YES, YES, YES! When writing your resume you began with your entire career in your hands. You then consolidated everything onto one or two pages to create your resume. Now, to write a powerful cover letter, consolidate your resume into one or two hard-hitting paragraphs that address the SPECIFIC needs of the company to which you are writing.

Well-written cover letters complement your resume and draw the reader's attention to the key points of your career most related to that company's or recruiter's needs. They are an essential component of any job seeker's successful search campaign and can make the difference between an interview and no interview.

To learn to write expert cover letters, refer to this book's companion title, **Best Cover Letters For $100,000+ Jobs** by Wendy S. Enelow (Impact Publications, 2001).

How should you present the fact that you are an "over-50" candidate?

First and foremost, do not "wave a red flag" announcing that you are an over-50 candidate. It's not the very first message you want to communicate to a recruiter or prospective employer. You don't want to lie, nor do you want to misrepresent yourself. However, it is not recommended that you start your resume with a statement such as "Over 30 years of experience ..." If you do, you will almost always eliminate yourself from consideration. The point of your resume is to open doors and get interviews, not tell your entire life story!

Do not kid yourself for one minute. Prospective employers are often concerned about hiring the "older" worker, no matter how well qualified and successful. Therefore, you must be careful in your use of dates. When you write that you graduated from college in 1964, you are immediately communicating the fact that you are an older candidate. In this situation, your best strategy is to include your degree with no dates.

The same thing can be said about your employment experience. If you began your professional career in 1966 and include that date on your resume, again you have inadvertently communicated, "I'm 55+ years old." That may not be the first thing you want to share with a prospective employer! Write your resume to sell your success, knowledge, and expertise, and leave your age behind.

For more information about how to incorporate your older experience into your resume while omitting the dates to avoid "aging" yourself, read the following section.

Should you include ALL of your work experience on a resume?

The answer to this question is a definitive "it depends." If you are 42 years old, then yes, include all of your experience, although you will most likely only briefly summarize your earliest jobs in order to comfortably fit everything onto two pages. However, if you are 58 years old, you have to make some difficult decisions about how far back in your career to go on your resume and whether or not any of the older experience is related to your current objective. This is a personal decision that you will have to make depending on your own specific situation.

It may be that you can find real value in your older experience; value that is relevant to your current career objectives. Perhaps you worked for well-known and well-respected companies, were promoted rapidly, accomplished great things, developed a revolutionary new product, or did something else fantastic. If this is the case, you certainly will want to include that information on your resume. Here are a few sample strategies for including experience from years past without using dates:

PREVIOUS PROFESSIONAL EXPERIENCE:

- Promoted through a series of increasingly responsible management positions with Acceleron Technologies, a $200 million laser products R&D firm.
  (focuses on fast-track career promotion)

- Previous professional experience includes several key positions with IBM, Digital, and Hewlett-Packard.
  (focuses on reputation of your employers)

- Reduced annual staffing costs by 28% in the first year and an additional 12% in the second year while HR Manager for the Chase Manhattan Bank's International Division.
  (focuses on your achievements)

By using these strategies, you are able to highlight the important aspects of your early career without drawing attention to length of employment and age. What's more, you have been up-front in disclosing that you do have previous experience and therefore have been totally above board and not hidden anything. Using one of these strategies will get you off on the right foot with a prospective employer. There is nothing worse than having to defend something you wrote on your resume while you are in an interview!

The Resume Writing Process

Everything in life has a process, and resume writing is no different. If you use the following structured outline, you will find that the task of writing and producing your resume is efficient, faster, and much easier.

1. Open a file in your PC and select a typestyle that (1) you like and (2) is easy to read. Type your name, address, email, and phone numbers (home, office, fax, and cellular). Include your office number only if you are comfortable accepting calls during the day and can speak in confidence. NEVER include your employer's 800 number. Your current employer should not be supporting your job search!

2. Type in all the major headings you will be using (e.g., Career Summary, Professional Experience, Education, Publications, Technology Qualifications).

3. Fill in the information for Education, Publications, Technology Qualifications, Public Speaking, Affiliations, Teaching Experience, and all the other categories EXCEPT Career Summary and Professional Experience. This information is easy to complete, requires little thought, and is generally just a listing of factual information.

4. Type company names, job titles, dates, and locations. Again, this information is easy to complete and will only take you a few minutes.

Now, take a look at how much of your resume you have already completed in just a few short minutes!

5. Write your job descriptions. Start with the very first position you ever held and work forward. The older jobs are easy to write. They're short and to the point, and include only highlights of your most significant responsibilities and achievements. Then, as you work forward, each position requires a bit more text and a bit more thought. Before you know it, you will be writing your current (or most recent) job description. It will take the longest to write, but once it is finished, your resume will be 90% complete.

6. Write your Career Summary. This is the trickiest part of resume writing and can be the most difficult. At this point, you may want to re-read the preceding section in this chapter on writing career summaries. Be sure to highlight your most notable skills, qualifications, and achievements as they relate to your current objectives and create a section that prominently communicates, "This is who I am and this is the value I bring to your organization."

7. Add bold, italics, underlining, and other type enhancements to draw visual attention to notable information. This should include your name at the top of the resume, major headings, job titles, and significant achievements. You may also insert lines and/or boxes to offset key information. But be careful. Overuse of type enhancements will instantly devalue the visual presentation and cloud a prospective employer's initial reaction. If you highlight too much, the resume appears cluttered and nothing stands out, clearly defeating your purpose.

HINT: Using bold print to highlight numbers (e.g., sales growth, profit improvement) and percentages (e.g., cost savings, productivity gains) is a great strategy. Someone picks up your resume and those numbers instantly pop out and grab their attention. You can use this same strategy to highlight other key information such as major clients, major deals and transactions, product names, honors and awards, and more.

8. Carefully review the visual presentation. How does it look? If your resume is two pages, does it break well between pages? Is it easy to read? Does it look professional? Even more important, does it convey the "right" message about who you are? At this point, you may need to adjust your spacing, change to a different typestyle, or make other minor adjustments to enhance the visual presentation.

9. Proofread your resume a minimum of three times. Then have one or two other people proofread it. It MUST be perfect, for nothing less is acceptable. Remember, people are meeting a piece of paper, not you. It MUST project professionalism, peak performance, and perfection.

Getting Started

You've read through all the preceding text of this book and now it's time for you to get started writing your own "best" resume. The very first step in writing a powerful and effective resume that attracts prospective employers and opens doors to new opportunities is to understand why you are the best.

- What is it that you have accomplished, delivered, produced, created, designed, managed, revitalized, or built that demonstrates your knowledge, expertise, and excellence?
- What have you done to positively impact financial performance of a company? Have you reduced operating costs, increased revenues, and improved bottom-line profitability?
- What have you done that's innovative and creative? What have you done to improve overall performance?
- What value do you bring to an organization? Why would someone want to hire you?
- Why are you better and more qualified than other candidates?

To help you answer those questions and more, refer to Appendix B for a series of exercises that will:

1. Help you identify your most significant skills and accomplishments.
2. Help you identify your most notable career achievements.
3. Help you clearly identify your career objectives.
4. Help you link your skills, knowledge, and achievements with your current objectives to create a powerful and winning resume presentation.

Your responses to these exercises are critical, for they are the foundation for everything that you include in your resume, where you include it, and how you include it. Just as important, these activities will help you identify information that you DO NOT want to include in your resume - information that is irrelevant at this point in your career and/or totally unrelated to your current career objectives.

If you follow all the instructions in this chapter and use the following resumes samples to help you write each section, you will be able to write your own "best" resume...a resume that will open doors, get interviews, and help you land your next great opportunity!

4

Best Resume Samples

Painting the "Best Picture"

Throughout this book I've written about the power you have in creating a resume designed to sell you into your next position. What information you include and how you include it is entirely up to you. Your challenge is to write a resume that focuses on your skills, qualifications, and achievements as they relate to your current objectives. You have tremendous flexibility in what you write, how you write it, and how you visually present it. That's what makes resume writing so challenging...there are no set rules!

The resumes that follow are all "real-life" resumes written for "real-life" job seekers, none of whom have earned a four-year college degree. Each resume was written with a specific objective in mind and developed to showcase the talents, achievements, and career successes of each job seeker. Most important, each resume opened doors, generated interviews, and helped land great new jobs!

Now, take the sample words, formats, styles, strategies, and concepts, and use them as the foundation for writing your own powerful resume. The opportunities are there...go get them!

MICHAEL R. BARNHOUSE

mrbarn@arc.org

289 Chester Hills Road • Leister, Pennsylvania 19089 • 614-382-3393

SENIOR EXECUTIVE – BANKING & FINANCIAL SERVICES
US, Asian, European & African Markets

Performance-Driven Business Executive with 20+ years of leadership experience. Dual career paths as both a Senior Banking Executive and a Senior Consulting Partner/Manager. Consistently successful in executing complex start-up, turnaround, and high-growth organizations facing complex regulatory, market, competitive, and operational demands. Dynamic presentation, negotiation, strategic planning, and operating management skills.

PROFESSIONAL EXPERIENCE:

President & Chairman – Nigerian Health Care   1997 to Present

Challenged to professionalize a fledgling operation and build to prominent national status. Recruited a team of professional directors, built relationships with leading medical personnel, and implemented corporate governance systems to define the organization's mission and objectives.

- Guided CEO in developing a strategic initiative to focus on future policy, government relations, and policy development. Currently facilitating implementation of a series of health programs, including the first-ever contract with the Nigerian Federal Government to design, implement, and manage a government-sponsored health initiative.
- Appointed Chairperson of the Community Awareness Program, a massive project to educate the population regarding the disease, its processes and its treatments. Favorably exploited mass-media advertising, marketing, and public service opportunities to extend market reach.
- Member of the Ministerial Advisory Committee to further government relationships.

Managing Director – Amelio State Corporation   1992 to 1996

Recruited by Spencer Stuart to assume full operating responsibility for a government-owned investment and pension plan fund administrator with over one million enrollees. Challenged to restructure and commercialize the organization, reduce inflated operating costs, recruit new management team, upgrade skill levels of workforce, and execute a successful turnaround.

- Achieved/surpassed all performance objectives for the entire operation. Increased FUM from $9 billion to $18 billion over four years and generated $96 million in income.
- Wrote off over $1 billion in assets within the first month (largest in the history of the organization) and effectively managed sensitive media affairs.
- Personally resolved two major problem contracts. Introduced incentives for $1.3 billion construction contract to facilitate early completion, saving over $70 million. Recovered $30 million on non-performing software and IT contract from US company.
- Restructured all manpower requirements, reduced staff from 850 to 450, and slashed annual operating budget by more than $30 million.
- Redesigned all plan administrative affairs, recruited and empowered new management team, oversaw development of streamlined business procedures, and reduced new benefits processing from three weeks to two days.

- Worked closely with major banks and investment firms to reduce Amelio State's fees while strengthening investment returns. Focused long-term investments in low-risk, high-yield markets while reducing reliance on non-performing investment programs. Introduced a new fund with investment choice, the first ever in Korea.

National Partner – Lewis & Dabney   1986 to 1992
International Banking Consultant – Michael Barnhouse & Associates   1983 to 1986

Founded successful international bank consulting firm advising clients on core strategies and operating methodologies in a deregulating Vietnamese banking environment. Broad responsibilities in strategy, operations, marketing, business development, regulatory affairs, and technology.

- Forged strategic alliance with **Tucker Gray** to service major client (Diamond Bank) and authored successful application to obtain Vietnamese banking license (one of only 16 awarded in the country). Subsequently identified joint venture partner to assist client in development of Vietnamese-based insurance company.
- Established joint venture with **Crosby-Davis Press** for the development of a new periodical (*Vietnamese Capital Markets*) to disseminate information and significant developments in capital markets following industry deregulation.
- Structured and negotiated a $120 million financing transaction to fund a major real estate development project for a multinational hotel and resort company.
- Guided local banking institutions to enhance their positioning and lessen the impact of foreign banks entering the Vietnamese market.

Firm was subsequently acquired by Lewis & Dabney in 1986. Retained as a National Partner to expand beyond traditional audit services and provide comprehensive strategic, operating, marketing, and regulatory services to banks and financial institutions throughout the country. Appointed to the International Banking Committee responsible for establishing and directing the firm's Worldwide Banking Practice Group. Major projects included:

- Advised the **Federal Airport Corporation** (government-owned entity operating all Vietnamese airports) on strategies to raise $600 million in funding to support expansion. Consulted with a team of L&D managers and client executives to initiate a fixed-rate Eurobond issue, obtain S&P rating, develop business plan, and solicit investment bankers.
- Retained by a major Vietnamese Bank (**Chen Ho Bank**) to resolve long-standing issues impacting profitability ($120+ million in bad debts, low morale, non-performing leadership, complex business processes). Devoted nine months to a complete restructuring of the institution at the Chairman's request. Developed new strategic plan that facilitated one of the most successful turnarounds in Vietnam's banking history.

Associate Director – Kenyan Bank Ltd.   1981 to 1983

Member of 5-person Senior Executive Team leading the start-up of a new banking operation to service middle-market customers throughout the country. Launched new venture to capitalize upon emerging opportunities resulting from deregulating industry.

- Credited with the successful start-up of the first new trading bank in Kenya in 50 years.
- Authored corporate policies and procedures, designed internal operations, drafted lending and credit policies, recruited/trained staff, and orchestrated country-wide marketing efforts.
- Instrumental in the negotiation and subsequent sale of the institution.

Vice President – Barnett Global Bank – International Division   1970 to 1981

Fast-track promotion through a series of increasingly responsible management positions in London, Brussels, New York, Kuala Lumpur, and Sydney. Specialized in the turnaround of non-performing operations worldwide.

- Revitalized corporate marketing and business development programs in **Paris** for the entire European continent. Redefined marketing strategies and tactical action plans, trained local staff, and generated some of the highest fees that the organization had ever produced.
- Completed successful two-year assignment in **Chicago** managing foreign credit programs for Southeast Asia and Australia. Ranked as the #1 graduate of New York's credit training program.
- Appointed as the youngest International Branch Manager to provide strong turnaround leadership and resolve long-standing credit and loan portfolio issues for the Bank's operations in **Singapore**. Replaced key management, upgraded competencies of 110-person staff, and transitioned market focus from multinational corporations to local exporters. Delivered phenomenal income growth as the fastest growing Barnett branch for five consecutive years.
- Orchestrated the Bank's initial entry into the highly regulated **Australian** market and built the largest foreign bank in the country. Led organization from start-up to $250 million in revenue.
- Developed strong expertise in cash management and liquidity. Lectured before the American Management Association and other prominent organizations on strategies to enhance internal cash management processes and performance.

<u>Early Professional Career</u> with **Luigi Bank** of Rome, Italy. Completed in-depth Bank Operations Training Program at HQ. Promoted and transferred to Ghana, West Africa to manage a volatile banking operation in the midst of a terrorist region. Credited with recruiting and training the first local women to join the Bank's regional workforce.

BOARD APPOINTMENTS:

Chairman of the Board, Parkinson's Disease National Association Ltd. (1997 to Present)
Managing Director, Prince Capital Ltd. – Private Equity Investment Firm (1997 to 1998)
Managing Director & CEO, Amelio Super Corporation (1992 to 1996)
Board Director, Minister Gold Mines Ltd. – Joint Venture with Exxon & Barnett Bank
             (1992 to 1996)
Board Director, Chemical Holdings Ltd. – Publicly Held Lease Finance Company
             (1976 to 1982)
Board Director, Chen Ho Group Ltd. – Second Largest Merchant Bank in Vietnam
             (1976 to 1982)

EDUCATION:

Educated in Australia.

AUSTIN BAKER

bakera@earthlink.com

135 Springtime Road
Agua Dulce, California 91350

661 287-3559
Facsimile: 661 287-3558

PRODUCTION MANAGER / COORDINATOR
Driving Organizational Change, Quality, and Continuous Improvement

Highly creative, meticulous, multitasked professional with strong technical background, providing hands-on leadership, direction, and focus with positive results and outcomes. Expert in analyzing existing operations and implementing strategies, processes, and technologies to improve organizational performance. Possess unique sense of innovation and resourcefulness with proven expertise in devising original solutions to complex problems. Effective troubleshooter whose strengths include:

- < Studio Recording Sessions
- < Project Scheduling/Budgeting/Controls
- < Creative Communications
- < Production Management
- < Equipment Troubleshooting
- < Logistics Management

Outstanding management, communication, and collaborative skills that help get the job done. Excellent retention of information. Hardworking and dependable with a strong work ethic. Work well under pressure without losing control. Understanding of total projects; always completed **on time** and **within budget**. Knowledge in handling difficult people.

Delivered multi-million-dollar improvements in productivity and operating efficiency, cost reduction, and earnings. Strong project management, information technology, human resources, and benchmarking experience. Sharp presentation, negotiation, and team building qualifications. Energetic and decisive business leader able to merge disparate technologies and personnel into a cohesive team-centered unit.

Computer literate: IBM and Mac (totally cross-platform); VisionPoint, Quickbooks, Excel (spreadsheet development); some Access and MS Publisher; MS Word; ProTools Editing.

PROFESSIONAL EXPERIENCE

THE FLAHERTY STUDIOS • Silver Lake, CA
Studio Manager (1994-1998)
Operations Manager (1992-1994)
Assistant Engineer / Supervisor (1990-1992)

1990 - 1998

Multifaceted assignment administering all aspects of production: clients, sessions, technical aspects, bookkeeping, and staff. Interacted with clients and throughout various production phases. Oversaw project operations from start to finish and ensured adherence to deadlines. Worked with production staff and engineers in an extremely fast-paced environment.

Handled entire studio setup: managed 3 assistant engineers and 15 employees, set up micro-phones, prepared recording equipment, retained recording musicians, participated in audio post-production work. Hired and trained studio personnel in studio equipment, terminated staff when necessary. Scheduled all staff (8 a.m. to midnight) for 3 studios and all equipment. Solved problems on technical levels even when engineers were at a loss. Resolved synchronization issues. Coordinated and facilitated work between wiring and equipment personnel.

Contracted singers and musicians for in-house production projects. Represented studio to clients, ensuring their needs were met. Assisted client in defining production goals and establishing parameters. Interacted well with people at different levels: creative, engineering, and difficult people.

Performed bookkeeping duties: A/P, A/R, client billing and collections. Negotiated employee healthcare benefit contract. Filed AFTRA, AF of M contracts, and processed payrolls for those sessions.

BAO BROTHERS, INC. • West Sacramento, CA   1986 - 1989
Bookkeeper
Full-charge bookkeeper.

EDUCATION

Associate of Arts, Computer Programming, Truckee Meadows Community College, Reno, NV
Courses in **Business Administration,** University of Nevada, Reno, NV
Courses in **Audio Engineering,** The Institute of Audio-Video Engineering, Reno, NV

PATRICE K. ALLEN

19 Old County Way
Chappaqua, NY 10514

(914) 453-9099
pkallen@coldrain.com

SENIOR MANAGER: CALL-CENTER & CUSTOMER-SERVICE OPERATIONS

**Fifteen-year record of improving quality, boosting revenue and profitability,
and delivering exceptional customer service and satisfaction.**

Experienced leader of customer-service operations and technology product/service delivery systems. Repeatedly built cohesive teams and achieved high standards of quality and productivity in constantly changing and competitive business environments. Provided turnaround leadership for operations in the US, Canada, Europe, and Asia; restored profitability and boosted revenues. Led essential training, product-development, and business reorganization initiatives. Record of achievements in:

- ✓ Quality & Productivity Measurement & Improvement
- ✓ Revenue & Profit Enhancement
- ✓ Training Program Development
- ✓ Product / Service Development, Testing, Refinement & Roll-out
- ✓ Project Management & Problem-Solving
- ✓ Start-up & Turnaround Operations / Merger Integration

EXPERIENCE AND ACHIEVEMENTS

WORLDWIDE TELECOM, INC., Jersey City, NJ

1984–Present

Senior Manager, Audioconferencing, 1996–Present
Manage 220-employee call-center operation, driving efforts to achieve continuous improvement in customer satisfaction, efficiency, and productivity to thrive in an environment of "doing more with less." Manage $22MM budget in 3 operating areas.

- ✓ **Boosted quality ratings to 99.5%** and maintained throughout mergers, heavy volume increases, and steady turnover of trained staff to higher-level positions in the company. Created true team atmosphere and continuously built staff skills through effective and comprehensive training.
- ✓ **Continuously improved productivity** — in 2002, increased reservations productivity by 26% and call-placement productivity by 53% — without negatively impacting quality.
- ✓ **Established an abundant, high-quality source for corporate personnel development,** as the starting point for all entry-level employees. Annually, promote 25% of employees to higher-level positions within the company.
- ✓ **Led special projects and strategic initiatives that supported business objectives:**

- – **Created highly profitable business unit** from unfocused telemanagement group. Set revenue goals, created training curriculum, realigned staff, aggressively tackled quality issues, drove product refinements, and established management structure and career pathing. Grew from negligible to $10MM revenue without increasing staff, and generated 40% profit.
- – **Turned around faltering Milan center.** Overhauled systems and procedures; improved communication; instituted training programs and cross-training initiatives. Efforts paved the way for revenue growth from $5.4MM in 2000 to $7.2MM in 2001.
- – **Assumed leadership of videoconferencing unit** during protracted search for senior manager. Instituted best business practices; put in place a stable management structure; launched training programs; transformed product development from engineering-driven to customer/market-centric; improved customer communications and satisfaction.
- – **Supported strategic product initiatives** — e.g., netconferencing, with revenue growth from $350K in 1999 to $7.2MM in 2001 — as a key member of the product-strategy team and leader of product testing and service support.

Director, Audioconferencing, 1994–1996
Promoted to lead operations for all of the company's 6 global audioconferencing centers — 3 in the US plus Canada, Milan (Europe), and Singapore. Developed strategic plans for performance improvement and capabilities growth; directly supervised 4 center managers; continued to serve as "resident expert" and troubleshooter for audioconferencing operations worldwide.
- ✓ **Improved call-center quality rating from 95% to 98%.**
- ✓ **Designed and implemented training curriculum and quality measurements** for call-center employees; subsequently expanded to phase 2 training to build on basic skills sets. As a result, employees "hit the ground running" and immediately provide skilled customer assistance.

Manager, Jersey City Audioconferencing, 1990–1994
Managed audioconferencing operations at company's flagship location; also served as troubleshooter/ problem-solver for global centers, stepping in as needed to improve performance and lead special projects.
- ✓ Untangled operational problems within Singapore office and oversaw installation of new computerized reservation system.
- ✓ Directed relocation of Montreal center to new facility.

Manager, Seattle Audioconferencing, 1989–1990
Chosen for clean-up/turnaround assignment at a branch office with a troubled history. Within a few months, restored order and reenergized staff, then focused on business growth.
- ✓ Successfully grew revenues.
- ✓ Spearheaded office relocation from downtown to suburbs to capture significant operational savings.

Manager, Dallas Audioconferencing, 1987–1989
Promoted to challenging management opportunity, directing ground-floor start-up of a new conferencing center in a new market for the company. Launched and completely staffed office; brought operation to productivity and profitability in record time.
- ✓ Generated $1MM in first-year revenue and turned a profit — dramatically outperforming projection of negative profitability and earning company's prestigious "Ace Award" for significant achievement.

Equipment Installation & Service Troubleshooter, 1985–1987

Receptionist, 1984–1985

EDUCATION AND MANAGEMENT DEVELOPMENT

AS Degree, Ocean County College, Toms River, NJ

Disney Management Training, Anaheim, CA

Lessons in Leadership — Tom Peters

Situational Leadership — Ken Blanchard

Corporate Training and Development Series — Corporate Diversity, Legal Context of Management, Preventing Sexual Harassment

PAUL ALLEN SMITH

827 Etowah ~ Royal Oak, MI 48333 ~ 244.999.1007

EXECUTIVE PASTRY CHEF

Breads / Candy / Pastries / Plated Deserts / Sugar Pieces / Chocolate Centerpieces

SUMMARY OF QUALIFICATIONS

➤ Over 20 years experience as a first-rate Pastry Chef.

➤ Excellent general knowledge of kitchen operations from pantry, sauté and broiler to ordering and scheduling.

➤ Launched new eatery employing various pastry concepts.

➤ Executive Pastry Chef for 4-Star hotels and restaurants… Developed menus… Artistically talented.

➤ Controls food & labor costs through planning, purchasing, production, and inventory management control.

➤ Experience in interviewing, training, scheduling, and supervising large staffs.

➤ Establishes rapport easily with all levels of staff, senior management, and guests.

➤ Prepares pastries for numerous venues from private parties to huge banquets serving up to 2,000 people.

➤ Excellent communication and interpersonal skills.

➤ Creative…innovative…team leader…dedicated… organized…detail-oriented…decision-maker…problem-solver…meets deadlines…safety conscious.

PROFESSIONAL EXPERIENCE

OWNER / EXECUTIVE PASTRY CHEF, MAIN STREET BAKERY, Royal Oak, MI   1993 - Present

Launched this retail/wholesale business that has inside service and carryout, as well as handling special orders for area country clubs, hotels, clubs, in addition to Cobo Hall, the Joe Louis Arena, and the Detroit Grand Prix, among others.

• Started from "0," increasing business each year, with last-year revenues topping $800,000.
• Produced large parties for presidential candidates Clinton and Gore when they were campaigning in Michigan. Also, cater parties for the owner of Little Caesars Pizza.
• Establishment has been accident-free since opening, due to strict safety enforcements.

EXECUTIVE PASTRY CHEF, DILLON'S CORONADO BAY, Coronado, CA   1992 - 1993

Provided pastries to two restaurants and a gourmet shop, in addition to supplying huge banquet facilities, accommodating up to 1,000 people. Ran a 24/7 operation and supervised nine employees.

PASTRY CHEF, BACK DOOR RESTAURANT, Washington, D.C.   1991 - 1992
Managed all pastry and bread production in restaurant serving 500 to 700 people per day. Supervised five employees.

- Served President George H.W. Bush and other Washington dignitaries.

PASTRY CHEF, DILLON'S VENTANA CANYON RESORT, Tucson, AZ 1990 - 1991 and 1985 - 1988

- Oversaw three dining rooms, catering service, and banquet facility capable of serving 2,500.

PASTRY CHEF, HOTEL CRESCENT COURT, Dallas, TX   1988 - 1990

- Headed a restaurant, pantry, gourmet shop, club, catering service, and banquet facility.

PASTRY CHEF, THE MANSION ON TURTLE CREEK, Dallas, TX   1982 - 1985

- Ran a 24/7 operation consisting of a restaurant and a banquet facility.

PASTRY COOK, THOMPSON FOOD ENTERPRISES, Harper Woods, MI   1979 - 1982

- Oversaw pastry-making facilities for four restaurants, catering service, and banquet facility.

PASTRY COOK, FRENCH GOURMET, Farmington Hills, MI   1979

- In charge of all cake batters and French pastries.

EDUCATION

The International Pastry Arts Center, received diplomas in *Breads, Doughs, Candy,*
        Chocolate and Sugar - Studied under Albert Kumin - former White House pastry chef

The Culinary Institute of America, received diplomas in *Advanced Baking* and
        Cake Decorating

The Wilton School of Cake Decorating, received diploma in *Master's Course*

ANTHONY P. ZORBA

777 Monteray Drive
Farmington, MI 48333
242.444.2244
apzorba@arc.org

CONSTRUCTION INDUSTRY EXECUTIVE

VICE PRESIDENT OF CONSTRUCTION / PROJECT MANAGER
LAND DEVELOPMENT MANAGER / CONSTRUCTION MANAGER

"Bottom-Line" Industry Expert with over 20 years experience in Design, Engineering, and Construction. Strong general management, mentoring, and team leadership skills. Decisive, determined, and profit-driven. Tough, but fair negotiator. Able to identify and implement strategies to reduce costs, increase revenues, strengthen customer relationships, improve business processes, and drive profitable growth. Expertise includes:

- Project Proposals & Presentations
- Contract Administration
- Subcontract Administration
- Trade Negotiations
- Legal Requirements & Permits
- Residential Construction
- Project Control/Management
- Purchasing & Materials
- Field Project Management
- CPM Scheduling
- Land Development/Planning
- Planned Communities
- Estimating/Bidding
- Construction
- Licensing
- Budgeting
- Architecture
- Home Building

PROFESSIONAL EXPERIENCE

BELVEDERE CONSTRUCTION, Southfield, MI
SENIOR PROJECT MANAGER, 1992 - Present

Handle all aspects of on-site construction projects, using critical path method, to include sales, marketing, land development, meeting with engineers and government agencies, estimating and bidding contracts, approving all bills, and overseeing progress billing related to residential and commercial projects. Supervise five people.

- Direct projects from initial planning and proposal stage throughout the entire design, engineering, and construction cycle, to staffing and facilities start-up. Projects include:
    - Total handling of a 50-unit, multi-family condominium complex.
    - Designing and building a $2 million retail center.
    - Heading the design and construction of a $500,000 retail center renovation.
    - Designing and building single-family homes ranging in price from $300,000 to $1 million.
- Conduct feasibility studies of undeveloped property with land planner for best use, and oversee due diligence issues.

ZORBA CONSTRUCTION COMPANY, Novi, MI
PROJECT MANAGER / SUPERINTENDENT, 1980 - 1992

Started out in family business with small projects. Over time, given bigger, more complicated projects with progressively increased responsibility, ending up as Project Manager/Superintendent. Performed estimating and coordinated bidding process for residential and commercial projects. Worked with land development and was responsible for all on-site supervision. Supervised 10 people.

- Researched, analyzed, developed, and implemented quality control measures that reduced the punch list by 50%.
- Investigated computerized scheduling, implementing a system that used the critical-path method.
- Oversaw the following projects from conception to completion:

  o Built a turnkey $6 million, 5-story medical facility, a $2.5 million design-built medical facility and an outpatient surgical center. Directed cost estimating, design review, CPM scheduling, change order review, on-site inspection, tenant relations, permitting, and on-site construction.
  o Handled all facets, including sales and marketing, for a 100-unit, multi-family project.
  o Instrumental in contracting and building one of the state's first tri-water heating and cooling systems, a closed-loop heat pump system which integrates fire protection.
  o Involved in the design and build-out of a Magnetic Resonance Imaging Center (MRI), the first independent one in the state of Michigan.
  o Design-built single-family housing ranging from $300,000 to $1 million.
  o Directed tenant improvement projects ranging from $100,000 to $3 million, and the building of a 100-unit, multi-family condominium complex.

EDUCATION

Construction Engineering, LAWRENCE INSTITUTE OF TECHNOLOGY, Southfield, MI

Terri McGrath

31 Lawrence Green, Lawrenceville, NJ 08648
(609) 771-3872 Home ▪ terrimcgrath@msn.com

PROFILE

☑ Versatile, creative and highly motivated **Design Management Consultant** with a passion for home textiles, furnishings, and interiors.
☑ Graduate Member of the Interior Arrangement and Design Association (3+ years).
☑ Results-oriented with strengths in project organization, budgeting, and strategic planning.
☑ Great interpersonal skills – talent for assessing needs and solving problems. Resourceful.
☑ Computer skills: Win NT/98, MS Word, Outlook, DOS, Internet, proprietary databases.

CREATIVITY & DESIGN

Design Management Consultant, Intelligent Interiors, Princeton, NJ   1999 – present

▪ Founded and currently manage the planning, development, and promotion of a residential room arrangement / space planning consulting business. Gained expertise through professional programs offered by the Interior Arrangement and Design Association (IADA).

▪ Create and implement unique and solutions-focused home furnishings arrangements, meeting clients' personal preferences and needs. Conceive and draft floor plans, create design proposals and determine all components of interior re-arrangement strategy: color schemes, furnishings, floor coverings, lighting, window treatments, and accessories.

▪ Research available accessories and furnishings, consistent with clients' budgets and priorities, to complement each room's new design concept. Recommend merchandise for the client to buy, selecting the best combination of style, quality, price, and availability.

PLANNING & ORGANIZATION

Closing Processor – Settlement Dept., Abstracts Corp., Lawrenceville, NJ   1992 – present

▪ Promoted from entry-level position to key role (primary loan closing processor) as this multi-million dollar title company grew to more than double its daily volume. Selected by company president to be in charge of department in his absence.

▪ Successfully interface with real estate brokers, attorneys, realtors, mortgage companies, staff, and government officials, as well as clients, in compiling, reviewing, and submitting financial and legal documents for closings in fast-paced, deadline-driven environment.

▪ Utilize finely honed multi-tasking capabilities, organizational skills, and diplomatic customer service abilities to personally generate 85% of daily in-house processings (8 – 15 per day) for up to $2 million in residential properties, as well as multi-million dollar commercial properties.

EDUCATION & TRAINING

Color Workshop, Interior Arrangement & Design Assoc. Conference, Chicago – 2001, 2002
Interior Arrangement Certificate, IADA – 1999
A.A., Liberal Arts, Mercer County Community College, West Windsor, NJ – May 1999

▪ ▪ ▪

ROB MINAKER

139 Carson Way, Ottawa, Ontario K1G 4S4
Home: (613) 279-2341 Email: rminakaer@sympatico.ca

ENGINEERING TECHNOLOGIST - MANUFACTURING
Specialising in Mechanical Design & Applications for Photonics

Self-directed professional with over 6 years experience in advanced manufacturing fields. High-energy self-starter who takes great pride in work. Excellent ability to quickly diagnose and analyse requirements for tool design. Exceptional interpersonal skills and effective customer relations. Skilled in assessing user needs, establishing project specifications, evaluating hardware/software solutions, then implementing electro-mechanical designs and applications.

Valuable team player who works closely with engineers to improve manufacturing processes. Core competencies include:

- Manufacturing Assembly
- Machine Programming, Operating, Inspecting
- Tool Design & Manufacturing
- Photonic & Optical Devices

- Research & Development
- Model Shop & Prototype Experience
- Machining & Design
- Process Control & Optimization

Photonics for Telecommunications Certificate

COMPUTER SKILLS
- C Language - Basic - CADKEY - Mastercam - Pro-Eng
- MS PowerPoint - MS Word and Excel - MS DOS

MACHINING SKILLS
- CNC Milling Machines - Lathes - Surface Grinders - Drill Presses - Hand Tools

EMPLOYMENT HISTORY

1999-2003, SURF PRECISION (A GSI Lumonics Co.), Ottawa, ON
Model Shop Machinist

Manufacturing Environment: Service and product development related to R&D of optics, optical coating, subassemblies, and optical testing. Major customers were private telecom companies, the Canadian Space Agency, and several educational institutions. 100 employees on site.

- Designed a prototype tool that increased productivity with consistent quality and repeatability.
- Analysed critical components and decided on the best way to manufacture.
- Controlled total manufacturing process from material selection to finished product.
- Learned specific requirements for optical shaping and coating.
- Shared expertise with co-workers to solve problems and improve tool design.

Sample Achievement
Challenge: A certain fixture in the manufacturing process was creating unnecessary delays and inefficiencies. Action: On my own initiative, I analysed the problem, then spent four hours designing and building a better fixture from scratch using an original concept while striving for simplicity. Result: My fixture minimized the error and handling of equipment (e.g., minimized alignment problems and deburring) that was used for the optical coating machine. It produced a far superior product. Manufacturing time was reduced by 20%, allowing machinists to work on other productive tasks.

1999, CAMFORD INDUSTRIES, Ottawa, ON
CNC Programmer/Machinist

- Quickly learned the variations of requirements for manufacturing tools used in telecommunications and aerospace industries.
- Selected to set up milling centers and quality control to increase production on the evening shift.
- Questioned customers on their needs and designed/modified hardware to meet their requirements.
- Assisted with troubleshooting, programming, and set-up challenges.

Sample Achievement

Challenge: Engineering was trying to develop a fixture for aligning a large precision component. Their intention was to make the part as quickly and repeatable as possible. Action: With my shop floor experience, I could see that this design would take too long to produce. Result: Simplified fixture design and minimized costly set-up problems while maintaining accuracy and repeatability.

1997-98, ALGONQUIN UNIVERSITY, Ottawa, ON
Model Shop Machinist

- Adapted to prototype requests that came from all areas of the engineering faculties.
- Replicated new tools from worn-out parts with minor improvements.
- Designed a sundial on the CAD system and then manufactured on the CAM system.
- Recruited for special physics project because of attention to detail and experience. Supervised two junior staff.
- Interfaced directly with the customer to understand requirements and ensure satisfaction. Assisted in R&D projects.

Sample Achievement

Challenge: Had to get a tool into a deep corner to cut the surface of a contour. No such tool was available. Action: Through programming and tooling, designed and built a special tool to do the job. Result: The client implemented my solution into their production line.

1995-96, NORTHLAND NETWORKS, Ottawa, ON
Model Shop Machinist (Co-op)

- Co-op program to manufacture telecommunications hardware as well as some broadband prototype components.
- Learned to create a variety of components for different types of precision molds.
- Interfaced with internal customers on their needs and manufactured or modified components.
- Learned the specific requirements needed in a research and development environment.
- Assisted in R&D projects.

PROFESSIONAL DEVELOPMENT

NORTHERN COLLEGE

Photonics for Telecommunications Certificate (*in progress*)	2001 – 2002
Laser Safety in the Workplace	2002
Manufacturing Engineering Technology Diploma	1996
Machinist	1995

MICHAEL R. REYNOLDS

entrepreneurforsuccess@aol.com

12 Kenzie Boulevard
Dallas, Texas 78993

Home: 581-990-8735
Office: 581-990-8709

ENTREPRENEUR / DEALMAKER / BUSINESS OPPORTUNIST
With Strong Operating Management Experience & Success

Dynamic entrepreneurial career as *President/CEO* of numerous new ventures, joint ventures, franchises, acquisitions, and investment opportunities that have generated total revenues of more than $3 billion and profits nearing $100 million. Combines vision and an innate talent for identifying prime opportunities with the ability to build operations, develop top-performing management teams, and build strong and sustainable market positions. Diverse industry experience. Core leadership qualifications include:

- Public & Private Investment
- Transactions Structuring & Negotiation
- Asset & Portfolio Optimization
- Risk Analysis & Leveraging
- Road Show Presentations
- Franchising, Leasing, & Consulting

- Multi-Site Operations / P&L Management
- Business Development, Marketing, & Advertising
- Strategic Alliances & Partnerships
- Real Estate Acquisition & Development
- Revitalizations, Turnarounds, & Divestitures
- Organizational Design & Development

Featured in People Magazine for entrepreneurial achievement.
Winner of the 1994 Keystone Award for fastest growing real estate firm of the year.

PROFESSIONAL EXPERIENCE:

President / CEO　　　**THE REYNOLDS COMPANIES, INC.**　　　1998 to Present
Privately held investment company

Founded firm to invest in a variety of public and private companies in the telecommunications, Internet, dot com, biotechnology, and consumer goods and services industries.

- To date, delivered an average 28% return on investment portfolio.
- Invested in a 5-site food service franchise, redesigned all core business and service operations, reduced costs and improved profitability by 45%. Doubled ROI in one year.
- Leveraged investments in several private placements and non-traditional financings with projected returns of better than 20%.

President / CEO　　　**THE REYNOLDS ALE COMPANY**　　　1995 to 1997
Start-up niche consumer product venture

Conceived a niche consumer product – Eagle Peak Ale – to "ride the coattails" of nationally known comedian. Launched a multi-year market research effort to evaluate the opportunity, obtained trademark, secured bank funding, negotiated manufacturing agreement with The Miller Brewing Company and launched new venture.

- Built trademark from concept into a $275 million company shipping 15 million bottles a year sold through 275 distributors in 32 states. Achieved unprecedented industry success.
- Paid off start-up expenses in 45 days to build a debt-free company with substantial profits.
- Licensed trademark to clothing manufacturer to produce t-shirts, hats, jackets, and other novelty items, contributing a 12% increase to annual revenues.
- Created the entire advertising, marketing, and product promotion portfolio for the product, including design of bottles, packaging, shipping cases, and all point-of-purchase materials.
- Hired investment banker to prepare offering memoranda, led road show presentations and positioned company for profitable PI. Transaction halted following industry decline.

| President / CEO | **THE REYNOLDS ORGANIZATION, INC.** | 1989 to 1998 |

Commercial real estate & business brokerage

Identified tremendous opportunity in the retail, commercial, and industrial real estate industry in the Denver metro area and launched new venture. Specialized in leasing, construction management, property sales, real estate consulting, and M&A transactions. Client base included national and international companies (e.g., McDonalds, Safeway, USPS, Mail Boxes Etc.)

- Grew to one of the most active and aggressive companies in the Denver market with up to $100 million in annual transactions (126% annual growth) with only 12 employees.
- Over 10 years, orchestrated 1,000+ transactions generating total revenues of over $1 billion.
- Ranked as the 10th largest commercial real estate brokerage in the Denver metro region.
- Expanded into the franchise consulting industry providing expertise in site selection, franchise sales, and franchise operations.
- Presented with, and accepted, an outstanding financial offer for the sale of The Reynolds Organization in 1998.

| President / CEO | **FISCHER FOOD SYSTEMS** | 1977 to 1988 |

Entrepreneurial restaurant venture

Launched first entrepreneurial venture at the age of 22. Negotiated $45,000 in financing from a local bank, set up the entire operation, and opened the doors.

- Built company from concept to $2 million in profitable revenues within first two years.
- Offset seasonality of business with the start-up of a wholesale division which manufactured and distributed to 125 restaurants, supermarkets, drugstores, and convenience stores throughout the region.

Subsequently expanded into the full-service restaurant business through a combination of start-up, franchise and joint venture opportunities. Directed every facet of each business, from design and construction to menu planning, staffing, marketing, advertising, and daily food service operations.

- Built a portfolio of 35 restaurants over an 11-year period with an average of 10-15 operating simultaneously. Generated annual revenues of $7-8 million with profits averaging 42%.
- Reconfigured portfolio to meet changing market demands and delivered an average 22% ROI on all divestitures.

EDUCATION: **AMERICAN UNIVERSITY**, Washington, DC
Business & Finance

PRESS COVERAGE:

- Featured in *The Washington Post, The Washington Business Journal, The Washingtonian Magazine, The Washington Intowner, Nation's Restaurant News, Beverage Industry Today, Beverage World, The Barley Corn Magazine, The Louisiana News Star, The Raleigh News & Observer,* and *The Prince George's Journal.*
- Appeared on more than 50 radio and television programs across the country.

BELLA DORNO

25481 Crocker Avenue   Downey, California 90242   323 798-1418

EXECUTIVE ADMINISTRATIVE OFFICER
PERSONAL EXECUTIVE ADMINISTRATIVE ASSISTANT
Driving Organizational Change, Quality, and Continuous Improvement

Meticulous, detailed, multitasked professional with experience planning and directing executive-level administrative affairs and support to Boards of Directors and senior management. Combines strong planning, organizational, and communications skills with the ability to independently plan and direct high-level business affairs.

Background encompasses managing cross-functional business affairs for small and large service organizations, providing hands-on leadership, direction, and focus with positive results and outcomes. Proactive in analyzing existing operations and implementing strategies, processes, and technologies to improve organizational performance. Possess unique sense of innovation and resourcefulness with proven expertise in devising original solutions to complex problems. Effective troubleshooter whose strengths include:

< Administrative Policies and Procedures	< Regulatory Reporting and Communications
< Board of Directors Meetings	< Executive Office Management
< Facilities Management	< Confidential Correspondence and Data
< Budgeting and General Accounting	< Special Project Management
< Purchasing and Vendor Negotiations	< Customer Communications and Liaison Affairs

Professional and articulate; work well with all levels of management in a professional, diplomatic, and tactful manner. Delivered improvements in productivity and operating efficiency, cost reduction, and earnings. Sharp presentation, negotiation, and team building qualifications. Outstanding interpersonal skills. Energetic and decisive business leader able to merge disparate technologies and personnel into a cohesive team-centered unit. Hardworking, dependable, trustworthy. Dedicated with a strong work ethic.

Proficient in the use of Word 2000, Excel 2000, and Access 2000. Experienced with shorthand and machine transcription.

PROFESSIONAL EXPERIENCE

EXECUTIVE ADMINISTRATIVE ASSISTANT   2001- Present
Downey Bank & Trust – Downey, CA

High-profile, executive-level administrative position supporting the Executive Vice President / Chief Lending Officer and other top management personnel throughout the organization. Scope of responsibility is diverse and includes Board affairs, customer communications, special events, regulatory reporting, and executive administration (assemble loan packages, collect reports, set appointments, keep calendar, screen calls).

- Executive liaison between Chairman, senior management, and employees to plan, schedule, and facilitate a broad range of corporate initiatives, company operations, and large-scale business functions. Communication is of the utmost importance in order to function independently and be self-starting in implementation.
- Built rapport with all departments and all branches. Recognized as principal consultant.
- Handle confidential operating and financial information; maintain corporate records and minutes.
- Maintain/update files for regulatory review, oversight, and approval.

- Organize all bank-sponsored projects:
    - American Cancer Society: Heart Walk, Relay for Life: selected as co-team captain, recruit people to participate, coordinate fundraising.
    - Fourth of July Parade: assist with float decoration, participate in annual parade.
    - Office holiday party: serve on the committee to organize and facilitate all activities, handle invitations.
- **Several commendations** from President and Board of Directors.

College Assistant, Communications Department   2001
Mission College, Mission, CA

Obtained significant experience in primary research; very resourceful in researching data and developing primary and secondary sources for Department Chair / Professor. Aided with brochure creation for the Communications Department. Provided general office support. Tabulated and recorded grades.

Administrator   1993 - 2001
Various community activities in Downey, CA

- Participated in reading programs at elementary and junior high schools.
- Acted as Recording Secretary at Franklin Roosevelt Elementary School Site Council Meetings.
- Planned and organized social events for high school sports team.
- Designed flexible administrative systems and processes for dissemination of reports to parents of confirmation students at Christ Lutheran Church. Transitioned from manual operations to complete automation.

Executive Assistant / Administrative Assistant   1990 - 1993
Sumitomo Bank of California, Business Development Offices, Los Angeles, CA

Executed complex administrative duties for Executive Vice President. Assisted in budget planning and monitored/analyzed monthly operating statement. Compiled reports using various research sources. Widely recognized as information source on executive policies and procedures as well as general personnel policies. Administered all personnel functions for office staff.

Executive Assistant   1979 - 1990
Crocker National Bank, Los Angeles, CA

Managed confidential correspondence, appointments, meetings, and schedules. Personally planned and coordinated bank and inter-company meetings. Performed executive administrative duties as outlined under current position.

EDUCATION

Currently pursuing **Associate of Arts, Business Information Management**
California State University, Los Angeles, CA

Diploma, Executive Secretarial Program
Patricia Stevens Career College and Finishing School, Milwaukee, WI

Numerous AIB Courses, Fred Pryor Seminars, and Internal Training Classes

Stella Faulkner

Senior-Level Executive ● Consumer Products ● Business Development

Executive Profile

A visionary executive with stellar record of successfully and consistently creating profits, fostering innovation, securing alliances, and managing change. Directly involved in every aspect of development, sales, and management of multi-million-dollar consumer goods manufacturers and finance firms.

Produce $50 to $60 million in annual sales; manage additional $70 to $80 million. Use cross-discipline background in finance and top-level sales to develop and implement profit-driven initiatives that open new markets, create new brands, reduce costs, and increase quality.

Command unmatched respect, clearly communicating a vision, reducing expense and time of execution, achieving goals consistently ahead of schedule, and increasing staff performance and allegiance to the highest levels.

Learn quickly, listen attentively, and act decisively, always accomplishing more than competitors, consistently creating competitive barriers to entry, and achieving extreme competitive advantage.

Areas of Expertise

- Top-tier key account sales development, strategy, and management
- Core management team operations...corporate change management
- Business creation and development...profit and loss oversight
- Vertical manufacturing configuration plans...merchandising strategies
- Joint venture / strategic alliance / acquisition identification and negotiation

Career Development

TEXTILE SOURCING, INC. (TSI), NEW YORK, NY   1992 to present
Executive Vice President / Vice President of Sales

TSI is a Fortune 1000 domestic/international (Mexico) vertical private-label knitwear/textile manufacturer selling to blue-chip manufacturers and retailers. Key customers include Nike, Adidas, Puma, Reebok, Guess, Polo, Patagonia, Calvin Klein, Gap, Old Navy, Banana Republic, Lands End, JC Penney, Target, and Eddie Bauer.

TSI is considered the industry leader, providing the most diversified range of products, quality, and services. Current revenues have topped $140 million, up from $35 million when hired nine years ago. Company employs 2,000 non-union workers and owns/operates all factories (12 in Pennsylvania, North Carolina, Virginia, and Mexico).

Manage entire company's P&L—directly for sales/marketing, and indirectly for manufacturing. Oversee $5 million to $10 million acquisition/capital improve-ment budget and $3 million sales/ marketing budget. Report to CEO.

● **KEY INITIATIVE**

Spearheaded TSI's transformation from a basic commodity producer into a full-service, vertical, diversified knitwear producer, creating the ability to win business and maintain/grow net margins.

In 1993, created a completely vertical environment that allowed every aspect of process, from design and conception, to finished product production, to be completed efficiently and offer customer value-added products and services.

Preserved TSI's core manufacturing base while providing value-added services that customers would normally seek elsewhere. Successfully insulated TSI from powerful commodity-based competition and created an agile one-stop-shop.

**122-77 Locust Ave., Auburndale, NY 11358   ●   phone: 718-488-9826
cell: 212-666-9009   ●   fax: 718-488-3232   ●   e-mail: textiles@arc.org**

Career Development (cont'd.)

- ### PERFORMANCE IN CORPORATE GROWTH / STRATEGIC AFFILIATIONS

Increased sales by over $60 million, creating net profits of over $8 million by creation of a cross-divisional strategic alliance. Personally nurtured and negotiated acquisition and managed configuration of two manufacturing facilities to manufacture broad range of products for Warnaco, a company that owns and controls, among other entities, Calvin Klein Jeans, CK underwear, Chaps, and Speedo.

Created hyper-growth during a period of competitor attrition, and increased net profits by over 50% by changing primary product / manufacturing focus from commodity-based product that inhibited TSI's ability to control pricing, and profit structure to full package production and reconfigured manufacturing.

In one year, created a $14 million+ business with Itochu and Nichiman—two of the largest trading companies in the world—by opening new markets for "Made in USA" products. This was during a time of extreme competitor attrition.

Created foundation for what is now a $30 million annual business producing a net profit exceeding 12%, by developing a Nike partnership to satisfy a number of specific product needs.

Produced blue-chip affiliations to develop customer-base stability for creation of minimal risk / maximum reward growth and capital investment. Identified industry leaders in several different markets, i.e. Active (NIKE), designer (Nautica), private-brand retail (Gap) etc., and worked a plan to win and secure their business. Initial affiliations fostered an avalanche of blue-chip customers including Tommy Hilfiger, Lands End, Calvin Klein, Adidas, Reebok, Guess, and Patagonia.

Added new sales of over $12 million, profits of $1.5 million, and additional manufacturing capacity of over 20,000 dozen/week by leading and closing an acquisition initiative for a Tultex textile factory and a Sara Lee sewing facility. Sales and profits continue to grow.

- ### PERFORMANCE IN COST REDUCTION / PROCESS IMPROVEMENT

Created an advantage of over $1.35 million in annual cost savings by using futures markets and negotiating skills to create a hedging program that saved, on average, $.05 per pound over competitors' buying ability.

Reduced manufacturing costs over 60% by building TSI's first Mexican manufacturing facility (pre-NAFTA). Led the move and executed the site selection.

Personally wrote over $60 million in annual business that did not require payment of sales commission (no reps used).

Decreased product development costs by 30%, and reduced unfocused, scattered, and costly product development cycle time—from 60-day average to less than 30 days—by eliminating the need for outside contractors, hiring a development manager, and molding a professional and effective development project team with complementary but diverse talents.

Increased sales by over $20 million over two years by creation of an incentive program that increased sales staff productivity.

Streamlined production-control reporting, providing extraordinary visibility for customers, and leading to almost no attrition of the customer base.

122-77 Locust Ave., Auburndale, NY 11358 • phone: **718-488-9826**
cell: 212-666-9009 • fax: **718-488-3232** • e-mail: **textiles@arc.org**

Career Development (cont'd.)

SWEATERS, ETC., NEW YORK, NY   **1990 to 1992**
Owner/Partner

$15 million domestic sweater manufacturer with mass-level and moderate- price junior and missy market customer base, Kmart, Wal-Mart, Costco, Mervyns, and Target. Employed 15, reporting directly to two partners.

Increased volume to $15 million from $5 million after acquired 33% interest in company in 1990. Sold interest in 1992.

SWARTHMORE BROKERAGE	**1984 to 1990**
Executive Vice President / General Partner	1987
Vice President, Sales	1985
Broker	1984

Money management and brokerage firm with international presence, specializing in managed futures and income fund creation / management.

As EVP, managed all sales functions and product development, overseeing a $2 million marketing and product development budget. Company had over $750 million under management and employed over 55 staff, all reporting to EVP.

Raised over $200 million in capital, and increased bottom line 20% by creating public and private investment funds (futures, equity, and equipment leasing instruments). Led teams working with Big Eight accounting firms and law firms to create registration statements and complete registration process.

Introduced the use of futures as a legitimate tool to effectively hedge commodity price variations for institutional use in the municipal markets. Won contract with Brooklyn Union Gas to use propane futures market to hedge price risk. Broke ground for public utilities acceptance of these markets/techniques as a risk-reduction strategy, and subsequently won several other multi-million-dollar hedging programs.

Conceived HMRI fund, one of the first medical equipment leasing funds, which purchased and leased stationary and mobile MRI units. Product produced an average return of over 14% as well as residual income. Value of the equipment sold at end of fund's life created a $9 million gain, increasing that year's profits by over 100%.

CATES AND JOHNSON   **1983 TO 1984**
Full-service brokerage firm.
Managed commercial hedging programs for petroleum concerns, reporting to the VP of commercial accounts.

Education

George Washington University, 1979 to 1982
Majored in Biology and Marketing

Professional

- Featured in the *Wall Street Journal* and *USA Today*
- Regular commentator on CNBC during Swarthmore tenure
- Keynote speaker at numerous finance and fashion industry conferences
- Held Series 7, 3, and 63 licenses

122-77 Locust Ave., Auburndale, NY 11358 • **phone: 718-488-9826**
cell: 212-666-9009 • **fax: 718-488-3232** • **e-mail: textiles@arc.org**

CAMILLO CASTELLI

123 Kennedy Street
Rocklin CA 95677
Email: camillocastelli@coldrain.com

Tel/Fax: 91 6609 0935
Business: 91 6609 3434
Mobile: 91 3979 1678

GENERAL MANAGER · PRESIDENT · CEO · PROJECT DIRECTOR

Clarity of vision, business acuity, and a personal passion for achieving results characterize personal performance over an impressive 20-year career progressing from trade apprentice to CEO-level roles. Competitive by nature, with a "big picture" focus that complements strategic and analytical talents for ongoing cost containment and process optimization. Outstanding track record in start-ups, joint ventures, and turnarounds; adept in managing multi-million-dollar technology projects, and weathering the turbulence and severity of today's global economic climate. An accomplished public speaker, team manager, and change agent-inspirational and energetic. Intuitively value human dynamics; skilled in building bridges, networks, and partnerships, uniting disparate views, and turning around stalled projects. Backed by a distinguished network of influential and senior-level business figures and politicians.

Key Credentials Include:

- Project Planning & Implementation
- Multi-Million Dollar Budget Management
- Contract Negotiations & Management
- Strategic Planning & Scheduling
- Infrastructure Modeling
- Business & Market Expansion
- Project Financing

- Outsourcing
- Human Resources Management
- Shareholder/Stakeholder Improvements
- Merger/Acquisitions/Alliances
- Team Building & Mentoring
- Cost Containment
- Customer Relationship Management

- Project Turnarounds
- Executive Level Staffing
- Revenue Generation
- Information Systems
- State-of-the-Art Electronic Technologies

Attuned to core business disciplines of Finance, Marketing, Sales, Engineering, Technology, Operations, and Logistics.

EXPERIENCE CHRONOLOGY

FSH INCORPORATED   1994-Present
Industry leader in fare collection and telecommunications equipment software, manufacturing, and implementations. Major clients include government, transport operators, banks, road tolling companies, and retailers.

Branch Manager and Legal Representative, FSH Inc. Italy (1999-Present)

Pioneered the establishment of an Italian company to support predicted revenues of •277.5 million stemming from the [then] newly secured contract to implement the Rome Integrated Smart Card Ticketing System. Despite the difficulties posed by legal challenges from unsuccessful tenders, no infrastructure or offices in Italy, and awkward work visa and permit administration, quickly established an influential network in diplomatic and political circles to fast-track each process, consolidate activities, and overcome operational obstacles.

Upon the successful establishment of the Italian presence, launched joint venture with the multinational SMK Corporation to form LRX-a company created to facilitate international operations and expansion. Considered an outstanding operational and logistical success, the Rome prototype is now seen as a formal template for future development into San Francisco, Singapore, and new projects globally.

Continuing to oversee the profitable management of the company, assumed multiple roles as Project Manager for the Rome Smart Card Project, and Operations Manager and Marketing Manager for ITS, as well as line managing human resources, call center, maintenance, and help desk and implementation functions.

Benchmarks & Milestones:

- **Selected by Board of Directors to assume CEO-level role** of Branch Manager and Legal Representative (institore e rapresentante legale) of FSH Incorporated's Italian Branch.
- **Within 8 months** of the contract signing, the trial system was developed and accepted by the client ATAC-Rome's public transport provider. Design, development, and installation works met the •44.3 million budget.
- **Identified additional revenue generating opportunities**, personally negotiating two lucrative, 8-year maintenance and upgrade contracts of •36 million with BNBD's General Manager.

FSH INCORPORATED - continued

- **Elevated market awareness** via a corporate marketing communications program generating intense interest from Greece, Austria, Germany, and Italian regions. Presented at transport conferences, and fielded inquiries from banks, government officials, highway-toll companies, IT engineering houses, and transport operators.
- **Protected company against any claims** made on the •27.7 million project deposit, by successfully negotiating extension to contract end date.
- **Strategically planned product expansion**, enlisting full company support for initiatives to propel the Smart Card to prominence as the standard card across Italy. As part of this full outsourcing agreement designed to assume the management of all ticketing business for the public transport operator, drove progress to the next level for taxicabs and parking in the City of Rome.
- **Championed a hierarchal human resources structure**, replacing expatriate executive staff with local executives to facilitate local employment and create a long-term, committed management team.
- **Delivered 10% operating profit** in 2002, slicing 25% from operating expenditures in 2nd quarter 2002. Current revenues are •19.4 million annually.
- **Managed manufacturing in Belgium and Perth**, and system engineering in Belgium, Perth, Melbourne, Hong Kong, and Rome, as well as overseeing worldwide activities.
- **Introduced BCMANSO Bank to company** and initiated a lucrative project financing deal for •44.4 million.

Project Manager, Special Assignment (1998-1999)

Hand-picked by CEO to contain rapidly escalating and negative publicity surrounding a corrosive acid vandalism issue that had quickly prompted steep declines in share prices.

- Triumphed over lack of resources, impossible deadlines, and disparate professional agendas, to establish a cohesive Disaster Recovery Operation Unit with a staff of 80 in just 9 days.
- Establishing a makeshift assembly line in the management car park, successfully located and transported rare and out-of-stock spare parts, and, as an extraordinary byproduct, generated $4 million in revenues.

Project Manager (System Development and Integration), Sydney Ferries, Australia (1998-1999)

Spiraling budget blowouts and long-overdue deadlines provoked a call to action from the Chief Operations Officer to wind down the $6 million Sydney Ferries project immediately. Settled quickly into project management role, assessing staff required for wind-down process, and commissioning engineers to produce details of outstanding works that provided the blueprint for dismantling and eliminating non-essential personnel from the site. Facilitated project shut-down within 10 weeks.

- **General Manager, Regional Operations (Victoria, Australia)** (1994-1998)
- Reported to: COO. Budget: $4 million. 10-year outsourcing contract generating $AUD 8 million annually.
- Won management praise for delivering project on time and budget, where 5 previous managers had failed in establishing the operation in tandem with the main project.

BROWNS ELECTRIC INC., San Francisco   1982-1994
Electrical engineering and contracting company specializing in communications and manufacturing.

Major Contracts Supervisor	(1990-1994)	**Team Leader**	(1986-1987)
Installation Supervisor	(1987-1990)	**Apprentice**	(1982-1986)

EDUCATION

Bachelor of Business (Business Management)   **A-Grade Electrical Mechanic**
San Francisco State University (2 years complete)   California Institute of Trades

Hundreds of hours devoted to ongoing professional development throughout career. Includes formal trade qualifications and courses as a Registered Electrical Contractor, Electrical Contracting, Estimating & Supervision, Legal & Accounting Principles for Electrical Contractors, Electronics, and Train the Trainer.

HENRY JASPER
hjpp2@arc.org

278 Meyers Drive
Fort Myers, FL 33299

Phone: 954-398-2939
Cell: 703-661-9903

SENIOR EXECUTIVE PROFILE

Business Development / New Ventures / Mergers / Acquisitions / Industry Roll-Ups
Emerging Information, Telecommunications & Internet Technologies
Bilingual in English & Spanish

Entrepreneurial Executive with a record of strong and profitable performance in the start-up, development, and management of emerging industries and businesses nationwide. Combines cross-functional expertise in:

- New Venture Funding/Capitalization
- Opportunity & Operations Analysis
- Seamless Acquisition Integration
- Financial Analysis & Due Diligence
- Advertising, Promotions, & Special Events
- New Product Development & Launch

- Industry Roll-Up & Consolidation
- New Market & New Industry Penetration
- Team Building & Team Leadership
- Executive Negotiations & Transactions
- Multi-Channel Sales Management
- Private Label / Co-Branding

Dynamic personality ... innovative and creative ... high-energy ... diplomatic.
Responsive to constantly changing market, industry, & business demands.

PROFESSIONAL EXPERIENCE:

TRANS-INTEL WIRELESS, Fort Myers, FL   1999 to Present
($20 million telecommunications & Internet services provider)

Business Development Manager – Mergers & Acquisitions

Recruited by CEO to provide executive leadership for corporation's aggressive business development initiative. Challenged to identify and develop opportunities to drive market and corporate growth through internal development, mergers and acquisitions of Internet Service Providers (ISP's) worldwide.

Manage a complex research, due diligence, and valuation process to identify prime candidates based on company size, management team, demographics, current and projected revenues, profitability, and other critical data. Prepare formal Board presentations outlining recommendations and specific action items.

- Identified and researched 12 potential M&A candidates with potential to bring an additional $12 million in revenue to the corporation over the next three years.

- Created formalized process to evaluate the viability of acquisition integration within existing corporate structure and culture. Implemented systems to facilitate seamless integration and forward motion.

- Spearheaded development and implementation of corporate Intranet to facilitate real-time communications between departments involved in M&A evaluation and analysis.

KODIAK COMMUNICATIONS TECHNOLOGY, Reston, VA   1991 to 1999

President/CEO

Launched entrepreneurial consulting venture specializing in business development, sales, marketing, and engineering services for emerging companies in the wireless and Internet technology markets. Built venture from concept into a firm recognized for technical and market expertise, with particular focus on the development and licensing of MMDS (wireless cable) and, most recently, ISP's.

- Managed 11 client projects with a focus on application and licensing of pioneering technologies as licensed by FCC. Created business infrastructures that generated $10 million in sales.

- Completed long-term engagement with Radar Communications, LLC to guide development, sales, and marketing of their nationwide toll-free "Personal Number" service. Instrumental in leading successful launch and developing national customer base for bundled services. Primary contributor in the selection, evaluation, and contracting of independent sales organizations nationwide.

- Instrumental in start-up and profitable growth of several ISP's, including Rayband Internet, a Louisiana-based computer company who recently sold their subscriber base for over $80 million.

- Orchestrated a number of high-profile regional ISP roll-out projects as the industry continued to develop and redefine itself.

GROCER AT YOUR DOOR, Springfield, VA   1997 to 1998
(Start-up wholesale food distribution company)

President/CEO

Identified market opportunity, developed business plan, invested capital, and launched the start-up of a new venture targeted to the high-end restaurant, hotel, and country club markets. Recruited and led a team of industry sales specialists to position Grocer At Your Door against well-entrenched competition. Established the entire operating organization.

- Built new venture from concept to 210 accounts and $1 million in profitable sales within 16 months.

- Negotiated the sale of the corporation to a major regional wholesaler at 12 times initial investment.

Previous Experience:

Director of Sales & Marketing	**T-QWEST**	1989 to 1991
Director of Sales	**Apollo Enterprises**	1986 to 1988

Key player in the start-up, development, and growth of two successful communications companies marketing FCC licensing opportunities. Directed investment banking, acquisitions, engineering, and large-scale business development initiatives. Built and led two top-performing field sales organizations.

- Delivered revenue and net profit increases averaging better than 32% annually.

EDUCATION: **Graduate** – American Academy of Dramatic Arts
                     Business & Economics Major – Northern Virginia Community College

ANDREW J. CARNABY, JR.
ajcjr@mindspring.com

66 Dover Dell Boulevard
Nashville, TN 37887

Home: 292.778.3982
Office: 292.988.3726

EXECUTIVE LEADERSHIP PROFILE
Chief Executive Officer / President / Executive Vice President
Start-Up Enterprise Ventures / Turnarounds & Revitalizations / High-Growth Organizations

High-performance leadership career building industry-leading companies nationwide. Extensive P&L responsibility for up to $500 million annually. Greatest successes in creating business infrastructures to support operations and meet customer/market demand. Cross-functional leadership expertise includes:

- Strategic Planning & Vision
- Marketing & New Business Development
- Information Systems & Technologies
- Customer Relationship Management
- Transportation & Distribution Operations
- Integrated Logistics & Supply Chain Management
- Multi-Site Operations & Facilities Management
- Personnel Training, Development, & Leadership
- Competitive Sales & Contract Negotiations
- Accelerated Revenue, Profit, & Market Growth

PROFESSIONAL EXPERIENCE:

ARNOLD HAYES HEALTH CENTER, INC., Nashville, Tennessee   1988 to Present
(Fully integrated logistics & supply chain management provider shipping $4 billion in products annually)

Chairman & Chief Executive Officer (1997 to Present)
Founder & President (1988 to 1997)

Launched entrepreneurial fee-for-service venture to penetrate the rapidly emerging contract logistics and supply chain management industry. Started business as a US division for a Canadian logistics company and, over the next 10 years, established nationwide presence with 40 major corporate accounts.

- *Corporate Growth & Revenue/Profit Performance*. Built company from start-up into a 300-employee corporation distributing over $4 billion in customer products annually. Delivered 10 years' average annual growth of 35% with 35%+ return on capital. Increased shareholder value year over year by 50%. Achieved the best operating ratios (e.g., ROS, ROE) in the industry.

- *Industry Prominence*. Created nationwide model for integrated logistics for the healthcare industry. Designed universal pricing algorithms and sophisticated costing models for double-digit gains in profit.

- *Business Development*. Captured key accounts including Astra, Bristol Meyers Squibb, Merck, and other emerging and leading players in the healthcare, biotech, pharmaceutical, OTC, and R&D industries. Directed two successful acquisitions ($55 million investment) to expand nationwide distribution network.

- *Organizational Design & Leadership*. Created the entire business infrastructure, all operating policies and procedures, finance and pricing division, HR systems, nationwide sales and marketing organization, and four state-of-the-art integrated logistics and supply chain management facilities.

- *Facilities Development*. Designed and built 10 new highly engineered buildings in 10 years. Structured and negotiated development, real estate, and leasing contracts totaling $250+ million.

- *Information Technology*. Invested over $35 million to create a best-in-class IT organization with fully integrated order processing, invoicing, marketing, distribution, logistics, and financial management systems. Expanded customer services to include integrated technology systems (EDI-structured) to enhance communications and product distribution/replenishment. Established data center in PA.

- ***Customer Management.*** Pioneered innovative customer service programs including a "cell-management" delivery service and a customer quality reporting system (SERVQUAL methodology). Consistently achieved "best in industry" customer satisfaction ratings.

GRANITE PHARMACEUTICAL DISTRIBUTORS, Milwaukee, Wisconsin   1987
($3 million regional logistics & distribution company poised for rapid growth)

Executive Vice President & Partner

Joined limited partnership to provide strategic vision, orchestrate process/business reengineering initiatives, prepare for capital financing offer, and position for long-term growth. Held full strategic planning, operating, and leadership responsibility for the entire business development, sales, and marketing organization. Concurrently, managed several new facility design/development projects. Reported to CEO.

- Pioneered innovative sales, marketing, and account development programs, and delivered 100% revenue growth within first four months. Surpassed all revenue and profit goals.

- Created the first formal strategic planning process to guide long-term growth and diversification.

WRAP DISTRIBUTION SYSTEMS, Milwaukee, Wisconsin   1978 to 1987
($500 million contract logistics company; subsidiary of publicly held MIRT Corporation)

Vice President – Marketing & Sales (1985 to 1987)
Executive Director (1984 to 1985)
Director of Operations (1981 to 1984)
General Manager (1978 to 1981)

Recruited to provide a new strategic business direction and renewed energy to drive the corporation into expanding entrepreneurial market sectors, divest non-performing operations and strengthen profitability. Promoted rapidly through progressive positions in Operations, Sales, Marketing, and General Management. Extensive experience in business development/diversification, marketing, advertising, warehousing, logistics, distribution, and production operations. Managed up to five independent operation units concurrently.

- Divested non-performing transportation business and launched the start-up of a brokerage service to consolidate shipments and improve volume pricing. Transitioned from concept into a $35 million service business in just two years.

- Established the first healthcare logistics business in the US. Grew to $25 million in annual service fees with a solid 10% profit margin. Delivered 40% return on sales and 50% return on equity.

- Introduced innovative premium services to meet customer demand, including integrated inventory, loss control, and order management systems. Significantly improved profitability.

ALIA MISTRA CORPORATION, Clare, New Jersey   1971 to 1978
(US subsidiary of French-based manufacturer of cosmetics & fragrances)

Corporate Manager – National Warehouse Administration (1976 to 1978)

Fast-track promotion through a series of increasingly responsible management positions in Customer Service, Production Planning, Finance and Inventory Management. Advanced to Corporate Manager with full operating responsibility for the entire US distribution and logistics organization. Youngest member of the Product Development Committee.

- Managed through a period of rapid expansion and internal change as US company grew from $26 million to $400 million in annual revenues. Specialized in the reconfiguration/revitalization of non-performing operations through process redesign and automation.

- Introduced 20-30 new products each year while getting products to market 50% faster. Participated in company's first-ever MRP implementation.

- Drove customer service satisfaction ratings to a consistent 99% for three consecutive years.

EDUCATION:

RUTGERS UNIVERSITY – Business Administration
IOWA STATE UNIVERSITY – Business Administration
WILLIAM PENN COLLEGE – Business Administration

PROFESSIONAL AFFILIATIONS:

Council of Logistics Management
Warehouse Education Research Council
National Wholesale Drug Association (Guest Speaker)

JEREMY C. RICHARDSON

236 York Town Court
Columbia, MD 21045

410.320.7698
jcr@coldrain.com

Career Focus

FINANCE INDUSTRY EXECUTIVE
(CFO / CEO / COO / EXECUTIVE VP)

*Chief Problem Solver · Corporate & Financial Planning · Strategic Partnerships
Banking Industry · Securities · Portfolio Management · Financial & Stock Analysis
Financial Controls · Start-Up & Turnaround Ventures · Business Development
Technology · Operations*

• Business Planning & Analysis	• Training Program Development & Staff Motivation
• Marketing & Sales	• Capital Budgeting & Profit/Loss Management
• Banking & Investment Products	• Risk Assessments & Loss Management
• Direct Marketing Experience	• Tax Planning & Compliance
• Alliances for Mutual Profitability	• Database Design
• Market Development	• Technology & System Integration
• General Business Management	• Strong Contract Review & Negotiation Skills
• Personnel Management & Administration	• Policies & Procedures Development

- Facilitate high-growth businesses. Analyze operations, formulate and implement difficult recommendations including innovative concepts to streamline processes, greatly improve productivity, and boost bottom-line profits. Accountable for P&L and large scale daily operations.
- Driven leader with desire to excel as top in industry. Accomplished and conquered all positions to date, e.g., ranked # 1 in a company of 2,500 as a financial specialist after only six months in position.
- Performance and hands-on management style: initiated a mentorship educational program and followed in the footsteps, on-the-job, of successful, high-speed CEOs of various firms.
- Consistently promote a "client service first" philosophy. Assemble, grow, and manage talented teams to deliver high-quality customer service and build accounts.
- Listen intently and accurately to assess customer needs and design, deliver, evaluate, and administer customized training materials and programs, financial requirements, sales packages, and IT solutions.
- Keen ability to project data, estimate probabilities and draw conclusions. Develop accurate sales forecasts and operational budgets. Manage multiple, diverse projects.
- Proficient use of various financial software including mortgage planning, investments, loans, Roth IRA, retirement, Evergreen Architect, TESS, MS Money, Excel, Word, and many others.

PROFESSIONAL EXPERIENCE

Financial Specialist, BB&T Bank, Maryland   1999 — Present

- ❑ Promoted from Branch Manager to Financial Specialist in 2000. Increased wallet share of existing customers and improved service measurement scores in all branches. Increased growth and retention, more than doubling goals at the half-year mark. Coach and mentor staff in complex compensation plans.
- ❑ Identify, generate, and grow revenue for new and existing clients. Observe and review operations. Create customer-service training programs and lead seminars. Conduct training in 35 branches. Trained personnel during a merger, maintaining high customer-service ratings. Resolve problems.
- ❑ Establish and manage a portfolio of affluent relationships. Member of community advancement executive team. Advise community businesses regarding financial requirements (401K programs, debt financing, payroll, direct deposits, retirement planning, expense and balance sheet analysis, etc.).

- ❏ Coach clients to define goals and objectives. Sell, manage, or work with a full spectrum of complex financial products, credit, and capital structures: real estate sales, auto loans, debt consolidations, small business leases, underwriting, loss management, trading, insurance policies, mutual funds, treasury bills, tax consulting, investments, portfolio management, securities, wire transfers, annuities, etc. Manage transactions worth $30M+ monthly. Lead sales planning meetings.
- ❏ Provide quality administration and regulatory compliance to individuals and corporations. Familiar with NYSE and NASDAQ requirements, tax and fiduciary law, and banking policy.

Owner/CEO, Construction Services, Baltimore, MD   **1995 – 1999**

- ❏ Formed and operated a construction repair company. Created alliances with insurance companies that provided claim repairs. Built a database of over 300 customers, providing steady sales and significant worth when selling the business.
- ❏ Managed all business requirements: company registration, claims, taxes, risk management, staffing, payroll, bookkeeping, equipment purchase/lease, customer service training, and quality control.

Sales Manager, Parts R Us, Columbia, MD   **1994 – 1995**

- ❏ Recruited by Parts R Us to turnaround underperformance and unmet sales goals gone unchecked for over one year. Evaluated current operations and cross-trained personnel, meeting sales goal within two months. Developed more commercial business in the first seven months than the entire previous year – increasing sales by 110%.
- ❏ Created relationships with numerous other auto-parts stores and auto dealerships, establishing Parts R Us as a primary supplier for parts and accessories. Personally managed supply orders and inventory while guiding the merger of the company. Assisted with conversion of nine other stores including systems integration, problems resolution, staffing, and local marketing.

COO/Owner, Mail and More, Silver Spring, MD   **1990 – 1994**

- ❏ Operated four franchise stores and supervised, trained, and evaluated 50+ employees. Trained new franchise owners. Managed staffing and created effective cross-training programs – so well received that other owners sent their staff for training. Managed capital budgeting, technology and system integration, accounting, customer service, expense planning, lease contracts, cash and asset management, and business requirements. Performed an extensive risk-management study.
- ❏ Created and sold new income products. Coordinated marketing for 43 area stores. Negotiated marketing contracts with local media.
- ❏ Quickly turned around one store producing negative cash flow; in five months improved cash flow 150%. Renegotiated leases and generated a 200% increase in sales in seven months.
- ❏ Lowered the cost basis of one store in 1.8 years by purchasing equipment for pennies on the dollar from a store going out of business and renegotiating leases – tripling bottom-line profits.
- ❏ Produced positive cash flow through due diligence visits, gaining exposure to key executives in growing companies, and spearheading marketing initiatives: direct mailings, market research, public speaking, etc.

PROFESSIONAL DEVELOPMENT & CERTIFICATES

- ❏ Currently enrolled in **College of Financial Planning to attain CFP and AAMS certificates.** Initiated an executive-level mentorship program: Enlisted the coaching and mentoring of CEOs, COOs, and marketing professionals of various firms and studied their work ethics, management practices, time management, organizational, and communications skills. Followed closely in their footsteps and learned directly from successful business executives, 1990.

Marcus R. Howe

1657 Notting Hill Road
Anaheim, CA 92807

714.998.7653
MRH@yahao.com

Accomplished Business Operations Manager
- Recognized as the Top Club Manager within the region -

- ☀ Food & Beverage Operations
- ☀ Inventory & Control
- ☀ Contracts & Negotiations
- ☀ Sound Business Practices

- ☀ Club & Restaurant Operations
- ☀ Business Partnerships
- ☀ Operating Budgets
- ☀ Strong Planning Abilities

- ☀ Policy Guidance
- ☀ Catering
- ☀ Public Relations
- ☀ Protocol

Significant Accomplishments

- ❑ Rapidly promoted throughout a distinguished food and beverage management career, culminating in the current position as Business Manager with scope of responsibility and business accountability for three clubs, two bowling centers, two hotels, one conference center, one golf course with club house, and one sports lounge. Control, develop, plan, review, and implement regulations for all facilities and special events (festivals, bazaars, and open-air concerts).
- ❑ Managed all phases of a $900,000 restaurant renovation.
- ❑ Significantly streamlined and improved operations increasing catering availability by 30% in a two-year period.
- ❑ Exceeded financial goals on numerous occasions: Exceeded FY99 budgeted goals for the bowling centers by 47% with savings of $105,000. Designed innovative customer service methods and developed expanded menus, exceeding budget projections by $42,000 for one function.

Professional Experience

Business Operation Manager, San Diego, CA (1999—Present)
Operation Manager, Spain (1996—1999)
Club Manager, Germany (1993—1996)
Assistant Manager, Richmond, VA (1992—1994)
Club Operations Manager, Colorado Springs, CO (1989—1992)

Business Operations

- ❑ Seasoned professional with comprehensive experience in directing all areas of community activities and facilities including contracts, financial planning programs, and administration for food and beverage management, customer service, billeting, golf club operations, community events, catering, and protocol. Develop long range plans. Determine resource requirements.

- ❑ Establish operating budgets and execute authorization. Set objectives for revenuue-making facilities including salaries, acquisitions, maintence/repairs, supplies, and construction costs.

- ❑ Review, interpret, and formulate policy, plans, and procedures applying a thorough knowledge of legal and regulatory requirements. Keen ability to analyze complex problems.

- ❑ Supervise over 200 personnel and direct-report facility managers responsible for providing top notch service in all facilities.

❑ Recruit, interview, hire, train, and evaluate subordinates. Develop and expect high-performance standards. Approve/disapprove personnel actions. Create innovative training and development programs. Prepare calendars. Successfully oversee multinational workforces and implement established EEO policies. Receive grievances and mediate solutions.

❑ Exercise stringent controls over accounting documentation, supply requisitions, and inventories. Prepare management studies and maintain statistical databases. Review programs, activities, facilities, revenue objectives, and budgets. Precisely analyze financial program data strengths and weaknesses and apply that information directly to budget preparations.

Communications

❑ Meticulously draft, edit, and review reports, policies and guidelines, contracts and purchase requests, and other written materials. Articulate press releases and correspondence. Manage PR matters. Attend community wide meetings as a business consultant.

❑ Effectively establish sterling rapport with community managers and officials maintaining open channels of communication.

Food and Beverage Management

❑ Direct menu planning and development, pricing, schedules and portion control. Closely monitor food and beverage inventory levels including alcoholic beverages. Supervise the purchasing and procurement of food items, supplies, and equipment.

❑ Established a Catering Manager position and subsequently recruited and trained the Catering Manager, significantly contributing to a financial turnaround in FY98.

❑ Expertly planned and orchestrated the fine details of social and business functions. Hosted over 140 events in a two-year period.

❑ Train food service professionals in proper protocol for serving dignitaries—place settings, seating, serving, wine etiquette, and so forth.

=== **Relevant Training** ===

- Catering Professionals, 2002
- EEO for Supervisors, 2001
- Budget & Accounting Seminar, 2001
- Catering Skills, 1999

- Internal Controls for Managers, 1999
- 5-Year Strategic Planning, 1998
- Division Chefs Course, 1997
- Food Management, 1996

=== **Languages** ===

Fluent German

ANNA RAY ARTHUR

12 Chelsea Avenue
Ames, Iowa 58372

Home: 502.399.3762   Email: ara29225@arc.org   Office: 502.980.3827

PROFESSIONAL QUALIFICATIONS:

- Inventory Control & Management
- Purchasing & Vendor Relations
- Accounts Payable & Accounts Receivable
- Sales & Financial Reporting
- Efficiency & Productivity Improvement

- Sales & Sales Management
- Customer Service Operations
- Office Management & Administration
- Recruitment, Interviewing & Hiring
- Employee Training & Supervision

Excellent communication, organizational and project management skills. PC proficient with Microsoft Word, Microsoft Excel, and Quick Books Pro.

PROFESSIONAL EXPERIENCE:

Business Manager   1995 to Present
ARMOUR POWER SERVICES, INC., Ames, Iowa

Independently manage all sales, customer service, general accounting, financial reporting, administrative, purchasing, inventory control, and staffing functions for a privately owned automotive service facility.

- Instrumental in supporting the company's rapid growth and expansion over the past five years, including a 100% increase in revenues and profitability.

- Developed and implemented an entire administrative process and structure to professionalize the business, improve productivity, and increase accountability.

- Designed a more efficient and cost-effective parts ordering and inventory management system.

- Automated manual accounting and financial analysis/reporting functions with Excel spreadsheets and other PC-based tools.

Owner & Business Manager   1992 to 1995
ANNA RAY'S CLEANING SERVICE, Ames, Iowa

Launched entrepreneurial venture and established a successful commercial and residential cleaning service. Responsible for sales, new customer development, and customer service. Coordinated scheduling, managed purchasing and inventory, and handled all accounting, billing, collection, and banking functions.

Merchandiser   1987 to 1992
MONTGOMERY SOUTHEAST, Montgomery, Alabama

Fast-paced position with a high-volume regional grocery distributor. Scope of responsibility was diverse and included customer service, order processing, customer complaint resolution, and inventory planning/control. Promoted two times in four years based on strong communication, organizational, and customer management skills.

Supervisor   1984 to 1987
QUICKEE MART, INC., Montgomery, Alabama

Managed a 50-employee retail operation generating over $6 million in annual sales revenues. Directed hiring, training, and employee scheduling. Coordinated product ordering with more than 30 vendors, controlled and documented inventory flow, and managed in-store loss prevention. Fully responsible for sales and customer service operations, daily sales reporting, and daily sales reconciliations.

Store Manager   1980 to 1984
EXXON OIL, Birmingham, Alabama

Held responsibilities identical to those with Quickee Mart, Inc. in this 15-employee operation. Managed during a period of significant growth in volume, customers, and revenues.

EDUCATION:

A.A. Degree in General Studies, Central Iowa Community College, 1999

A.A Degree in Marketing, Central Iowa Community College, 1996

Business Management Certificate, 1989

Certificate, National Association for Convenience Stores, 1986

Seminars in Sales, Communications, Time Management, & PC Software

VOLUNTEER WORK:

Advisory Committee Member, Jamison Boys & Girls Home

References Provided Upon Request

RONALD R. JACKSON

700 Maple Ridge Road
Auburn, Maine 04210

Telephone: (207) 777-7777   **rjackson@sprintmall.net**

CAREER PROFILE:

Business Entrepreneur / Seasoned Manager with an impressive record of success in varied businesses and financially related projects/programs. Outstanding communicator with proven abilities in staff and employee assessments, training, supervision, and management. Very dedicated and hard-working individual with an innovative and creative-thinking approach to problem-solving and generating new ideas with diversity as the cornerstone of overall abilities.

Transferable Skills Include:

- Experience working in public and private sectors.
- Ability to communicate on all levels in writing and orally.
- Thrive in an environment requiring extensive people contact.
- Successful entrepreneur having owned and managed two separate businesses.
- Diversified sales skills (retail sales, service sales, and varied customer service).
- Varied manufacturing knowledge and expertise (negotiations, price quotes, pricing/costing, sales, fabrication, material handling/inventory control, expediting, shipping and receiving, and customer quality control and assurance).

EDUCATION:

Husson College, Bangor, Maine	**Business Administration, 2 Years**
Edward Little High School, Auburn, Maine	**Diploma**

Continuing Education:
- *Varied Business Seminars & Recreational Workshops.*
- *Class B – Bus/Coach Drivers License.*

WORK HISTORY:

Shipping Manager
- *Quality Painting, Inc. (Auburn, Maine)*   1996 - Present
    ~ Currently oversee all shipping and receiving requirements.
    ~ Assume plant-manager level duties and responsibilities as needed.

Seasonal, Awning Division Manager
- *Ameri-Tents & Awnings (Auburn, Maine)*   1996
    ~ Oversaw all sales and installations.
    ~ Ordered supplies, distributed materials, and supervised staff.

(Continued on Page 2 of 2)

WORK HISTORY: (continued)

Owner/Manager
- *Pop's One-Stop (Greene, Maine)*   1987-1996
    - ~ Grew a small "Mom & Pop" store to achieve large-volume sales.
    - ~ Hands-on owner; oversaw all business functions and management through financial, sales, and customer service.
    - ~ Business included full-kitchen facilities with the capacity to seat 28.
    - ~ Store offered a large variety of dry goods for sale to customers.
    - ~ Maintained 4 pumps for customer gas sales.
    - ~ Employed 7 full-time and 4-6 part-time people.
    - ~ Sold this successful business for reasons other than business related.

Owner/Manager
- *City Auto Body (Gray, Maine)*   1984 -1989
    - ~ Grew this automobile repair facility to a full-time and profitable business employing 6 full-time certified technicians.
    - ~ Implemented new environment programs to safeguard employees against hazardous waste.
    - ~ Arranged for upgrading employees by helping them to become certified in varied related areas.
    - ~ Sold business to devote more time to growing Pop's One-Stop.

Varied Positions in Various Areas   Prior to 1984
- *Parks & Recreation Director for a Municipality (2 years)*
- *Recreation Director for a Private School (2 years)*
- *Ski Resort Asst. Manager/Manager/Operator (8 years)*
    - ~ Opened and operated a ski facility.
    - ~ Hired, trained, and supervised a staff up to 28.
    - ~ Directed entire staff that worked with 90-100 campers (ages 7-13).
    - ~ Served as a Certified National Ski Patrol Examiner & Certified Lifeguard.
    - ~ Served on the US Olympic Nordic Grooming Team.
    - ~ Conceptualized, introduced, and implemented many and varied programs in public and private sectors for youth and young adults.
    - ~ Drafted and implemented annual budgets for multiple activities.

PERSONAL DATA:

- In addition to excellent work ethics and history, offer total flexibility in current career goals and requirements ... Open to change ... Willing to travel, commute, or relocate ... Available for immediate interviews ... Outstanding references available upon request.

• • •

PATRICIA HUGHES

214-345-8831 (home)
214-333-9871 (cell)

1458 Skyway Drive, Dallas, TX 75208

Energetic **MANAGEMENT PROFESSIONAL** skilled in building motivated teams enthusiastic about achieving company goals. Cross-functional experience in general management, human resources, and customer relations.

Strengths:

Accounting: Extensive A/P, A/R, procurement, and inventory control experience. Strong ability to work with cross-functional teams to accelerate profit gains.

Management: Exceptional communication and interpersonal skills. Talent for selecting the right person for the right job based on individual strengths, and leading them to exceed company goals. Excellent organizational and problem-solving capabilities.

Customer Service: Tactful and diplomatic. Innate ability to find common ground with everyone and foster long-term, profitable relationships.

Computer: Expertise in Windows 95 and 97; Microsoft Word, Excel, and PowerPoint; PeopleSoft Finance; and Great Plains Dynamics.

CAREER EXPERIENCE

NATIONAL RV SUPPLY, INC., Dallas, Texas – 1999 to 2002
Contractor
> Assisted Controller in day-to-day operations. Developed processes for tracking orders, monitoring inventory, purchasing, and disseminating information to internal departments.
> > ➢ Developed an inventory management system and revitalized purchasing process to streamline operations and significantly increase efficiency.

SOUTHWEST PROPERTIES, INC., Houston, Texas – 1997 to 1999
Property Manager – 1998 to 1999
> Challenged to launch a new department charged with overseeing all tower construction, site maintenance, repairs, and monitoring. Served as the liaison for landowners, utility companies, and field implementation personnel. Ensured lease compliance with all regulatory agencies.

> > ➢ Hired, trained, and managed a 6-person staff. Created and implemented a duplicatable process to ensure timely project completion and regulatory compliance.

> > ➢ Created a comprehensive database to track lease activity and payments, reducing waste and controlling costs.

> > ➢ Implemented processes enabling sales and technical departments to work together seamlessly.

ASR Manager – 1998
> Promoted after one month to hire, train, and manage a 5-person staff serving as the principal point of contact in all sales process phases. Consistently met or exceeded company goals and objectives. Reported directly to the COO.
> > ➢ Empowered staff to rise above the "Girl Friday" image and serve as a liaison for the sales department, freeing the sales team to generate increased sales.

➢ Collaborated with internal departments to conduct hands-on training promoting a thorough under-standing of the tower construction process.

➢ Authored an in-depth procedure manual for all company departments, detailing the step-by-step process and time frame for completing various projects. The manual was later adopted as a viable sales tool.

Account Support Representative (ASR) – 1998

Recruited by the CEO to be part of a team providing continuous communication between customers, National Account Managers, and field, engineering, and implementation person-nel.

SPRINT COMMUNICATIONS, L.P., Orlando, Florida – 1995 to 1997
Purchasing Agent – 1997
Finance Assistant – 1995 to 1997

Dispatched by Personnel One for a one-day temporary assignment and immediately hired as a full-time employee. Point of contact for the corporate accounting department in Houston, Texas.

➢ Key team member participating in the phenomenal growth of the company which expanded to 500 sites with eight retail locations in West Central Florida.

➢ Developed and implemented a comprehensive procurement process adopted as the standard practice company-wide.

PERSONNEL ONE TEMPORARY SERVICES, Tampa, Florida – 1994 to 1995
Administrative
Diverse temporary assignments culminating in job offers at 96% of the businesses.

SEAHAWK DEEP OCEAN TECHNOLOGIES, INC., Tampa, Florida – 1993 to 1994
Administrative Assistant
Conducted administrative, clerical, and A/P and A/R functions; coordinated travel arrangements; assisted in mobilizing boat operations and communicating with stockholders.

EDUCATION

Completed 90 credit hours towards Bachelor of Arts degree
University of Maryland at Baltimore County, Baltimore, Maryland

TRAINING & DEVELOPMENT - SEMINARS

AMA/Padgett Thompson Management Skills
AMA/Padgett Thompson Accounting and Finance

PROFESSIONAL ORGANIZATIONS

American Business Women's Association * Tampa Business & Professional Women's Association

VOLUNTEER ACTIVITIES

Metropolitan Ministries – Organized highly successful food and clothing drives.

WILLIAM A. NORRIS

2322 Oak Terrace
Newark, New Jersey 02983

Phone: 912-933-2637   Email: wand@erels.net   Cell: 809-661-9889

MANAGEMENT PROFILE
Health Care Practice Management / Group Practice Management

Fifteen plus years of general management responsibility in fast-paced, high-volume health care operations. Combines strong organizational, leadership and administrative talents with the ability to build staff camaraderie and improve staff performance. Energetic, self-motivated, and results-oriented. Multi-tasked with excellent project management skills. Proficient with Windows 98, Microsoft Word and Excel, Quicken 2000, and Medmaster.

—Multi-Site Medical Practices	—Billings & Collection Management
—Marketing & New Business Development	—Financial Planning, Analysis, & Reporting
—Medical & Administrative Staffing/Training	—Lease & Contract Negotiations
—Office Technology & Medical Equipment	—Purchasing, Inventory, & Supply Management
—New Practice Start-Up & Growth	—Patient Relations & Communications

PROFESSIONAL EXPERIENCE:

LANDERS EYE CARE INSTITUTE, Kissimmee, Florida   1991 to Present

Business Administrator (1999 to Present)
Business Associate (1995 to 1999)
Office Administrator (1991 to 1995)

Fast-track promotion through a series of increasingly responsible business management positions during the turnaround and profitable growth of this 5-site group medical practice. As Business Administrator, hold full operating, billing, collections, financial reporting/analysis, administrative, human resources, marketing, advertising and technology responsibility. Joint P&L responsibility with physician-owners.

- Achieved/surpassed all profit objectives. Consolidated business and financial operations, closed non-performing locations, and realigned the entire administrative function. Built revenues from $1.2 million to $3.7 million and pre-tax profit margins from 9% to 43%.

- Computerized the entire organization (including Medicare and Medicaid billings) for total cost savings of more than 45% annually. Introduced best-in-class practice management systems and procedures.

- Professionalized administrative, clerical, and medical staffs. Introduced a series of training, reward, and incentive programs to sustain improved performance. Cut 55% from A/P operating costs.

- Member of 4-person management team responsible for feasibility analysis, design, construction, staffing, and operations of new $1.1 million surgery center. Personally negotiated 30-year, $900,000 mortgage paid in full within four years. Delivered full ROI within 11 months.

- Designed and directed an ongoing marketing, advertising, and business development initiative to increase the visibility of the practice, expand referral network, and increase market penetration.

- Sourced vendors, evaluated products, and purchased over $50,000 in equipment and technology.

EDUCATION: **Curry College**, Milton, Massachusetts
             Graduate, 45+ hours of continuing professional education in medical management

RANDIE SULLIVAN

239 Ascot Boulevard #212
Tampa, Florida 33283

Phone: 291-938-2837
Email: Randie229@arc.net

PROFESSIONAL OBJECTIVE:

Professional Sales, Special Events, or Public Relations Position in the Hospitality Industry.

PROFESSIONAL QUALIFICATIONS PROFILE:

Sales, Marketing, & New Business Development – Excellent experience in sales and marketing with strong presentation, negotiation, and sales closing skills. Consistently successful in outperforming competition by building trust and rapport with clients. Solid sales performance in corporate, industrial, and consumer markets. Entrepreneurial drive, energy, and enthusiasm.

Customer Relationship Management – Well respected for ability to develop and retain long-term client relationships. Work one-on-one with accounts to identify needs and respond with the design/delivery of appropriate services. List of 100+ references of long-term satisfied clients.

Public Relations & Special Events – Planned/managed numerous special events in cooperation with corporate, government, and public sector partners. Excellent skills in planning complete events, from theme to marketing to the entire scheduling, logistics, and event management function. Extensive public speaking, volunteer training, and organizational leadership experience.

Media & Press Relations – Outstanding skills in fostering and managing positive relationships with local, regional, and national media. Skilled media communicator with extensive public speaking and on-air experience. Earned personal media coverage for special events and entrepreneurship in *Kiplinger's*, *LA Times*, *Chicago Tribune*, *Family Circle*, *Redbook*, and others.

PC Technology Skills – Proficient in the use of Windows 95 & 98, Microsoft Word, PowerPoint, Excel, PageMaker, QuickBooks, WordPerfect, Corel Draw, and Act.

PROFESSIONAL EXPERIENCE:

Special Events & Public Relations Consultant   1997 to 2002

Dedicated the past five years to several major projects and contract assignments:

Special Events Consultant – City of Safety Harbor, Florida. Marketed the concept and won approval from the City of Safety Harbor to plan and direct the first-ever community clean-up initiative – Clean-Up 2000. Recruited, trained, and managed over 700 volunteers from civic associations, youth groups, and schools to complete 42 city-wide projects. Partnered with area businesses for corporate sponsorships and city agencies for operating support.

Special Events Director – Founded new organization, Sparkle USA, to educate economically disadvantaged children. Created unique concept to teach youth in homeless shelters about personal and environmental hygiene. Completed six events over the past two years.

Author – Wrote and published book entitled ***Spring Cleaning for Health & Happiness*** which sold 30,000 copies. Launched a massive PR and marketing campaign nationwide, traveled throughout the country for book tours and signings, and managed all administrative functions.

President, General Manager, & Sales/Marketing Representative   1977 to 1997
Maids of New England

Launched new business venture and built to one of the largest cleaning companies in the Northeastern U.S. Single-handedly managed the entire sales, marketing, and business development function for the company, building customer base from ground floor to more than 250 commercial, industrial, government, and consumer accounts. Built staff to more than 60 completing over 100 projects per week.

- Drove sales growth from start-up to $2.3 million in profitable revenues each year.
- Designed print advertisements, promotional materials, and other marketing communications to increase market awareness and expand customer base.
- Negotiated corporate and government fee-for-service contracts.
- Professionalized the business and the industry with standardized service, quality, cost, and performance requirements. Provided organization with a substantial market advantage.
- Established all business systems for purchasing, logistics, scheduling, customer service/management, fleet management, billing, accounting, collections, and long-range business planning.
- Presented with opportunity to sell the business and negotiated an extremely profitable exit agreement.

EDUCATION:

194 College Credits – **UNIVERSITY OF BOSTON**
Marketing, Public Relations, Management, Administration, Humanities, and Social Services
Graduate, Tom Hopkins Sales Training
Graduate, Tony Robbins Sales Training

PROFESSIONAL & CIVIC MEMBERSHIPS:

National Speakers Association	Safety Harbor Chamber of Commerce (Volunteer)
Florida Speakers Association	Public Relations Society of America (Past)
Florida Publishers Association	Sierra Club

LESLIE JEAN LASLOW

HUMAN RESOURCES SENIOR EXECUTIVE

In senior Human Resources positions with the world's best known gaming/entertainment companies, delivered unique solutions that transformed corporate goals into profitable reality, built effective HR and operations systems, and managed rapid and sustained business growth.

- As Senior Vice President and Vice President with TCN/Gaming Inc. and United Entertainment, managed multi-millions-of-dollars and directed the HR strategies for thousands of employees in multiple locations on four continents. Directed core management activities far surpassing typical Human Resources functions, including key components of TCN's sale and of Gaming World's acquisition and subsequent sale.
- With 20 years of management experience in gaming and hospitality, offer a valuable grouping of cross-functional skills specific to the unique needs of these businesses. Thoroughly familiar with industry-related labor issues, regulatory requirements, security, employee satisfaction, staff development, and complex cultural integration.
- Developed numerous programs to support corporate goals and create lean yet effective operating conditions. Programs include creation and implementation of change-management concepts to introduce a "One-Company Mentality" that merged best practices of corporate policies and cultures resulting in improved systems, employee relations, and customer service.
- Recognized by company leadership and peers as a "smart, industrious, tenacious, and decisive leader and visionary." Manage Human Resources as a value-add, not a resource drain. Quickly assess situations, rapidly crafting solutions, building teams, organizing actions, and creating profit and/or efficiency with each project's conclusion.

AREAS OF EXPERTISE

- Multi-Million-Dollar Budget Oversight
- Mergers, Acquisitions, and Sales
- Accelerated Growth Management
- High-Performance Executive Teams

- Labor Relations and Negotiations
- Regulatory Compliance
- Corporate Security and Policies
- HRIS Systems Implementation

- Development and Training Programs
- Executive Staffing and Recruitment
- Compensation and Benefit Programs
- Employee and Customer Relations

CAREER HISTORY

TCN Corporation – Gaming Division, Las Vegas, Nevada • 1993 to Present

TCN Gaming/Gaming World, Inc. has annual revenues of $1 billion and nine worldwide locations with 19,000 employees.

As Corporate Senior Vice President, Human Resources ('96 to Present), report to Chairman/CEO for Gaming World, Inc., serve as key member of corporate executive management team, and handle work far surpassing typical HR management responsibilities. Promoted following TCN Corporation's acquisition and gaming unit consolidation of Gaming World, Inc.

- Managed key components of sale of company when Gaming was sold twice in nine months. Frequently called upon to handle acquisitions, mergers, downsizings, consolidations, and cultural integrations, as company's corporate objectives altered.
- Directed human resources worldwide at nine locations with approximately 19,000 employees. Managed 14 VP-level direct reports, 100 indirect reports, a $10 million budget, and HR teams at nine operating units.
- A key achievement was development/implementation of HR strategies to support company's growth, with emphasis on cultural integration focused on employees' acceptance of "One-Company Mentality" formed from four- to-five distinct business cultures.

As Corporate Vice President, Human Resources ('93 to '96), was originally recruited by TCN Corporation to lead Human Resources function for new gaming business unit, reporting to Executive Vice President of the Gaming Division. Direct reports included five corporate HR professionals as well as indirect reports located at all properties.

- A key achievement was core management involvement in maturation of this new business unit, including the development of human resource strategies, executive recruitment, benefits, compensation, training, and labor relations.
- Aided in opening of five new locations by 1996 (and the acquisition of three others by 2000 while Senior VP). Developed properties in Nevada, Mississippi, Indiana, Peru, Canada, and South Africa.

1832 Linden Tree Lane, Las Vegas, Nevada 89117
Phone: 702-900-8363 • Fax: 702-990-3666 • Cell: 702-651-3869 • Email: LJLaslow@arc.net

CAREER HISTORY (continued)

United Entertainment Inc., Las Vegas, Nevada • 1984 to 1993

United Entertainment operates 17 casinos in 17 markets, employs more than 40,000 employees worldwide, and is one of the most recognized and respected names in the casino entertainment industry.

As Regional Vice President, Human Resources ('90 to '93), was promoted and selected to aid in company's 1990 "regional emphasis" reorganization as a member of the newly established regional executive management team. Personally managed all HR issues for new region and directly supervised a staff of 35.

- A key achievement, as executive team member, was the consolidation of redundant functions, standardization of business practices, and reduction of cost structure within two months and without negative impact on staff morale and customer satisfaction.

As Director, Human Resources ('86 to '90), was selected to join new senior management team for an under-performing property, supervised a staff of 21 direct reports, positively impacted business/financial results, and enhanced customer/ employee experiences.

- A key achievement was the introduction of a new human resource philosophy including formalized training/ development programs for all levels, reward and recognition systems, customer satisfaction systems, and employee feedback vehicles.

As Corporate Director, Personnel & Employee Benefits ('84 to '86), was recruited for newly established corporate role and reported to the Executive Vice President / Chief Operating Officer. Managed development of corporate human resource policies and programs, supervising a staff of 10. Introduced new uniform employee benefits strategy including health and welfare, retirement, and employee assistance plans impacting 9,000 employees.

- A key achievement was the management (including strategy, communication plan, and outplacement) of corporate headquarters' decentralization and rightsizing (from 250 employees to 50) as well as the complete development and standardization of corporate policies and employee benefit programs.

Real Holdings Corporation, Reno, Nevada • 1979 to 1984

Multi-faceted company including real estate development, lodging, and casino holdings in Arizona, Nevada, and New York.

As Director, Human Resources, managed HR functions for 2,500 employees including staffing, training, compensation, benefits, employee relations, and labor relations. Supervised a staff of 15 direct reports.

- A key achievement was the negotiation and administration of eight complex labor agreements.

PROGRAM DEVELOPMENT

Designed and implemented these successful programs: United's *"Better People Strategy,"* a toolbox that assisted the company in growing rapidly without losing internal brand identity. • Gaming's first *uniform management bonus program.* • Gaming's and United's *uniform employee satisfaction system.* • Gaming's first *executive development program* • United's first company-wide *labor management system.* • Industry's first *behavioral-based customer service training system,* eventually adopted by United company-wide as a "standard" practice. • Redesign of a *uniform/global benefits strategy* for 19,000 Gaming and 9,000 United employees. • United's, Gaming's, and Real Holdings *compensation systems.* • Gaming's *management / executive bonus plan.* • United's *customer satisfaction system.* • Gaming's *cultural integration strategy.* • United's/Gaming's *service/profit chain philosophy.*

EDUCATION

Business Administration Program, University of Miami, Miami, FL, 1972 to 1975

University Nevada Business School • four-week program in *International Executive Development*
Penn State Business School • three-week program in *Executive Development*
Babson School of Executive Management • one-week program in *HR Leadership*
Harkson Institute • two-week program for *Leadership Skills Certification*
Columbia University • four-week program in *Industrial Relations*
United • two three-week programs: *Excellence in Management* and *Excellence in Leadership*

SUSAN J. LAWTON

201 Sky Blue Path ▪ Laurel, MD 21042 ▪ 410.224.9820 ▪ sjlaw@arc.net

CAREER FOCUS

HUMAN RESOURCES PROFESSIONAL / EXECUTIVE ADMINISTRATOR / OFFICE MANAGEMENT

PROFESSIONAL AND PERSONAL VALUE OFFERED

▪ Interpersonal Communication Skills	▪ Planning & Problem Solving	▪ HRIS
▪ Office Administration & Operations	▪ Planning & Organization	▪ Benefits
▪ Employee Relations	▪ Personnel Administration	▪ Security

▪ Skilled executive-level administrator and personnel manager with full accountability for HR budgets, government clearances, and office organization. Oversight direction for operational functions including accounts receivable, accounts payable, bank reconciliations, order entry, purchasing, shipping & receiving, payroll, commissions calculations, HR issues, event planning, travel coordination, hiring & terminations, and files management.

▪ Detailed researcher—analyze complex information from multiple sources. Quickly identify and resolve problems in the earliest stages. Extremely reliable and consistent. Apply a clever use of resources and tools ensuring optimum operations. Promote quality awareness. Implement highly effective and innovative communication methods.

▪ Proficient with Word, Office Suite, QuickBooks Pro, Outlook, Access, and Excel.

PROFESSIONAL EXPERIENCE

Technology Corporation, Ellicott City, MD 1996 — Present
Senior Manager of Human Resources, TSSI Clearance (1997 to Present)

❑ Selected for promotion to create and implement an HR function for this fast-growing technology company. Research and incorporate successful HR strategies. Administer all benefits and HR functions including insurance programs, 401k plan, vacation policy, applicant tracking, payroll, and company functions. Enforce EEO regulations.

❑ Researched, analyzed, purchased, and set up an HRIS system, streamlining administrative functions and bringing the office to current-day technology.

❑ Developed an effective approach for hiring and retaining key technical personnel, doubling the engineering staff in only one year, by working with a broker and significantly expanding the benefits package, conducting new employee orientations. Schedule exit interviews with all departing employees to confirm such issues as COBRA and gain valuable insight into the reasons for separation.

❑ Drafted employee policies and published the first-ever employee manual, providing legal protection to the company. Designed an employee-appraisal program, trained managers, and provided implementation guidelines aimed at establishing and maintaining a climate of mutual understanding between employees and management. Coordinate and participate in corporate planning meetings, ensuring corporate goals are reflected in HR strategies.

❑ *Facility Security Officer (FSO) (1996 to Present), Collateral Duty:* Initiate and track all required personnel security clearances. Maintain meticulous logs and up-to-date files for accurate referencing. Work closely with Defense Security Service (DSS) representative. Prepare for and participate in annual DSS inspections to ensure company compliance.

Office Manager (1996 to 1997)

❑ Directed all administrative and operational functions. Successfully automated check-writing processes, resulting in accurate tracking of payables and a more professional company image. Analyzed and purchased voice mail for existing telephone system, providing a more efficient and cost-effective method of handling incoming calls. Researched and negotiated leases for all office equipment and products.

❑ Coordinated company relocation. Selected moving company and scheduled/implemented moving procedures without interrupting daily operations. Chose color scheme, furnishings, and decorations. Committee Chair for the purchase of new telephone system to meet the needs of growing company.

RTM Technologies, Inc., Baltimore, MD 1995 – 1996
Human Resources Manager and FSO/Document Custodian—Secret Level

❑ Selected for promotion to enhance employee relations and provide depth to the corporate human resources role. Effectively expanded the HR function beyond its administrative duties to allot time for employee interaction and counseling and designed a progressive disciplinary and counseling plan to address existing personnel problems. Proposed an annual HR budget pertaining to training, equipment, recruitment, and administrative costs.

❑ Worked closely with the parent company's VP of HR to develop exempt and non-exempt pay grades, successfully revising the salary review system to ensure equitable distribution of funds budgeted for salary increases.

RTM Technologies, Inc., Baltimore, MD 1995 – 1996
Personnel Manager

❑ In approximately two-year periods, successfully progressed in an upward career track from Administrative Assistant, Sales Coordinator, Marketing Coordinator, Office Manager, Executive Assistant, Executive Assistant & HR, and Personnel Manager.

❑ Managed office administration, coordinated trip accommodations, maintained calendars, answered phones and greeted guests, and attended to executives' needs. Handled sensitive information with utmost confidentiality, working in a high-stress, busy office environment.

❑ Upon resignation of personnel manager, assumed personnel administrative accountability. Independently resolved long-standing issues on insurance premium reporting, 401k, and employee record keeping.

❑ Directed and managed employee relations issues. Supervised the merit review and appraisal process. Infused discipline and order to the personnel action process and assisted with interviewing and hiring personnel. Administered hiring and termination paperwork.

PROFESSIONAL ASSOCIATIONS

Society for Human Resources Management, Member

PROFESSIONAL DEVELOPMENT

Completed numerous courses, seminars, and in-service training sessions in such subjects as Human Resources and Law, Labor and Employment Law, Computers, Interviewing Techniques, and Security.

LUIS SILVA

3822 W. 103rd Street • Olympia, Washington 98501
(360) *898-3726* • LSilva111@emall.com

SENIOR INFORMATION TECHNOLOGY & SYSTEMS EXECUTIVE

Real Estate Industry

Chief Information Officer designing and optimizing technologies to drive outstanding business performance. Catapulted company to the 2002 Real Estate Technology Leader in Olympia with reputation rivaled by companies in substantially larger markets. Project-management expertise in website and web-application development. Proven track record implementing innovative cost-savings strategies in effective manner. Direct experience in hardware/software, network design and management, team leadership, and budgeting. Pragmatic problem solver with keen skills in negotiation, communication, and business acumen. Accomplished in supervising contractors.

PROFESSIONAL EXPERIENCE

REYNOLDS & NIGHT REALTORS, Olympia, Washington   1996 to 2003
Newly formed company resulting from A. B. Night / F. G. Reynolds merger creating the largest real estate company in Olympia metro area with 2,000+ agents and 35 sales offices.

Chief Information Officer (Reynolds & Night Realtors), 1/02 to 1/03

Directed successful merger and spearheaded integration of two stand-alone company MIS divisions including e-mail, websites, accounting systems, and agent-productivity programs. Evaluated technology needs and recommended implementation after determining cost efficiency.
- Combined the two company portal websites.
- Oversaw extension of programs to agents resulting in the training of more than 800 agents in three weeks.

Chief Information Officer (A. B. Night Residential), 2/96 to 12/01

Established and maintained wide area network for 300 computers and 1,000 users. Built and maintained two company websites, one for the general public, plus one for agents and staff. Directed development of agent-productivity tools. Managed five technical staff. Progressed in company from Vice President and Director of Technology positions.
- Saved company $200,000 by decentralizing call center with virtual cooperation made possible by wide area network.
- Earned numerous awards and recognition with origination of Olympia premier real estate website that generated 9.5 million hits per month in December 2001.
- Created first agent portal site in Olympia that functioned as central source of agent-productivity tools generating 900 unique weekly visitors; grew into preferred method for corporate communication with agents.
- Developed web-based agent-productivity programs that accelerated business for agents with buyers and sellers.

Continued on Page 2

WORLD DATA, INC., Kansas City, Missouri   1991 to 1996
Software development company producing CMA report tool that was purchased by title companies and distributed to real estate agents.

President
Created and maintained software that daily downloaded data from 66% of the Missouri Multiple Listing Services (MLS). Grew business from servicing one to twelve counties within five years by sourcing and signing contracts with the MLS and title companies. Automated reporting process to increase volume at lower cost.
- Established an industry benchmark with new process previously manageable only through access to tax records.

ACCESS DATA, INC., Overland Park, Kansas   1988 to 1990
Software development / consulting company.

President/Owner
Wrote custom applications and performed database conversion/analysis for clients contracted under a guaranteed-hours program.
- Maintained one client for two years while developing custom quotation, billing, and tracking software.

DATA ONE SYSTEMS, INC., Overland Park, Kansas   1981 to 1988
First company to assemble computer data storage products to sell by nationwide mail order.

President
Negotiated supplier contracts with 55 clients from Fortune 100 companies. Engineered several cost-effective products that improved company's competitive position. Increased sales volume by creating advertising for placement in the newly emerging computer magazines. Hired, trained, and managed a staff of 50 employees.

PREVIOUS PROFESSIONAL EXPERIENCE included progressively responsible management positions in the insurance industry.

EDUCATION

Electrical Engineering / Management Degree Program, Iowa State University, Ames, Iowa
Completed 60 credit hours.

Technical Skills
- Microsoft: SQL Server / Exchange 2000 / 2000 Server / Proxy Server
- Working knowledge of Cisco routers – 3600, 2500, 800 series
- Statistica (Statistical Analysis)
- Crystal Info / Reports
- Web Site Activity Analysis
- Citrix
- Firewalls
- Industry-specific and general accounting programs

REGINALD L. KRAMER

#47 Arthur Penn Boulevard * Green River, Montana 77893

Home: 484-389-2610
Office: 484-990-1010

Email: rlk23@voyager.net
Fax: 484-990-1011

SENIOR INFORMATION TECHNOLOGY EXECUTIVE
Chief Information Officer / Vice President / Executive Consultant

High-profile leadership career partnering IT with business operations to achieve organizational success. Expert in developing and deploying appropriate technology tools, systems, and solutions to drive performance, process, quality, revenue, and profit improvement. Strong strategic orientation with the ability to build advanced technology architectures, infrastructures, and operations for diverse applications. Outstanding relationship management and executive liaison skills. Keen focus on customer relationship management and retention.

Consummate "general manager" with experience in staffing, budgeting/finance, facilities, administration, purchasing, warehousing, and supply chain management. Strong planning and leadership skills.

PROFESSIONAL EXPERIENCE:

Executive IT Consultant (1994 to Present)

Executive Consultant on IT strategy, business solutions, organizational effectiveness and performance/ process improvement for client corporations throughout North America. Highlights:

- **Canadian Electric Light Company Limited.** Retained for 3-year assignment as the Senior IT Executive and Year 2000 Chairman. Led efforts as part of corporate-wide initiative to increase market penetration and grow through acquisition. Developed IT strategy, introduced new technologies (e.g., routers, PCs, networks) and replaced core business systems. Led Y2K compliance for both technology and service delivery. Managed $10+ million investment.

- **Alaskan Petroleum Limited** (*equivalent of US Fortune 50*). Evaluated internal IT infrastructure and cost overrides, recommended aggressive outsourcing project, and led the entire outsourcing, vendor selection, and contract negotiation process.

- **United Farmers of Wyoming** (*150+ store cooperative*). Developed new technology strategy, restaffed IT organization, implemented PC and networking technologies, and facilitated a significant improvement in organizational efficiency while reducing net operating costs.

- **Secrist Office Products Ltd**. (*largest retail office products distributor in US*). Evaluated organizational processes and technologies as part of a massive sales improvement program.

Chief Information Officer & Vice President of Administration (1992 to 1994)
Director of Administrative Services (1990 to 1992)
Director of Information Systems (1989 to 1990)
Systems Development / Programming / Systems Operations (1979 to 1989)
ALBERTA UTILITIES CORPORATION – Canada

Promoted through a series of increasingly responsible IT management positions to CIO and VP of Administration. Scope of responsibility included the IT organization, Controllers Office, Purchasing, Warehousing, Building Operations, Fleet, Office Services, and Administration. Led successful initiative to transition culture from monopoly to a fast-moving, customer-driven, competitively focused private enterprise. Extensive involvement in team building and training to facilitate positive change.

- Youngest Vice President in the 45-year history of the corporation.
- Managed operating and capital budgets totaling over $10 million annually.
- Developed and led a team of 500+ (including 150 IT personnel).

Credited with the strategic design, development, and implementation of millions of dollars in technology advancements to strengthen company performance, streamline processes, reduce staffing and operating costs, and build a best-in-class IT organization. Major projects included:

- Orchestrated project teams in the design, implementation, and delivery of numerous customer information and support systems (e.g., billing, invoicing, inventory, service, financial reporting) to automate core business processes and enhance customer interaction.

- Introduced an internal economy program that charged for IT services to each department and introduced outsourcing for non-critical operations. Positioned IT as a competitive entity within the organization and benchmarked against industry leaders for cost and performance.

- Forged a unique partnership with Digital Equipment and structured/negotiated $10 million contract with $10 million in capital expenditures and 120 staff. Delivered double-digit savings in operating costs, a 50% reduction in capital costs, and a 22% reduction in staffing needs.

- Partnered with the Texas state government and three other corporations to leverage joint resources for the development/deployment of advanced GIS technologies. Saved each corporation a minimum of $5 million annually in operating costs.

- Directed construction of new $4.5 million office building equipped with advanced building automation tools to maximize productivity. Redesigned staffing patterns and introduced new technology tools to optimize performance, quality, and service competencies. Resulted in a 20%+ reduction in staffing requirements. Ranked #4 in worldwide survey for cost of service.

- Implemented robotics technology into warehousing operations and reduced inventories 20%.

- Pioneered new technologies that reduced staff 75% in drafting and technical departments.

EDUCATION:

Graduate – Executive Management Development Program, University of Eastern Ontario
Graduate - Managing Relationships Program, Niagara Institute

PROFESSIONAL AFFILIATIONS:

Chairman, Information Subcommittee, Lester Wise Academy, Montana

Led team responsible for design/installation of technology infrastructure to support a new 1,000-student educational center designed to be a leader in the use of technology-driven education.

Past Chairman, Computing Information Section, Texan Electrical Association
Past President, Data Processing Management Association
Instructor – Systems Development, Cranston Institute of Technology
Member, Council of Management Information Executives, Conference Board of North America

ANDERS P. ENNISON

8450 Scented Pine Lane
Garner, North Carolina 27529
(919) 347-7870 - Phone
anderspe@l9.com

DIRECTOR / BUSINESS DEVELOPMENT EXECUTIVE / GENERAL MANAGER
Customer Service, Telecom & Information Technology Management Focus

---

Executive management or business development leadership position with a progressive growth company in the technology/telecommunications industry that values strategic vision, team building, customer service program direction, quality controls, and innovative action plan implementation skills.

* **Technology Services Leadership**	* **National Services Management/Strategies**
* **Customer Service Program Design**	* **Major Project Management/Customer Relations**
* **National Support Organization Direction**	* **Project Planning/Capital Budgets Decisions**
* **Quality Control/Assurance**	* **Customer Forum Development**
* **Service Support Process Management**	* **Budgeting/Cost Controls/Billing Process Control**
* **Sales/Customer Engineering Management**	* **Marketing/Sales/Revenue Generation Strategies**
* **Customer Satisfaction Metrics**	* **Vendor Relations/Contract Negotiations**
* **Training/Coaching/Team Building**	* **Internal/External Organization Liaison**
* **Facilities Resource Optimizations**	* **Process Automation/Operations Management**
* **Customer/Client Relations/Networking**	* **Sales/Service Team Correlation/Streamlining**
* **Client Communications Liaison**	* **Technical Direction/Company Focus & Expansion**

PROFESSIONAL EXPERIENCE

LEVEL 9 COMMUNICATIONS, Chapel Hill, NC
Director, Information Systems (2002- Present)
* Recently appointed to restructure development teams who create and support tools into the IS function from customer service. Currently responsible for providing the Information Technology needs for the TICON Customer Service, Engineering, and Sales Engineering functions. Provide management to system architects developing long-term tools, strategies, and migration plans for customer service requirements. Also provide strategic tool planning and architecture support for design teams, aligning current tool sets with correct processes. Utilize knowledge of engineering process, from sales engineering to network engineering.

Director of TICON Customer Service (1991-2002)
* Helped grow revenue from $250 million to over $1.9 billion. First-year service revenues (that we created in 1999) were $10 million and effectively doubled the second year.
* Created customer forums or user group meetings, chaired/hosted and orchestrated the meetings, and focused on customer service in conjunction with sales teams. Developed strategic partnerships between Customer Service, Sales, and TICON customers, effectively increasing customer satisfaction.
* Successfully provided correlation between the sales and service teams in 1991 so that every salesperson had only one service person to work on his or her accounts. Instilled belief that *the sales force owns the customer and the service team owns customer issues,* increased sales and customer satisfaction by 20% per contract.
* Established a national team to support and win customers through various channels throughout the United States - Amherst, MA; Seattle, WA; Chicago, IL; Tucson, AZ; Atlanta, GA; and Miami, FL.
* Successfully implemented telecommuting in the organization with 25% of the department opting to work from home. Plan increased customer satisfaction by 17% while significantly reducing costs by $8.6 million.

PROFESSIONAL EXPERIENCE, cont.

*   Customer satisfaction ratings from the these key accounts were above 89% from 1995 through 1998 and 99% in 1999 (top 5% of all account ratings).
*   Attained 42% employee satisfaction results with 84% participation when Level 9 utilized The Zogby Organization's employee opinion survey process in 1999.
*   Created vision and direction for the organization; established a clear mission and set the direction for TICON Customer Service operations. Made significant operational changes since the group and function did not exist prior to 1991.
*   Managed financials and project cost controls, with budgets from $1.5 million to $15 million annually, never exceeding budget. Successfully recruited leaders from competing companies, adding 19 of the top 50 people in the organization.
*   Provided comprehensive support directly to Customer Executives for all Level 9 products including Switching, Wireless, Optical Access, and Data.
*   Directed a team of up to 58 Customer Service professionals across the United States and the Caribbean, providing a single point of contact for 650 independent telephone companies, CLECs, and ISPs.
*   Served as prime interface into VP/C-levels for large customers' maintenance and support organizations.
*   With a customer base of 300 + small to medium-sized companies, including P-Coms and WillTel, the account base needed to present technical and maintenance information consistently and cost effectively. To increase customer service, implemented user group meetings. The user groups consisted of regional and state groups.
*   Capitalized on changes in the business environment such as customers starting to purchase multi-product networks. Implemented a project management team that grew to 15 project management professionals.
*   Created service support processes with other service entities to ensure product or organizational boundaries did not impact business customer service levels. Provided contributions to the development and implementation of an effective call center strategy. This strategy encompassed all aspects of the service call center, increasing and streamlining the total cycle of service interventions by ensuring an accurate and prioritized service call-tracking and dispatching process as well as pre-diagnosis of all service requests.

Technical Director, Switching Technical Support Services (1989-1991)
*   Major customer base included key regional Bell operating companies (Bell South, Nynex, Bell Atlantic, Southwest Bell, Pacific Bell, US West, Ameritech) and 750 smaller companies.
*   Successfully reduced customer-trouble reports from 3,400 open and overdue in 1989 to 150 open and overdue in 1991 while reducing the workforce by 13%.
*   Represented Level 9 at the semi-annual National ESAC meetings as the primary speaker, discussing call reports reduction performance. Received personal appreciation comments from several Bell company leaders.
*   Responsible for directing a workforce of 15 senior managers and 315 technical engineers supporting all Level 9 network switching customers nationwide.
*   In a technical support role, had 315 people in my direct team with another 59 spread across the country. Created the NORTHSEAM which required engineers on regional teams to talk to a core engineer on the phone in order to refer a problem in to the team. Core engineers couldn't return a problem to the regional engineer without talking to the person who sent the original problem, and the problem couldn't be closed without the customer agreeing to the solution.
*   Recognized as the customer service technical interface to the top maintenance management positions in the Bell companies. Provided 24/7 emergency technical support for all switching customers in the United States.

Held the following positions in support of installation for Level 9:

Director, Installation Services (1985-1989)
Senior Manager, Installation Technical Support for Southeast and Southwest (1983-1985)
District Manager, Installation - Northwestern (1979-1983)
Field Engineering Technician (1976-1979)

LEVEL 9 INTERNAL MANAGEMENT TRAINING PROGRAM

* Customer Service Market Management – 2000 & Beyond Program
* Pay for Achievement – Personal Incentive Program
* Jeff Hereema – The Human Elements of Successful Management
* Interpersonal Skills for Managers
* Effective Information Presentation Workshop
* Accounting Practices at NTI
* Effective Listening for Managers and Employees
* Management Supervisory Orientation
* Fundamentals of Management
* Level 9 Marketing Leadership Forums I & II

TECHNICAL PRODUCT SKILLS SUMMARY

Skill base includes:

* DMS, 10, 100, 250, 500, 300   * Most Data Products: Passport, CVX
* DMS Family Remotes: OPAQs, RLMs, RLCMs   * All Access Products: Accessnode, DMS 1
* Succession Products   * Voice Mail Products
* All Optical Products: OC3, 12, 48, 192   * Wireless Products: MTX, Network Installations

SUMMARY OF QUALIFICATIONS

* 20 + years of experience in the technology industry including serving as **Director of Information Services** and **Director of IOC Customer Service** for Level 9 Communications. Outstanding management career including nationally recognized operations in customer service and sales program effectiveness.

* Thorough management training. Known as an excellent communicator providing clear direction to employees. Created new organizations to ensure success before opportunities became issues.

* Background focuses on customer support, new business and revenue generation, business solutions design and implementation, team leadership, and major customer/client management. Multi-dimensional experience in multiple areas: telephony, communications, network management, sales, service, operations, corporate staffing, and customer support center design and direction.

* Extensive knowledge of the telecommunications business and the demands on service providers from customer service experience. Worked closely with service-provider operations teams. Successfully managed a nationwide technical-support organization for two years and a nationwide service organization for a combined total of 10 years.

* Demonstrated Customer Service Center process management and orchestration at director level, providing technical direction, focus and decision-making for all IT/IS operations. Served as liaison to sales, engineering, and customer support elements/systems support.

* Recognized as an outstanding leader, team leader, project planner, and project developer with visionary leadership skills transferable to senior-level positions in service, finance, sales, and customer service. Designed programs that correlated sales and support services to increase productivity and customer satisfaction.

References Available Upon Request

ALAN C. GROSSMAN
alan_gross@pacbell.net

12 Deerborne Drive • Los Angeles, California 94920 • 560.980-3828

TECHNOLOGY INDUSTRY EXECUTIVE

Building innovative technology ventures into well-established and profitable market leaders with stable workforces and long-term employee loyalty.

- Information Technology & Internet Business Ventures
- Software Licensing, Development, & Deployment
- Sales, Marketing, & Business Development – US & International
- Business Operations Design, Development, & Optimization
- Finance, Accounting, & Cash Flow Management
- Banking & Venture Capital Funding
- Acquisitions & Internal Funding
- Investor & Shareholder Relations
- New Product & Service Development
- Customer Development & Retention

PROFESSIONAL EXPERIENCE

Founder & Chairman   **MEETING.COM / MEETING INTERNATIONAL**, Irvine, CA

Forecasted the emergence and phenomenal growth of the Internet, launched innovative business to create a global communications network for affinity groups, and built new venture from concept into a 100-employee organization currently generating over $1.5 million in profitable annual revenues. (7 years)

New Business Start-Up & Growth. Leveraged technology innovation into a workable and marketable solution, established operations, and built into a successful and profitable organization. Subsequently revised business plan, technology services, and delivery models to keep pace with changing market and client demands.

Market Positioning. Designed and implemented one of the first service models to provide an international electronic forum for groups with common interests to use the Internet as the best vehicle for real-time group communications. Subsequently positioned company as the leading third-party provider of distance learning, currently hosting 100+ online campuses with 45,000 users in both educational institutions and corporations.

Partnerships & Market Success. Created a collaborative partnership with the University of Alabama to create virtual classrooms providing distance learning and educational services. Built their student base from 50 to 6,000 over four years and positioned the University as the largest online campus in the world.

Sales, Marketing, & Business Development. Established a firm presence within the niche affinity market and acquired clients across diverse business sectors (e.g., educational institutions, corporate/nonprofit boards of directors, branch office associations, international companies, religious organizations).

Technology Infrastructure. Created a sophisticated environment for both PC and MAC environments, integrating email, modem, audio, and visual technologies.

Business Infrastructure. Built the entire corporate infrastructure, sales and marketing organization, financial and accounting systems, a quality-driven customer service function, and all day-to-day operations. Recruited talented management team and technologists, maintaining an extremely stable workforce within the volatile California marketplace.

Founder & CEO   **GROSSMAN BUSINESS SYSTEMS**, Los Angeles, CA

Built entrepreneurial venture (mainframe data services) from start-up to $30 million in annual revenues with 225 employees. Doubled revenues each year for 14 consecutive years, building GBS into the largest privately held technology company of its kind in the Western US. (21 years)

Technology Products & Services. Identified and optimized market opportunity for the delivery of mainframe data services (transaction processing, order entry systems, database design/administration, direct mail operations), software licensing, and packaged application services. Created a sophisticated internal technology infrastructure with state-of-the-art hardware platforms, software, and applications.

Venture Capital Funding. Structured an innovative VC funding program exchanging technology for corporate stock to acquire all requisite technology hardware and software to build and grow GBS while avoiding any long-term corporate debt obligations.

Acquisitions & Corporate Development. Launched an aggressive acquisition program to acquire technologies and gain market share. Structured and negotiated six successful acquisitions, all internally funded with no initial out-of-pocket expenses. Facilitated integration of technologies, clients and personnel into existing corporate infrastructure.

Sales, Marketing & Business Development. Built customer base to over 2,000 clients, including numerous Fortune 500 companies (e.g., Apple Computer, Motorola, PG&E, Pacific Telephone, INTEL Corporation, US Leasing, Pacific Stock Exchange, Ziff Publishing, Centex Communications, Princess Cruises, OCTEL, HUD). Positioned GBS as a cost-effective, efficient, and modern alternative to internal client IT operations, justified cost and created "win-win" relationships. Retained core customer base for over a decade.

Market Positioning. Established GBS as one of the largest and most modern data centers in the region with 5,000+ terminals worldwide. Consistently outpaced competition with innovative technology products, services, and support programs to dominate the competition and sustain double-digit profitability.

Infrastructure Development. Built the entire operating infrastructure, sales and marketing organization, and financial function. Recruited and led six-person team of corporate officers and division vice presidents to guide business growth and operations. Achieved and sustained a stable workforce despite industry volatility.

Corporate Sale. Presented with extremely profitable divestiture opportunity and negotiated/closed company sale in 1989. Retained by the Board of Directors to assist with transition over the next year.

PROFESSIONAL AFFILIATIONS

Governor, International Council for Computer Systems & Technologies (1999 to Present)
Chairman & Founder, Computer Committee, Finnish Club (1989 to Present)
Finance Committee, Finnish Club (1988 to Present)
Associate, Kennedy Institute on War and Peace (1999 to Present)
World Presidents' Organization (1990 to Present) / **Young Presidents' Organization** (1981 to 1990)
Finance Committee, Los Angeles Yacht Club (1995 to 1998)
Founder & Director, Monterey Research Institute (1979 to 1997)

EDUCATION

TOLEDO UNIVERSITY / OHIO STATE UNIVERSITY – Accounting & Statistics

MELISSA HASTINGS

22 Mars Road
Rocklin, CA 95677

Email: chastingsc@coldrain.com

Telephone: (917) 665-9090
Mobile: (917) 631-6661

IT PROJECT MANAGER • ADMINISTRATIVE SPECIALIST • OFFICE MANAGER

Energetic, intuitive leader, motivated by tight deadlines and the pressure of excellence. Consistencies of problem-solving, decision-making, and methods of attacking issues logically have become hallmarks of employment over a diverse and progressively ascending career. A forward thinker, strategic planner; outstanding ability to multitask and juggle several projects simultaneously—with no discernible sacrifice to system quality or customer service levels. Lead by example; promote and expect high professional standards that endorse a "can do" team environment and the willingness to "go the extra mile."

- Business Process Reengineering
- Procedure Optimization
- Workflow Management & Prioritization

- Staff Recruitment, Training, & Supervision
- IT Purchasing & Negotiations
- Project Coordination

- Budget & Resource Allocations/ Projections
- Technology Management
- Help Desk Support

TECHNOLOGY SYNOPSIS

Applications: Microsoft Office 97-2002, MS Project
Databases: MS Access
Internet: Internet Explorer; Netscape Navigator
E-Mail: Lotus Notes, Outlook 97-2002, Eudora, Netscape Mail
Platforms: Windows 2000 /NT/95/98/ME
Multimedia: Media Player, Quick Time,; Real Player
Networks: Cisco VPN Altiga, Cisco Wireless Aironet, Network Backups, Net Store, TTIL 5.0
Intranets: Citrix ICA

EMPLOYMENT CHRONOLOGY

THE EXPORT CORPORATION

Feb 02–Present

Office Manager, Management Information Systems Department

Report to: Manager, Information Systems & Technical Services
Budget: $1 million (Operational & Project)
Environment: Multiple departments with 190 desktops, 50 laptops, and Windows 2000 LAN. Provide support for all internal systems, system development, and help-desk functions.

Confronted upon commencement with undocumented software and equipment, and an ad-hoc approach to maintenance reports and expenditure monitoring.

- **Spearheaded centralization process to consolidate all software and equipment registers** via a user-friendly and accurate database producing "at-a-glance" reports on maintenance contracts, budget allocations, and department expenditure trends.
- **Successfully bargained with seasoned negotiators on purchase of competitive hardware and software products.** Consistent record of success in winning discounted prices and value-added options for items up to $50,000.
- **Key contributor in large-scale desktop rollout project**; collaborated with IT manager to strategically plan time frames, and coordinate resources and technical personnel. Praised by departmental managers for keeping them "in the loop" by regularly communicating issues, priorities, and project expectations.

ROYAL BANK OF CANADA, **Business Analyst (Contract)**

Sep 01–Feb 02

Researched, categorized, and recorded all company software and licensing information, from internal applications through proprietary office suites. Delivered completed inventory of 600+ items within deadline, linking to all license and support chains.

PDP INSURANCE CO., **Support Analyst**   Aug 99—Mar 00

Multifaceted role offering Level 1 and 2 desktop support for 300 end users on issues surrounding Microsoft Office Suite, Novell, patching equipment, new hire builds, software installations, peripheral equipment, Internet, and internal clients.

- Coordinated numerous multi-phased PC and peripheral relocations as the company consolidated and downsized operations. Conceived and documented schedules, and synchronized technical staff to attend outside business hours to lessen impact on daily operations. **Relocations proceeded seamlessly, with no data lost and no interruptions to end users** during business hours.
- Refined help-desk support system to reroute inquiries instantly to help-desk operators.
- Principal point of contact between external engineers and customers. Fielded inquiries from customers on the progress of issues, and freed engineers from customer contact to concentrate on producing technical solutions.

HORWATH CLARK WHITEHILL, London, **Senior Project Coordinator (Contract)**   Jan 99–Aug 99

Project: PMS – Project Management System. An automated timekeeping system for accounts and administrative support personnel to process and bill time to clients.

Led team of 3 in devising, testing, and rolling out new automated timekeeping function, designed to facilitate fundamental infrastructure change, replace antiquated paper system, and reduce staff headcount in an environment resistant to change. Managed project timelines, resources, and objectives, developed test case plans and training programs, chaired weekly progress meetings, and fielded inquiries from staff. Project was a resounding success, **delivered on time and within budget**.

- **Devised learner-friendly training program** that represented the different levels of computer literacy from novice to advanced users. Presented training courses and conducted in-house change management seminars, winning positive audience feedback for clarity of communications and knowledge of subject matter.
- Presided over system testing prior to going "live." Resolved system bugs, documented changes and fixes, converted data with no errors, and provided post-live support that transitioned users to new system and reinforced training.

CHRISTIE'S AUCTION HOUSE, London, **IT Trainer**   May 97–Jan 99

Offered help-desk support on DOS-based internal applications and Microsoft Office for over 1,500 end users across London and Europe. Transformed computer novices to advanced users of internal systems and Microsoft Office packages through one-on-one and advanced training.

SYNTEGRA, London, **Support Analyst**   Apr 96–May 97

Responded to ISDN line and gateway faults. Identified and prioritized issues for escalated resolution in a critical environment necessitating high-security clearance for the billions of pounds in transactions passed daily. Principal point of contact for fielding customer inquiries, complaints, and support.

- **Produced "Front-Line Support Guide," a step-by-step blueprint** for handling customer-support issues, monitoring progress, and maintaining lines of communication to circumvent customer ill will.

PRIOR EMPLOYMENT:

- **Human Resources/Assistant,** Whitehorse Financial Services (1994–1996). **Receptionist,** Vale Veterinary Group (1992-1994)

EDUCATION

Certificate of Information Technology   Johnson College, London UK

Secondary Schooling, UK   Graduated with A Levels; 3 CSEs; 5 O Levels

DARRELL A. SIMPSON

135 Northline, Redford, MI 48222

333.777.4444 • maverik@arc.net

SYSTEMS ANALYST / BUSINESS ANALYST / PROJECT LEAD / TEAM LEAD

Accomplished **Systems Analyst** and **Computer Support Professional** skilled in all facets of desktop and application systems, sales support, planning/design, programming, installation, configuration, and maintenance. Over 11 years of experience and business knowledge in the marketing, manufacturing, and customer service sectors.

Analytical thinker with exceptional project management, organizational, interpersonal, and communication skills, as well as demonstrated ability to manage multiple priorities in fast-paced environments. Ability to convey complex solutions to end user in a simplified manner. Strong leadership qualities and dedicated team player.

COMPUTER EXPERTISE

Operating Systems: MS Windows NT/95, MS-DOS, UNIX, and Novell NetWare
Programming Languages, MicroFocus, COBOL, SQL, Xerox VIPP, Assembler, Fortran, C++, Oracle, JCL, FoxPro, Magic
Application Software: MS Office 97 (Word, Excel, PowerPoint, Access, Outlook), Visio
Hardware: IBM-Compatible Microcomputers, NT Servers, Xerox 6135 DocuTech Printers, Honeywell 7000 Mainframe, High-Speed Online Inkjet Printers.

PROFESSIONAL EXPERIENCE

SYSTEMS ANALYST, GRANGE MARKETING SERVICES, Detroit, MI (1994 - 2002)

Hired as Junior Programmer and promoted to Systems Analyst after four years. Maintained existing applications and designed, coded and tested new ones requested by client to meet customer requirements. Worked on high-visibility projects for Ford dealerships, interacting closely with print, production, and sales to ensure smooth operations. Revised ISO 9000 documents with Quality Department. Supervised and mentored four junior programmers.

Large Applications
- (FDCC Program) - Provided technical and systems support to sales department and in-house project facilitators. Produced weekly packing slips for shipment of marketing material to all dealerships in the United States, including Alaska and Hawaii. Programming changes were made each week to meet shipment needs for 4,000+ dealers.
- Recognized by client for outstanding performance on monthly reporting project.

Interdepartmental Support
- Gathered job specifications and necessary requirements from sales, production, and print departments to ensure produced marketing materials met client expectations.
- Collaborated with outside vendors such as UPS, Airborne, and Xerox to upgrade systems and analyze/correct problems. Also, set up new and consolidated existing templates for batch-label runs.
- Heavily involved in conversion from mainframe to client server for Y2K compliance.

Sales Support
- Quoted new jobs for Sales Department.
- Accompanied sales team in gathering specifications and project details, offering technical assistance as needed.

HELP DESK TECHNICAL REP, LASER CORPORATION, Westland, MI (1993 - 1994)

Supported sales reps throughout country, setting up, testing, and sending collection letters to customers. Received information from sales to personalize letters to meet client specifications.

- Worked extensively with customers to provide the products they wanted and to make collections easier.

DATA SECURITY/AUDIT COORDINATOR, ELECTRONIC DATA SYSTEMS, Northville, MI (1985 - 1992)

Worked on-site at a GM engine manufacturing plant, acting as liaison between analysts and the IT operations equipment to prevent downtime. Provided technical support for printers and PCs throughout the plant.

- Oversaw ACF2 system that handled employee IDs for the various levels of password access.
- Trained end users in logging on and accessing the system.

Previous positions at EDS as a Team Lead at Troy Print Center and as a Courier.

EDUCATION

Enrolled in **B.S.** for *Computer Information Systems*, Madonna University, Livonia, MI - expected graduation 4/04

* One of six recipients in 1996 to receive award for highest GPA in major (CIS) - continually on Dean's List

Associate in Science, *Computer Science*, Henry Ford Community College, Dearborn, MI

GLENN C. MARTIN

805-225-7949 • gcm@email.com
1382 White Tail Lane • Bakersfield • CA • 93307

SENIOR PROJECT MANAGER

Systems Engineering and Design ... Internet Technology & E-commerce ... Strategic IT Sourcing
Technology Solutions & Systems Integration ... Cross-Functional Technology Teams

Fast-track management career; combine visionary leadership with technology expertise to analyze needs, define parameters, and lead cross-functional teams in the development of cost-effective solutions. Excel at assessing and proactively responding to changing organizational needs. Excellent communication, troubleshooting, and interpersonal skills; diligent and detail-oriented. Strong commitment to deliver timely, accurate, and quality work.

TECHNICAL EXPERTISE

Microsoft
Windows 2000 Directory Services Infrastructure • NT Server 4.0 Enterprise Technologies
TCP/IP on Windows NT 4.0 • Internet Information Server • SQL Servers 7.0 and 2000
Visual Basic 6.0 for Applications • Project 2000

E-Business
Disaster Recovery/Business Continuance • Security • Strategic IT Sourcing • Managed Services Collocation
Network Monitoring & Management • Streaming Content • B2B E-commerce
Scalable Data Storage

CRM/ERP Solutions
SAP • PeopleSoft • Siebel • Oracle E-business suite • Microsoft Great Plains • BEA WebLogic WebMethods •
CommerceOne • SAS

Networking
Firewall • VPN • Load Balancing • XML & SSL Acceleration • DNS • Caching
Interconnecting Cisco Network Devices (ICND)

NOTEWORTHY CAREER HIGHLIGHTS

Challenge: Turn around failing customer relations to retain Dell's largest customer. **Action:** Developed an aggressive recovery strategy to foster communication and resolve all outstanding conflicts. **Result: Within 6 months of takeover, reduced response time by 500%; increased customer service scores from 1.33 to 5 (on a scale of 1-5); and drove revenue increases by 400%.**

Challenge: Automate and streamline the vote-history research process. **Action**: Led a cross-functional team in reengineering the existing flat-file system to a relational database with a web browser interface allowing for execution of queries and drill-down reports. **Result: Realized annual savings of more than $240,000 and increased reporting accuracy to almost 100%.**

Challenge: Distribute timely corporate communications to targeted interest groups and constituencies. **Action**: Drove the compilation of a 2.5-million record database, automating the transmission process through integration with fax and email services. **Result: Instant transmission of corporate message to targeted audiences which significantly expanded constituent and interest group awareness. Increased published news stories by 800% within first year of launch. Negotiated a 200% reduction in provider fees.**

Challenge: Automate administrative tasks and accelerate approval process. **Action**: Conceptualized, planned, designed, and coordinated a secure, confidential corporate Intranet. **Result: Reduced administrative staff time by 50 hours per month; cut management approval processes in half; and saved more than $6,000 in paper costs within the first year.**

Challenge: Create a database solution providing shared access to multiple customers while decreasing customer cost and increasing profitability. **Action**: Designed and implemented a shared SQL server solution providing access via ODBC from a customer web server. **Result: Significantly reduced capital costs and increased monthly profits from $8,500 to $25,000 per server (over 300%).**

Challenge: Unite a sales department floundering from lack of direction and product knowledge, and reduce 3- to 5-month delivery time. **Action**: Created a sales and marketing plan clearly defining products and services. **Result: Addressed all potential problems up-front through a new business prospect review meeting, and reduced product and service delivery time to less than 30 days.**

PROFESSIONAL EXPERIENCE

DELL SERVICES, Bakersfield, California – since January 2001
(Strategic IT sourcing services)

Channel Account Manager
Redefined project objectives, rebuilt customer relations, accelerated product development cycle, reduced costs, and drove revenue increases for the company's largest client, Merrill Lynch Consulting.

- Instituted a direct service and support policy that fostered responsive problem resolution and reduced overhead by 500% within 6 months.
- Reengineered server standby operations, reducing costs by 50% and saving the company and its customers more than $10,000 per month for each hot-cold SQL configuration.
- Drove system reconfigurations that permitted the timely delivery of easy-to-understand SLA reports.

ILLINOIS STATE ASSEMBLY, Chicago, Illinois – 1995 to 2000

Director of IT – 1999-2000
Senior Technical Project Manager – 1997-1999
Deputy Director of IT – 1996
Network Administrator – 1996
Hired as a **Systems Engineer** and fast-tracked into a management position within one year. Developed strategic IT objectives and directed a $7-million computer services operating budget. Provided visionary leadership to cross-functional teams to ensure cost-effective business solutions were delivered to customers on time and within budget.

EDUCATION / TRAINING

Completed all MCSE coursework
Certified Project Management Professional (PMP) – anticipated October 2003

Completed 100+ hours towards **Bachelor of Arts in Business Administration** – anticipated May 2003
Kansas State University, Manhattan, Kansas

PROFESSIONAL AFFILIATIONS

Project Management Institute (PMI)

JACQUES CAPPELLINI

1000 Hollow Nut Road • Bronxville, New York 10983

Residence: 914-887-3428   Email: jcapp@arc.org   Business: 212-909-1766

INTERNATIONAL BUSINESS EXECUTIVE
Executive Vice President / Managing Director / COO / CEO
US, Latin America, Asia & Australia

Twenty-year leadership career building profitable international business organizations, including start-up ventures, acquisitions, turnarounds, and high-growth organizations. Expert strategist, analyst, planner, team leader, negotiator, and business driver who has delivered dramatic gains in revenues, profits, and market share in both developed and emerging nations. Fluent in English, Portuguese, and Spanish. Cross-functional management responsibility for:

- Profit & Loss Performance
- Multi-Site Operating Management
- Strategic Alliances & Partnerships
- Product Design & Development

- Marketing & Business Development
- Infrastructure Development & Optimization
- Mergers, Acquisitions, & Joint Ventures
- Information & Telecommunications Technology

PROFESSIONAL EXPERIENCE:

CRESCENT EMERGING MARKETS LTD. – New York   1998 to Present

President & CEO

Recruited by shareholders of this start-up technology venture (collects and disseminates data on publicly traded companies in 62 emerging market countries) to redesign product development, sales and marketing strategies, build organizational infrastructure, and competitively position for long-term, profitable growth. Selected from a competitive group of top-level executives based upon extensive experience in the planning and leadership of related technology and information provider organizations.

- Built infrastructure, reorganized management team, recruited staff, and positioned company for $6 million in annual revenues by 2002 and $14 million by 2004.
- Accelerated product development cycle and managed database development through completion.
- Established and built a multi-tiered, third-party distribution network to expand market reach.
- Structured and negotiated $1 million in financings to support current cash requirements.

RAND-CENTRAL AMERICA INC. – New York   1993 to 1998

Executive Vice President / COO – Latin America (1996 to 1998)
Senior Vice President – Latin America (1993 to 1996)

High-profile leadership position as a member of Rand's Executive Management Committee and Rand America Holdings Executive Committee. Full strategic, operating, marketing, business development, and P&L responsibility for all Latin American operations. Scope of responsibility included regional managers, country managers, marketing directors, financial director, technical director, HR manager, and a staff of 400+.

Challenged to reinvent the Latin American business organization and create a market-driven acquisition program to capitalize upon emerging business opportunities. Clients included major US and international banking and capital markets institutions and local financial and media organizations.

- Achieved/surpassed all financial objectives. Increased revenue from $40 million to $85 million, profits from $4 million to $13 million, and market penetration (terminals installed) by more than 200%.
- Relocated Latin American HQ to New York City to enhance synergy between all Americas operations.
- Restructured entire organization and supporting infrastructure. Hired new management and marketing talent, shifted decision-making responsibilities to the country level, and repositioned market focus.
- Identified opportunity, structured and launched Rand's first commercial broadcast television venture, a 24-hour Spanish language news channel broadcasting in the US, Spain, and Latin America.

RAND-CENTRAL AUSTRALIA – Sydney   1990 to 1992

Managing Director – Australia & New Zealand (1991 to 1992)
Regional Applications Manager – Southeast Asia (1990)

Promoted and given full responsibility for the marketing, development, operations, and P&L performance of Rand's business organizations throughout Australia and New Zealand. Led through a multidisciplinary organization comprised of a wholly-owned subsidiary, a company-owned subsidiary, and a third-party distributorship.

- Despite country-wide market instability, delivered 5% revenue and profit growth while strategically repositioning Rand as the company of choice with all major accounts.
- Negotiated long-term contracts with Australia's four major banks, generating $24 million in annual sales.
- Appointed to Board of Directors of local software firm acquired by Rand to guide software development.
- Facilitated the merger and integration of Condel into Rand's Australian operations, eliminated unprofitable business lines, and repositioned for continued market growth.
- Reconfigured product mix, upgraded technology, and expedited all customer conversions. Transitioned product focus to more advanced technology with lower volume, higher quality, and improved profitability.
- Downsized operations in New Zealand and increased margins to 45% on $12 million in annual sales.

RAND-CENTRAL ASIA – Hong Kong   1988 to 1989

Marketing Manager

Recruited to Rand to conceive, create, and implement a completely new Information Management Systems strategy and business throughout the entire Asian market. Scope of responsibility extended from product planning, design, and development to market launch and ongoing customer support.

CRESCENT STAR BANK – Hong Kong   1985 to 1987

Vice President – Asia/Pacific Operations & Systems – Global Trading & Treasury Division

Led design, engineering, and execution of new systems architecture, advanced technologies, and global LAN to support operations throughout Asia Pacific (total of 12 branches and more than 500 employees).

CRESCENT STAR BANK – New York   1983 to 1985

Vice President / Group Project Manager – Global Trading & Treasury Division

High-profile HQ position leading the design, development, and implementation of advanced technologies, networks, and applications across all core financial, trading, and treasury systems.

BANCO MARA / CRESCENT STAR BANK – Lima   1968 to 1983

Senior Vice President – Systems Planning & Development

Fast-track promotion through a series of increasingly responsible MIS management positions to final promotion as Senior Vice President (equivalent to CIO) for one of Peru's largest financial institutions.

EDUCATION:

UNIVERSITY OF MICHIGAN	Strategic Planning (1994)
NORTHWESTERN UNIVERSITY / KELLOGG	Executive Development Program (1984)
ESCOLA NACIONAL DE QUIMICA	Mechanical Engineering (1967-69)

PERSONAL PROFILE: Peruvian Citizen … US Permanent Resident.

DIANE REED

803 N. 10th Street
San Jose, CA 95110

(408) 225-3421 Home   d_reed@msnn.com   (408) 936-2424 Cell

International Marketing Manager

PROFESSIONAL SUMMARY

Motivational global marketing evangelist with 15 years of proven results. Strong ability to create and communicate a call-to-action. Proven ability to increase sales, build brand awareness, and promote a company's image. Ability to keep both the big picture and all of its facets in mind. Strong ability to build enthusiasm around object of marketing. Ability to successfully relate to and work with diverse people, adapt to cultures, and travel extensively. Outstanding communication skills as a trainer, educator, and motivator. Unequaled professional who embraces change and thrives on challenge.

Collaborative Marketing: Established marketing relationships with big players such as Intel, Microsoft, and Sun Microsystems.

Budget Management: Managed seven-figure marketing budget. All projects delivered within or under budget.

Innovative Techniques: Successfully approached circuit board marketing as B2C product.

International Relationship Building: Traveled worldwide, successfully developing key markets and relationships.

PROFESSIONAL EXPERIENCE

CADENCE DESIGN SYSTEMS, INC., San Jose, CA   1999–2003
Manager, Worldwide Field Marketing
Worked collaboratively to define product direction and technology enhancements to create market-driven, solution-based tools. Traveled to Europe and Pacific Rim to meet with customers and the Cadence Design Systems field organizations in a marketing evangelist role.

- Worked collaboratively to successfully launch (both externally and internally) four products within an 11-month time period.
- Successfully collaborated to enter into joint marketing relationships with Intel, Microsoft, and Sun Microsystems.

HEWLETT-PACKARD COMPANY, Palo Alto, CA   1993–1999
Corporate Director of Marketing
Managed the Hewlett-Packard products and services branding campaign by creating the most effective, visible, and consistent marketing communications of any printed circuit board company in North America. Closely collaborated with trademark attorneys to protect intellectual properties, logo, and name. Assisted in investor relations activities, including compliance with SEC regulations and communicating with shareholders, financial media, and financial analysts. Assisted in developing prospectus for 1996 IPO.

- Instrumental in company growth from two to 19 divisions domestically and internationally. Revenues increased from $50 million to $240 million.
- Managed and allocated annual marketing budget which grew from $50,000 in 1992 to $1.5 million. Met budget on every project.
- Innovator of new approach to circuit board marketing as a not only B2B product but also as a B2C product.
- Developed global marketing and international collateral for Israel, Singapore, Hong Kong, Malaysia, Japan, China, Scotland, Ireland, and England. Traveled frequently to these regions and developed ongoing relationships with key influencers, including editors and publishers of trade magazines in Asia, Israel, Europe, and the United States.

109

Professional Experience, Continued

HANOVER CORPORATION (sister company of Hewlett-Packard), Menlo Park, CA   1994–1995
Director of Sales and Marketing

Managed sales and marketing for start-up company while on loan from Hewlett-Packard. Developed company positioning and image from start-up phase to completion. Developed collateral to launch initial product. Assisted in development of English/Hebrew user manual. Completed the mission of helping create a company and making it attractive to an outside buyer.

UNITED AIRLINES, Chicago, IL   1986–1993
On-Duty Manager, In-Flight Operations (1990–1993)

Handled all in-flight irregularities and onboard crises from a crisis communications/damage control standpoint. Served on various task forces to develop better ways to serve customers while saving the company money.

Corporate Sales Development and Marketing Associate, UA Headquarters   (1986–1990)

Researched ways to improve customer satisfaction and boost return on investment. Made recommendations on event sponsorships, product endorsements, and co-op endorsements with other companies.

EDUCATION

Working toward **B.S. in International Business/Marketing,** San Jose State University, San Jose, CA

Additional Professional Development Coursework:

High-Tech Marketing, Everest Advisory Group, 2001
Value Selling Workshop, Value Vision Associates, 2000
Value Differentiation Workshop, Value Vision Associates, 2000
Working Collaboratively, Leadership Dynamics, 2000
Fundamentals of Finance and Accounting for Non-Financial Professionals, American Management Association International, 1998
Conflict Management Skills for Women, SkillPath Seminars, 1998
Strategic Planning for High-Tech Markets, Oregon Graduate Institute, 1998
Winning Technology Leadership, Ivey Business School, Executive MBA Program, London Ontario, Canada, 1996

PROFESSIONAL AFFILIATIONS

American Marketing Association
Women in Technology, Inc.
American Electronics Association

■ ■ ■

Charlotte Tybee

520 Mountain Ridge Road   Gold Canyon, AZ 85219   CT400@coldrain.com   ☏ 928.998.2312

What I can offer Trentco as your newest Asset Management Specialist

❑ Leveraging inventory expertise to benefit management across the board ❑ Translating inventory **data** into information that builds and keeps profits ❑ Designing, building, and managing inventory systems from scratch ❑ Transforming accountability systems into tools that keep your company competitive ❑ Recruiting, training, and retaining excellent teams

Recent work history with examples of problems solved

❑ *Hired away by executive management to be* **Corporate Fixed Assets Manager,** BB Services, Scottsdale, Arizona   Aug 98 – Apr 02

BB offers communications, cable, telephone, & high-speed Internet in five Southern states.

Managed an inventory worth more than **$18M**. Indirectly supervised 20 equipment control clerks.

Sought out to **build our company's entire inventory system from scratch** — starting with no training, no employees, no building, and no vendors. Did it all, from buying the building to writing every procedure to hiring the staff. **Payoffs: Up and running well in just months** — a rare feat.

Traveled to five locations to apply the lessons I mastered throughout our company. **Payoffs: Transformed rooms of thousands of randomly stacked items into a system that others could maintain even after I left.**

Found and fixed an inventory problem that cost us millions of dollars for more than five years, after others' solutions had failed. Tracked the glitch to a training deficiency in customer service. Won full management support for my plan, which had **nearly no additional costs. Payoffs: In six months, losses dropped to zero** and stayed there.

Soon noticed that the cost of our vendor-provided repairs was too high. Persuaded management to adopt my suggestions to boost vendor quality and accountability and **save** money. **Payoffs: Significant savings** from the first year. **Quality of customer service rose sharply,** a key item in our very competitive market.

Transformed data into information that **saved us millions**. Found our techs weren't trained to identify reparable items reliably. My tested plan got management's strong support. **Payoffs: Repair and accounts receivable costs dropped fast.** Customer service and employee morale much improved.

❑ **Assistant Manager,** Auto Electric Service Company, Phoenix, Arizona   Jan 97 – Aug 98
Auto Electric was the local AC Delco distributor.

Managed an inventory worth **$200K**.

Did my homework to persuade seasoned owner to move from manual to computer-based inventory control. Applied what I learned in a different industry to **give his company confidence to accept change**. *Payoffs:* Stock levels, reorder points, inventory accountability, and customer service at **top-notch levels in just six months.**

❑ Converter Control Clerk *promoted over three more senior people to be* Repair Supervisor and **Warehouse Manager**, Cablesys of Arizona, Phoenix, Arizona
Jul 83 – Dec 96
Cablesys was a cable TV provider.

Had full responsibility for hundreds of line items stored in a 10K ft² warehouse.

Stopped a major inventory loss that had gone unchecked for years. For the first time, held all 60 repair professionals accountable for the $1,500 in tools we issued each of them. Coordinated closely with other divisions, then wrote the procedures. *Payoffs:* **General Manager bought my plan unchanged; thousands of dollars saved.**

Made time to learn our sales department's special needs. Worked closely with them to make our inventory support their marketing campaigns. Did my homework, then **convinced management** that investing in **inventory levels linked to sales** projections was **sound business.** *Payoffs:* Huge — and lasting — **drop in customer complaints.**

EDUCATION

❑ Two years of college coursework at Arizona State University, Tempe, Arizona   78 – 80
Paid my own way. **Dean's List.**

COMPUTER SKILLS

❑ Expert in Word and Excel; proficient in **proprietary inventory control software suite** and Internet search protocols; working knowledge of Quicken.

Page Two

WARD JOHNSON

23223 White Oak Drive   Long Beach, California   714 302-6332

Results-oriented, dedicated, honest, hands-on **INVESTIGATOR** with 20+ years experience. Combines strong field experience with outstanding qualifications. Expert in law enforcement training and interagency relations. Unique combination of intuitive and analytical abilities. Enthusiastic, highly motivated, and resourceful; can be counted on to get the job done. Professional, articulate, and self-confident. Meticulous and mature team player, yet decisive in self-implementation, to complete any task in a precise and timely manner. Intricate knowledge of how to deal with people from various socio-economic backgrounds. Outstanding writing skills. Computer literate.

Combines strong training, resource management, budgeting, and technology skills with excellent performance in liaison affairs, negotiations, investigations, and data analysis. Keen negotiation, problem-solving, crisis management, and relationship management skills. Quick and effective problem-solver while dealing with new concepts, systems, and procedures. Powerful presentation and communication skills.

Expert in the use of advanced technologies for research, reporting/documentation, competitive intelligence, information management, and other applications. Strengths include thorough knowledge of California Penal Code; civil law experience; organizational and administrative management; and leadership skills. Strong knowledge of general police duties including:

Evidence Collection/Protection	Resource/Protection Programs	Investigation/Search Procedures
Security/Emergency Response	Defense Management	Traffic Control/Operations
Apprehension/Advisement of Rights	Court Testimony	Dispatching

EXPERIENCE

Fast-track promotion since 1991 based on consistently thorough outstanding work notwithstanding increased responsibility with tighter deadlines.

INVESTIGATOR   2001 - Present
Officer Involved Shooting (OIS) Section, Critical Incident Investigation Division
Long Branch Police Department (LBPD)

> Selected to serve in this newly formed OIS section. Investigate citywide officer-involved shootings, upper body control holds, law enforcement activity related deaths, and in-custody deaths. Conduct highly sensitive, confidential administrative investigations involving in-depth interviews of involved and witness officers, civilian witnesses, victims, and suspects. Ensure tactical, drawing, and exhibiting of firearm, use of force (UOF), and all related issues are thoroughly addressed prior to reports being written and submitted to UOF Review Board for adjudication before being submitted to the Chief of Police and Police Commission.

> Astute at recognizing areas in need of improvement, with the vision to develop action steps and see them through to a prompt and successful completion. Determine if a crime has been committed. Use database researches, cameras, and recorders. Participate in multi-car vehicular surveillance. Provide accurate, concise, and timely reports.

> Frequently assigned more complex/intricate cases and original jurisdiction investigations. Act as liaison between local law enforcement, Police Commission, and District Attorney's Office. Knowledge of criminal law.

> Earned **numerous commendations** for outstanding service and report writing.

INVESTIGATOR 1996 - 2001
Law Enforcement Injury Investigation Section, Detective Headquarters Division (DHD), LBPD

Recruited to investigate and supervise citywide officer-involved UOF incidents resulting in the suspect(s) being hospitalized, all officer-involved animal shootings, and non-tactical accidental discharge shootings without injuries. Reconstructed shootings. Edited and supervised writing of all reports prior to submission to UOF Review Board for adjudication. Thorough knowledge of criminal and civil procedures.

DETECTIVE II (Supervisor) 1995 - 1996
Gun Detail, LBPD

Supervised police officers and detectives.

DETECTIVE I 1994 - 1995
Gun Detail, DHD, LBPD

Conducted investigations which often led to filing criminal charges when federal, state, and local firearm regulations were violated, as well as inspections of pawn shops, sporting goods stores, and private individuals who held federal firearms licenses.

PATROLMAN / FIELD SERGEANT 1991 – 1994
Long Branch Police Department
Supervised 6 to 30 officers simultaneously.

Prior to 1991

EDUCATION

Courses in Business Administration, California State University, Long Beach
Graduate, Los Angeles Police Department Academy
P.O.S.T. Training: Standard, Intermediate, Advanced, Supervisory
Numerous courses in supervisory skills, weapons, rules and regulations

Deborah Dulaney, AIC

1776 Patriot Lane, Bridgewater, NJ 08807
(908) 575-5555 § debdulaney@msn.com

Executive Staff Support / Office Management / Administrative Management
Legal & Insurance Industries ▪ Knowledge of Medical Transcription & Terminology

---

CAREER PROFILE

☑ More than 15 years' experience in legal and insurance settings. Promoted through increasingly responsible positions to office administration and senior-level executive staff support.

☑ Accustomed to independent decision-making authority. Strong project management, supervisory, organizational, and problem-solving skills. Associate-in-Claims Certification.

☑ Keen understanding of business priorities…a genuine team player committed to doing whatever is necessary to help executives and companies be successful. "Make-It-Happen" person.

☑ Proven professionalism acting as prime interface between senior attorneys and high-profile business clients, staff, boards of directors, vendors, and governmental agencies.

☑ Dependable, loyal, discreet, and tactful, with impeccable integrity and professionalism.

PROFESSIONAL EXPERIENCE

McCafferty, Holden, Goldman, & Levinsen, PC, Woodbridge, NJ   1993 – present
Legal Secretary to Partner – Asbestos Dept. (1999 – present), **Legal Assistant**   (1993 – 1999)

Oversee and manage office administration, scheduling, legal documentation / record keeping, and account billing for busy, growing Asbestos Department with four major clients in oil production, electrical supplies, manufacturing, and plumbing supplies.

- Efficiently manage 500 – 600 active case files (complex multi-plaintiff and multi-defendant cases with 300 – 350 sub-files) by creating and utilizing computerized spreadsheets, tables, and progress charts to track case activities. Add 390 – 400 new case files annually.

- Saved $16,200 monthly in attorney's billable time by independently reviewing files, composing legal pleadings, briefings, and correspondence. Completed all reviews, motions, and briefs for 57 asbestos cases within 10 business days – three days prior to court deadline.

- Streamlined turnaround time for receipt of new files, initial documentation creation, actual billable accounting, and working time from 96 hours to within 24 hours.

- Doubled departmental productivity by promoting the benefit of additional staff, after careful needs assessment and review of office procedures. Participated in hiring, and successfully trained, supervised, and coached support staff to achieve team results within aggressive deadlines.

- Designed and developed case management forms, efficiently presenting case-file information for attorney's review at court hearings, and reducing the need for large, complicated case files.

Edison Lakes Insurance Company, Edison, NJ   1988 – 1993
Paralegal to Senior In-House Counsel / Claims Adjuster
Recruited by mid-sized insurance firm with subsidiaries nationwide to assist senior-level attorney.

- Prepared legal documents for auto, property, personal injury, workers' compensation, and homeowners' claims. Interviewed claimants and witnesses, obtained and investigated medical records, and recorded statements for relevant case-file information.

- Selected to evaluate and settle all claims for the small claims department. Attained track record of speedily settling claims (in less than three days). Negotiated and developed reliable network of body shop repair facilities and other vendors for auto and property claims.

McCormack & Lasher, Princeton Junction, NJ   1986 – 1988
Office Manager / Paralegal

- Oversaw daily operations of busy general practitioner's office. Provided key administrative support for pre-trial activities, interviewing clients and witnesses to collect vital information for legal documents. Attended and assisted attorney in all depositions and trials.

- Interviewed, hired, trained, and managed five clerical support staff, coaching them in developing and maintaining good client relationship management skills and customer service.

CERTIFICATIONS

Certificate in Human Resources, Somerset County College, Somerset, NJ   2002

✓ Human Resources Management	✓ Training & Development	✓ Recruiting & Selection
✓ Compensation: Salary & Benefits	✓ Problem-Solving	✓ Employment Relations
✓ Equal Employment Opportunity	✓ Decision-Making	✓ Public Speaking

Medical Secretarial & Transcription, Carroll County Technical Institute, Carrollton, NJ   1997
Associate-in-Claims Certification, Insurance Institute of America, Malvern, PA   1990

EDUCATION

A.A.S., Paralegal / Legal Assistant Program, Mercer Community College, Trenton, NJ   1990

CONTINUING EDUCATION:
- ☑ Rutgers University Business Seminars, New Brunswick, NJ   2001 – 2002
  Management and Human Resources Seminars in Administrative Management, Team Leadership, Project Management, Payroll Management, Supervision, and Budgeting.
- ☑ Human Resources (2-day course), Legal Council of America, Princeton Junction, NJ   2001

COMPUTER SKILLS

✓ Windows XP	✓ MS Office XP	✓ MS Word	✓ Case Master (database)
✓ Windows 98/NT	✓ WordPerfect 6.1	✓ MS Excel	✓ TABS (billing system)
✓ Internet Explorer	✓ MS PowerPoint	✓ MS Access	✓ MS Outlook

PROFESSIONAL ASSOCIATIONS

Association of Trial Lawyers of America ▪ American Society of Legal Office Managers
National Notary Association – Notary Public

WILLIAM GRAYSON

122 Madison Street
Radford, VA 28938

wmgrayson49@yahao.com
Phone: 804-599-0982

MANUFACTURING INDUSTRY PROFESSIONAL
Cross-Functional Experience in Production Management, Process Design, & Quality Engineering

More than 15 years of increasing responsibilities in fast-paced, quality-driven, customer-focused manufacturing operations. High-energy, enthusiastic, and dependable team player and team leader who excels in challenging and competitive environments. Highly developed problem-solving skills with ability to "think outside the box" and deliver innovative solutions to operating challenges. Multi-talented with a broad base of experience in:

- Multi-Product Manufacturing Operations
- Product Redesign & Manufacturability
- Test Engineering & Failure Analysis
- Vendor Sourcing & Relationship Management
- Performance Improvement & Optimization

- Technical Training & Team Leadership
- Quality Improvement & Leadership
- Cost Reduction & Avoidance
- Technical Troubleshooting
- Technical Reporting & Documentation

**PC proficient with Microsoft Excel, Access, Outlook, and Word.
Experience with PowerPoint, Project, and other application-specific software.**

PROFESSIONAL EXPERIENCE:

GTE, Radford, Virginia   August 1992 to December 2002
(Acquired by Crisp-TTI in October 2000)

Manager (2000 to 2001)
Quality Engineer (1999 to 2000)
Production Supervisor (1997 to 1999)
Lead Technician (1993 to 1997)
Technician (1992 to 1993)

Fast-track promotion through a series of increasingly responsible production, operations, quality, and management positions with one of the world's leading telecommunications companies. Advanced based on consistently strong gains in production yields, operational efficiency, and quality ratings across diverse product lines. Recruited, trained, and supervised teams of up to 70 employees on three different shifts.

Successfully managed through a period of accelerated company growth and then through a multi-tiered reorganization, acquisition, and diversification.

- Led production ramp-up of new product and **increased output by 200%** to meet short-term increase in customer demand. Concurrently, **reduced scrap by 87% and failure rates by 12%, positioning production area as #1 in the company**.

- **Increased production yield by 300% within six months** after assuming responsibility for a poorly performing production line. Redesigned core planning, scheduling, staffing, and production functions to streamline processes and expedite output.

- **Launched new product into production**, managed vendor relationship, coordinated partnership with industrial engineering team, eliminated recurrent product failures, and **obtained final test yield rating of 98%**.

117

- **Revitalized non-performing engineering, operations support, and manufacturing areas challenged with personnel, material, quality, and cost problems**. Implemented immediate solutions to restore production and performance, achieve financial objectives, and meet client/ production obligations.

- **Improved product quality ratings by 7.5%** through design/implementation of a well-targeted and goal-driven quality improvement plan. In addition, improved rates of escape in one key production area (SMA) by 100%.

- Participated in the **design/redesign of more than 14 telecommunication products** to enhance product quality, manufacturability, and field performance/reliability.

- Spearheaded successful implementation of several **plantwide ISO 9000 initiatives** for FY00. Introduced innovative training, software development, and document processes to extend quality efforts throughout all core operating and business departments within the organization.

- **Benchmarked manufacturing and quality processes** and facilitated the transfer of specific processes from corporate headquarters to Radford production plant.

- **Consistently improved production yields** where others have previously been unsuccessful, **strengthening GTE's relationship with its customers** and consistently meeting production milestones and deadlines.

SMITH & GREEN, Lynchburg, Virginia   April 1988 to August 1992

> **Electronics Technologist** coordinating maintenance, repair, technical troubleshooting, and design improvements for a variety of production and quality control equipment for the nuclear industry.

UNITED STATES AIR FORCE, Germany   April 1984 to April 1988

> **Radio Maintenance Technician** responsible for installation, operation, and maintenance of ground-based radio communication systems. Transmitted highly sensitive command and control information (voice and data) in tactical field situations.

EDUCATION & PROFESSIONAL TRAINING:

- 1,500+ hours of technical training from equipment manufacturers worldwide
- 400+ hours of professional training and development courses
- **Distinguished Graduate** – Junior Management Training
- **Honors Graduate** – USAF Ground Radio Maintenance School
- **Honors Graduate** – USAF Basic Electronics School
- Miscellaneous college courses, including Maintenance Planning & Scheduling, Architecture, Business, and Human Relations

PAUL L. MICHAELS

233 Fox Runn Drive
Portland, Oregon 79382
(313) 289-9338   plmike@arc.net

SENIOR MARKETING & BUSINESS DEVELOPMENT EXECUTIVE
US / Europe / Asia-Pacific / Australia / Latin America

Fifteen-plus-year management career leading marketing and business development organizations world-wide. Full P&L responsibility. Member of several US and foreign boards of directors. Cross-functional expertise in:

- Strategic Planning, Vision, & Execution
- Field Sales & Marketing Leadership
- Organizational Development & Teaming
- Training & Leadership Development
- Global Distribution Network Management

- Merger & Acquisition Integration
- Joint Ventures, Partnerships, & Alliances
- Product Development & Commercialization
- Technology Licensing
- Client Relationship Management

PROFESSIONAL EXPERIENCE:

CONRAD ASSOCIATES – Portland, Oregon   Present

Marketing & Business Development Consultant providing expertise in product development and commercialization, market penetration, technology licensing, joint ventures, and strategic alliances. Guiding principals in developing marketing strategy and optimizing business relationships to drive profitable product launches and long-term revenue growth.

REYNOLDS MEYERS GREEN – Osaka, Japan   1995 to 1996

Managing Director of Marketing (*Concurrent with VP – Commercial Development*) leading the successful turnaround and repositioning of an fully integrated marketing organization (resulting from the merger of three independent pharmaceutical manufacturers). Scope of responsibility included marketing, business development and product commercialization for a $1.5 billion organization.

- Created a new, strategically focused marketing organization leveraging best practices of all three companies. Defined new market position, accelerated product development,introduced an American-style sales process and leadership training programs, and created regulatory approval strategy. Reduced organizational staffing levels by 20%.
- Member of the **Board of Directors** and Executive Committee of Osaka Reynolds Meyers Green. Member of the **Board of Directors** of Meyers Green UK.

NOTE: Key leadership role in development and leadership of new venture company with German parent, French management, and Japanese sales organization. Orchestrated cross-cultural change management programs to create America-style operation leveraging best practices of all companies.

MEYERS GREEN – Nippon, Japan   1992 to 1995

Vice President / Commercial Director with full strategic, operational, and financial responsibility for sales, marketing, operations, distribution training, and third-party alliances for the Japanese subsidiary of US pharmaceutical manufacturer. Directed a staff of 1,000+ and a $150-million operating budget. Joint P&L responsibility with President. Member of the **Board of Directors** and Executive Committee.

- Captured a 20-point gain in market share for #1 product line (total share of 50% +). Achieved a 5% improvement in established product line with $2 million profit improvement despite overall market decline. Introduced innovative sales training and development programs.
- Eliminated one layer of operating management while improving organizational productivity 10%.
- Led successful acquisition and integration of $200 million Japanese company into existing organizational infrastructure. Introduced sophisticated marketing and corporate image programs.
- Orchestrated major expansion of field sales organization (100% growth over three years).

MEYERS GREEN – Omaha, Nebraska   1989 to 1992

Vice President – International directing all business activities in Asia (excluding Japan) and Latin America. Held full P&L responsibility for both subsidiary and licensee/distributor organizations, including strategic planning, finance, manufacturing, sales/marketing, human resources, and product distribution. Managed 200 direct reports, 1,250 indirect reports and a $20 million annual budget.

- Redesigned European, Asian-Pacific, and Latin American licensee/distributor organizations, increased sales $10 million and improved net profit contribution by $5 million.
- Drove market share growth of major product in Australia from 35% to 50% through transition from prescription to OTC status. Created multimedia consumer marketing and ad campaigns.
- Established renewed market presence in Korea with innovative concept and no financial risk.
- Launched new licensee owned/financed manufacturing plant in Pakistan to retain market presence.
- Divested Philippine subsidiary, negotiated licenses, and improved annual profit nearly $1 million.

NOTE: Member of Corporate Transition Team for 1989 Meyers Benston / Green Industries merger. Renegotiated contracts, realigned global distribution network, and successfully integrated/leveraged worldwide sales and marketing organization.

GREEN INDUSTRIES PHARMACEUTICALS – Toledo, Ohio   1989

Director – Global Commercial Development, a one-year corporate staff position managing strategic planning, marketing, and development for two of the company's largest and most profitable products. Headquarters management representative for global launch with $100 million in first-year sales.

GREEN INDUSTRIES PHARMACEUTICALS – Korea   1981 to 1988

Managing Director – Asia (1985 to 1988)
Regional Manager – Asia (1983 to 1985)
Marketing Manager – Asia (1981 to 1983)

Fast-track promotion to final position managing all sales, marketing, staffing, training, product management, and product launch programs for Green's Asian operations (11 countries excluding Japan). Achieved significant gains in productivity and profitability. Solidified market position.

<u>Early Professional Career</u> with Gardner Enterprises in Australia. Promoted rapidly from **Medical Sales Representative** to **National Training Manager** to **National Sales Manager** to **Director of Sales & Marketing**. Company was acquired by Green Industries in 1981.

EDUCATION: **BA of Commerce Program** – McKensie University – Melbourne, Australia
                      Graduate, 200+ hours of Professional, Management & Leadership Training

MAGGIE GRUNERT

12 Osborne Street
Manassas, Virginia 22109

(804) 332-9809
maggieg@yahao.com

PROFESSIONAL QUALIFICATIONS:

- Sales, Marketing, & Business Development
- Customer Presentations & Negotiations
- Contract Closings & Transactions
- New Product & Service Launch

- Customer Relationship Management
- Competitive Market Positioning
- New Account Development
- Public Speaking & Events Management

PROFESSIONAL EXPERIENCE:

Marketing & Training Coordinator   1998 to Present
SPIZ GROUP, Alexandria, Virginia

Fast-paced sales and business development position marketing advanced health, safety, and environmental training programs to industrial manufacturers and producers, construction companies, and environmental organizations throughout a 6-state region. Operate in a consultative sales role, educating clients on OSHA regulations, compliance requirements, and specific training opportunities.

- Instrumental in increasing revenues 2,000% over three years. Personally involved in presentations, bids, negotiations, and contracts for more than 400 new clients/contracts.
- Forged strong working relationships with key accounts through expertise in identifying specific needs and delivering appropriate programs and services. Brought in more than 500 qualified leads each year.

Marketing Representative   1993 to 1998
MAGGIE'S SPECIALTY PRODUCTS, Alexandria, Virginia

- Marketed specialty products to corporate and institutional clients throughout the Eastern and Mid western US (Virginia to Oklahoma). Independently managed the entire sales process including developing marketing strategies, managing key account relationships, preparing bid proposals, negotiating pricing, and coordinating a series of high-profile special event programs.

- Personally negotiated and closed key contracts with the National Institute of Health (NIH), American Diabetes Association, Babcock & Wilcox, Capitol Events, Society for Maternal-Fetal Medicine, and a state-wide political campaign.

Marketing & Advertising Representative   1982 to 1992
GROTON DAILY NEWS, Groton, Connecticut

Top-ranked revenue producer in an extremely competitive commercial market. Launched a series of innovative marketing and business development campaigns, penetrated new sales territories, nurtured key account relationships, and introduced an entire portfolio of new advertising products and concepts.

- Won the "Most Sales Award" as the #1 revenue producer in the organization.
- Delivered solid revenue growth of 25% annually for 10 consecutive years.

EDUCATION & CERTIFICATIONS:

Associate of Arts in Marketing, Southern Massachusetts College, Boston, Massachusetts
Certificate in Marketing, Tate-Radcliffe School, New York, New York
Certificate in Meeting Planning, Boston Trade School, Boston, Massachusetts
Certified Meeting Planner, Professional Convention Management Association

Meridee Petry

2210 Greenway Drive
Princeton, NJ 08540

603-951-0999
Meridee@earthlink.net

Medical Office Management / Clinical Services Support

✓ **Clinical, Customer Service, and Call Center Management** – Research and analysis, inbound service operations, customer communications, after-call work, fulfillment, product and launch support, and management reporting in multi-channel, customer-focused environments. Customer affairs specialist.

✓ **Project Management** – End-to-end planning for initiatives, resource management, coordination of internal and external resources, communications with cross-functional teams/stakeholders, and problem solving.

✓ **Communications** – Effective verbal skills with strategic partners, internal and external customers, and management. Experience interfacing with key clinical sales account representatives and vendors.

✓ **Training** – Provide software training and support for medical office staff end users, as well as central billing office call center. Facilitate flawless operation of billing system through system upgrade training.

PROFESSIONAL EXPERIENCE

WOODBRIDGE MEDICAL CENTER, Woodbridge, NJ   2002 – present
Premier health organization of the Woodbridge Healthcare System, providing medical, diagnostic, surgical, behavioral health, rehabilitative, and preventive health services for inpatients and outpatients.

Office Manager, Delaware Valley Family Healthcare Center
Direct and maintain smooth operations of busy medical branch office (21 physicians). Assure cost-effective operations, meeting patient and residency-training program needs. Monitor and conduct activities directed by State of New Jersey licensing boards, and provide direction for meeting state regulations and JCAHO standards.

JOHNSON CLINICAL SERVICES, INC., Princeton, NJ   1993– 2001
Senior Customer Service Group Leader
Promoted from Customer Service Representative to lead 20-member customer service unit responsible for order fulfillment, including billing and delivery. Trained, supervised, and scheduled customer service staff, including new-hire training. Served as liaison between customer service and management.

- Directed high-volume 800-line inbound service operations (order processing) from regional sales reps, hospitals, purchasing agents, and physicians. Resolved account escalations, promoting customer satisfaction. Gained in-depth knowledge of pharmaceutical products, pricing, order fulfillment, claims, and credits.

- Served as first point-of-contact with 65 regional account managers in East and West Coast territories, answering product-related inquiries, researching customer issues, and resolving order discrepancies. Initiated daily product update meetings via telephone for enhanced account relationship management.

- Maintained and updated product database of current, divested, discontinued, and future pipeline products, and generated executive management statistical reports monitoring daily call volumes and breakdowns.

EDUCATION

Medical Office Management Certificate, Middle Valley Community College, Clinton, NJ – May 2002
A.A., Computer Applications, Mercer Community College, Trenton, NJ – May 1993

Computer Skills – Well versed in Medical Management, Windows NT/2000, MS Office 2000 including Word, Excel, PowerPoint, MS Project, Access, MS Outlook, Visual Basic 6, Visio, and SQL Server 2000 Database.

CAMPER BRYCE
cbryce@coldrain.com

30000 The Old Road No. 35
Frazier Park, California 93225

805-537-5956

NETWORK ADMINISTRATOR / TECHNICIAN / PC SUPPORT PROFESSIONAL
Making technology accessible to people

MICROSOFT CERTIFIED SYSTEMS ENGINEER (MCSE) and **MCP** with extensive international and diverse technical experience in the IT field, emphasizing network administration and PC support, and user support of batch and on-line programs for a variety of business, accounting, customer service, and financial reporting functions. Particularly effective in the management of complex systems projects requiring extensive research and testing. Extensive disaster recovery and migration work (Network Engineering).

Creative, results-driven, hands-on expert in the design, development, and delivery of cost-effective, high-performance technology solutions to meet challenging business and multimedia demands. Strong background in all facets of project life cycle development from initial feasibility analysis and conceptual design through documentation, implementation, user training, quality review, and enhancement. Well-versed in the documentation and installation of sophisticated networking and client/server technologies.

Energetic and decisive business leader able to merge disparate technologies and personnel into team-centered business units. Solid technical training, team building, management development, and customer service skills. Positive motivator able to focus efforts of others.

Experience applicable to diverse industries, markets, and opportunities.

SYSTEMS AND PROTOCOLS

Network Planning	System Integration	Switches & Hubs
Frame Relay Networking	Software Configuration	Router Configuration
Telephony & Fiber Optics	Hardware Configuration	Network Firewalls
Microsoft Platforms (back office suite)	Exchange 2000	SQL Server
Windows NT, XP, TCP/IP	SMS	UNIX
Macintosh	MAI Basic 4	FORTRAN
IBM	LAN	WAN
MS Exchange/Scheduler MS Access	Visual Basic/Access	SQL, C
Internet Information Server	RPG	COBOL

Proficient in various scripting languages such as shell and batch, as well as major application packages (e.g., Microsoft Word, Excel, Access, Lotus 1-2-3, dBase III Plus, and several others).

PROFESSIONAL EXPERIENCE

SENIOR NETWORK CONSULTANT   1995-2003
Votixx Systems, Inc. – Bakersfield, CA

Southern California's premier Microsoft Solution Provider

Directed a team of PC technicians, network administrators/analysts, and help-desk personnel in the management of all facets of information technology. Designed and deployed new systems including Windows NT and Windows 2000 based servers running SQL Server, Exchange, SNA Server, and SMS Server. Migrated data and operations from various legacy systems such as Novell NetWare. Created and wrote programs for clients either as stand-alone applications or as aids to migration of production data in Visual Basic/Access and SQL. Trained clients' staff on use and maintenance of deployed systems.

Critical contributions:
- **Networking:** Planned and integrated 40+ office Windows NT and multi-domain with over 100+ servers. Administered primary and backup domain controllers, file servers, print servers, and email servers.
- **Computer Network Security:** Implemented policies for employee use of Internet and email. Authored technical policies and procedures for technical manuals.
- **Technical Support:** Provided technical support and end-user training to internal and external customers on network, software, and computer systems.
- **Vendor Relations:** Negotiated all hardware and software purchases for company, successfully saving thousands during new network integration.
- **Project Management:** Full P/L responsibility; established budget (projected manhours and equipment); involved in hiring process; handled all scheduling; ensured projects were completed **on time** and **within** (quite often **under**) **budget.** Participated in cross-functional project teams and team meetings. Regularly attended trade shows.

Clients included:
CREATORdirect
Windows 2000 and Exchange 2000 deployment from Windows NT 4.0 and Unix-based SMTP mail. Implemented primary mail server in clustered environment and provided support for clustered SQL server.

Kabang.com
Designed and assisted in programming of membership system for website using Digital Rights Management (Windows 2000 Active Directory and SQL Server).

University of Southern California / Marshall School of Business
Deployed Exchange 5.5. Designed and executed long-term coexistence strategy for existing NT-based mail system. Change was effectuated with no downtime.

Saudi ARAMCO, Kingdom of Saudi Arabia
Designed and implemented Exchange 5.5 to handle all 35,000 worldwide employees. Migrated 20,000 users from Microsoft Mail on Novell NetWare servers. Provided support for deployment of servers outside Kingdom and trained operations staff of ARAMCO. Delivered early and under budget for this $4-million project which was performed on a fixed-price contract.

Los Angeles Times
Designed and wrote a distributed Access application for Circulation Department to assist in tracking of rack sales and calculation of individual delivery route performance against sales goals for calculation of bonuses.

Mattel
Designed worldwide implementation of Exchange and assisted with implementation of Windows NT from NetWare and Exchange from MS Mail for corporate headquarters in El Segundo, along with desktop deployment of Windows 95 and Office 95. Changed network protocols from IPX/SPX to TCP/IP.

Southern California Gas Company
Led user-interface project designing and implementing Microsoft Mail for approximately 10,000 users in corporate headquarters and 10 field offices. Implemented Exchange as backbone for mail-transport system as well as interface to SMTP for corporate email.

Technicolor
Conceived and executed corporate mail backbone system; provided support to mail administration team.

SENIOR CONSULTANT   1994-1995
Information Technology Solutions – Lake Piru, CA

Programmer/Analyst for implementation of PeopleSoft Asset Management System. Participated as member of design/development team for Work-In-Progress module for Asset Management System.

DATABASE ADMINISTRATOR / DATABASE ANALYST   1990-1994
Packard Bell Electronics – Salt Lake City, UT

- Database administration/analysis for Technical Support, Manufacturing, and Technical Documentation divisions.
- Aided with telephony applications as member of design/development team (customer call logging, telephone call-back messaging).
- Executed beta testing and implementation of Windows NT and SQL Server.
- Wrote application launch program.
- Handled disaster recovery after Northridge earthquake.

Prior to 1990

Programmer/Analyst	Credit Managers Association of California	Los Angeles, CA
Consultant	Independent Consultant	Pasadena, CA
Administrative Assistant	Liquid Carbonic Industrial/Medical Corporation	Irwindale, CA
Sales Representative	ComputerLand	West Covina, CA
Senior Computer Operator	Pasadena Star-News	Pasadena, CA

TECHNICAL EDUCATION AND CONTINUOUS TRAINING

Windows NT, Windows 9x, Windows 2000, Windows XP
SQL Server 6.0, 6.5, and 7.0
Exchange 4.0 Beta
Beta Tester for Windows NT, Windows XP, SQL Server and Exchange
MAI Basic 4, Business Basic
IBM on RPGII
Fortran IV on IBM/360 Mainframe (Courses at California Institute of Technology)

Caroline Mayes
network engineer

4444 San Luis Rey Court
San Jose, California 95101
℘ 408.345.8723
✉ cmcyber@yahao.com

SUMMARY OF PROFIT-BUILDING CAPABILITIES

❑ Finding and solving the right problems — the first time ❑ Discovering, winning, and keeping customers ❑ Mastering steep learning curves with my own professional development programs ❑ Providing solutions that keep pace with customers' growing needs

IT CERTIFICATIONS AND EXPERIENCE TO LEVERAGE YOUR SALES

CCNA	MSCE 2000	CNE 5.1
CCDA	MCSE NT 4.0	Expecting CCNP in Oct. '03

❑ Installing, servicing, and upgrading network software and hardware – comprehensive server support – security systems – VPN solutions – Windows NT and Windows 2000 network administration – WAN support – integrating routers, switches, VPN concentrators, wireless network devices – into reliable, effective tools

IT SKILLS THAT SAVE TRAINING COSTS

❑ Cisco: Expert with PIX firewalls; proficient with routers, VPN concentrators, wireless networking devices
❑ 3Com: Proficient with routers and switches
❑ WAN: Proficient with Frame Relay and T1, ISDN; working knowledge of PPP
❑ Operating Systems: Expert in Novell Netware 3.x, 4.x, 5.1, DOS 6.22; Proficient in Windows 3.x, 95, 98, NT 4.0, 2000, XP
❑ Supporting software: Proficient in Network Associates Sniffer Pro 4.5, Visio 2000, MS Exchange server, the entire suite of MS Office applications; working knowledge of Cisco Network Designer

RECENT WORK HISTORY WITH EXAMPLES OF PROBLEMS SOLVED

❑ **Systems Engineer**, Sierra Computer Resources, San Jose, California, Sep 00 to Present
This Fortune 500 company sells, installs, services, and leases computer equipment to commercial, health care, financial, educational, and government customers. Annual sales: $925M.

Results: Regularly **meets or exceeds revenue goals**. Earned three raises in less than two years.

Responded quickly when a major customer's in-house engineers had tried — and failed — to fix a tough, profit-robbing network problem. Chose just the right diagnostic tool, then offered strongly supported solution. *Results:* **Problem disappeared and never returned. Customer got maximum capability with a limited budget.**

Guided an account that came to us after they had committed to an expensive, unworkable network. Earned the trust of the network administrator and senior management. Then designed a scalable, capable system to meet their needs. *Results:* **Generated $40K** from this account alone.

❑ **System Administrator** and **Network Manager**, Arista Services, La Morada, California, Aug 99 to Sep 00
Arista is a leading clearinghouse processing, transferring, and settling billable records between wireless operators worldwide.

Solved a problem for a customer who didn't speak English well and was located 3,000 miles away in a time zone 6 hours later than ours. I had never seen this problem before and all the usual tools failed. With no OJT, I quickly mastered an advanced diagnostic tool. *Results:* **Operations returned to normal fast. Customer couldn't be happier**.

Discovered our server didn't offer virus protection the very morning a malicious program was crippling systems worldwide. Bought us time by educating 20 users spread over two states. Then found a safe way to inoculate our systems. *Results:* **Seamless operations. Avoided very costly corrective action.**

❑ **Owner and Operator**, Focused Microsystems, Oakland, California, 88 to 99
My company built, installed, and maintained systems that ranged from single PCs to small networks. I built this company from the ground up, attracting hundreds of accounts – some large – across California.

Transformed an old, abandoned shell into our newest, full-service 5,500 ft² location. With only one helper, did it all from cleaning out trash to building an entire technical support center. **Results: Maintained dominance in a very competitive market** despite the enormous drain on available manhours.

❑ **Computer Technician** at Ronco Office Equipment and Chappell Computers, Mendocino, California, 86 to 88

EDUCATION AND PROFESSIONAL DEVELOPMENT

❑ Associate in **Industrial Electronics Technology**, Mendocino Technical College, Mendocindo, California, 87
Paid my own tuition by working full time while carrying a full academic load.

❑ "Advanced Techniques in Designing, Installing, and Managing Windows 2000 Networks," Pomery Computer Resources, two weeks, Mar 01
One of only two selected, from ten eligibles, to have this training funded by my employer.

❑ "Supporting Windows 4.0 Server Core Technologies," New Horizons, one week, Feb 97

Karen M. Peters

71 Canal Street, Princeton, NJ 08540
(609) 951-8392 Home ▪ (609) 203-1990 Mobile ▪ karnpetrs@earthlink.net

SUMMARY

Office Administrator. Sixteen years' experience in diverse and challenging payroll, accounting, and health benefits administration roles. Expert liaison skills with colleagues and professional staff. Effectively interact with executive administrators to problem-solve and advance organizational goals. Proven track record in:

✓ Financial Records Management	✓ Payroll Administration	✓ Risk Management
✓ Health Benefits Coordination	✓ Leadership & Team Building	✓ Communications
✓ Project/Operations Management	✓ Financial & Tax Reporting	✓ Service Training & Support

Proven ability in supporting operational structures, and establishing efficient accounting and payroll systems. Skilled at learning concepts quickly, working well under pressure, and communicating ideas clearly. Diplomatic and professional at all times. Keen understanding of priorities…a genuine team player. Notary Public.

KEY SKILLS

☑ **Payroll Administration.** Effectively introduced and maintained efficient payroll systems, processes, and procedures, ensuring compliance with all regulations with high-pressure, time-sensitive environments. Gained expertise in setting up and maintaining in-house and online computerized systems for payroll and reporting.

☑ **Time Management.** Demonstrate excellent organizational skills, with ability to prioritize and multi-task. Conscientious in following through on commitments and meeting deadlines. Noted for detail orientation.

☑ **Customer Service and Communications.** Key player in health benefits orientations for new employees. Initiated quarterly "Money Talks" staff newsletter. Adept at interfacing with individuals at all levels.

PROFESSIONAL EXPERIENCE

BURLINGTON TOWNSHIP BOARD OF EDUCATION, Pemberton, NJ   1992 – present
Head Payroll Bookkeeper / Health Benefits Coordinator - Recruited to provide accounting/ technical data guidance and leadership for payroll administration. Train, evaluate, and supervise assistant payroll bookkeeper.

- Prepare $1.25-million semi-monthly payroll for 620 teachers, substitutes, administrators, and support staff, guaranteeing the accuracy, integrity, and secure maintenance of payroll information. Transitioned manual records and systems to computerized payroll administration and online bill paying, meeting a tight deadline.

- Effectively reconcile, process and maintain proper salaries and complex payroll deductions, interfacing with HR department as well as outside government agencies. Streamlined and organized $25-million tax, pension, and health benefits programs to assure timely submittal of monthly, quarterly, and annual reports.

- Recognized as "in-house expert" for payroll, deductions, and health benefits, resolving 95% of employee inquiries on the spot. Initiated and write quarterly staff newsletter to inform employees on these issues.

- Chosen to develop a standardized payroll risk management system, ensuring confidential records, as well as secure identification methods. Collaborate with finance controller in payroll distribution, including line-account budgeting and reporting, as well as dispersal of payroll monies from the General Ledger.

- Initiated and currently head 6-member project management team for Distinguished Staff Awards Program, focusing special attention on the accomplishments of support staff.

PROFESSIONAL EXPERIENCE

ATLANTIC TOWNSHIP BOARD OF EDUCATION, Atlantic City, NJ   1986 – 1992
Payroll Supervisor

- Reconciled, processed, and dispersed $72,000 semi-monthly payroll for 1,500 employees, supported by two part-time clerical staff. Calculated time sheets for the entire school district. Interfaced with personnel to verify employment records for accurate payroll and tax (federal and state) records management.

- Established records and procedures for streamlined record keeping and bill paying of payroll deductions, including FICA, unemployment, tax-sheltered annuities, savings, credit union, garnishments and support, union dues, and federal and state taxes.

- Chosen to deliver new employee orientation for health benefits, pension and tax purposes. Set up a "one-stop" center for supplying appropriate forms, as well as instruction on accurate, complete submittals.

- Gained in-house reputation for expertise in details of payroll, payroll deductions, and health benefits issues.

EDUCATION & DEVELOPMENT

Ongoing Professional Development including:
Office Administrator Training Program, Burlington Township School District, Pemberton, NJ2001 – 2002
Comprehensive training in communications, customer service, risk management, process improvement, time and stress management, advanced technology and job-specific training.

NJEA / NEA / BCEA Workshops on Communications, Supervision, Leadership, and Stress Management 2002
State and Federal Tax Workshops, Division of Pensions and Benefits, Trenton, NJ   2000
Workers' Compensation and Payroll Taxes Courses, New Jersey Law Center, New Brunswick, NJ   2000
Accounting Courses, Burlington County Adult Community School

Graduate, Center City High School, Philadelphia, PA

PROFESSIONAL AFFILIATIONS

☑ The League of Women Voters   2001 – present

☑ Burlington Business & Technical Association (BBTA) – President   1998 – present
Elected to newly formed professional association for Burlington Township professional and support staff. Wrote constitution and bylaws. Serve as member of Membership, Grievance, and Negotiations Committees, as well as representative to monthly President's Council meetings.

☑ National Education Association (NEA), New Jersey Education Association (NJEA)   1998 – present

COMPUTER SKILLS

Well-versed with Microsoft Office 2000 (Word, Access, Excel), Windows 2000/NT, Microsoft Publisher 2000, Internet Explorer, and computerized online banking services.

▪ ▪ ▪

Tanya McGrady

47 Old Glastonbury Way
East Hartford, CT 06128

tmcgrady@snet.net

860-474-0903 Home
860-603-2309 Mobile

Office Manager / Administrative Manager

Boosting efficiency, profitability, and management productivity.

Consistent record of achievements and contributions during 10+ years in diverse, challenging administrative-management roles including Executive Assistant to the Governor of Connecticut, Administrative Manager of the state's prison libraries, and Operations Coordinator critical to a private-sector business evolution.

Work effectively on deadline and in time-sensitive, stressful situations; possess a sense of urgency and quick decision-making skills. Well organized, proactive, and thorough, with well-developed communications skills and a history of extremely productive working relationships with peers, staff, and management.

Expertise

- Office Administration
- Human Resources Administration
- Personnel Records Management
- Policy, Procedure, & Manual Development
- Budget Management & Reporting
- Purchasing & Supply Management

- Project Management
- Procedural Streamlining
- Cost Reduction & Efficiency Improvement
- Technology Implementation
- Team Leadership / Staff Management
- Customer & Constituent Service

Experience and Achievements

Executive Operations Coordinator, 2000–2003   Employers Insurance of Connecticut, Hartford, CT

Improved operational procedures, organizational structure, and efficiency for newly privatized worker's compensation insurance company. Directed administrative activities for company that, at peak, employed 400. Coordinated travel schedules and insurance audits; assigned staff based on client needs and staff capabilities; assisted with confidential investigations; served as worker's comp administrator for the company's internal claims; initiated, led, and managed multiple special projects and assignments.

- **Rescued the budget-management process** when entire 5-person budget department returned to state employment. Fully absorbed duties without hiring additional staff, saving the company more than $200K annually through staff elimination.
- **Saved countless hours of attorney time** by drafting new company policies that were approved by legal department with minimal changes and subsequently implemented company-wide.
- **Streamlined budget reporting** and created meaningful, accurate reports for senior management.
- **Contributed to technology transition** from Hyperion to Oracle financial software.
- **Developed the company's first accurate organizational charts.**
- **Coordinated smooth and 100% successful reinsurance meetings.**

Administrative Manager, 1997–2000   Connecticut Department of Corrections, Hartford, CT

Recruited by Director of Prisons to take long-vacant position and bring leadership, organization, and operational improvement to the Department's libraries and compliance-monitoring process. Managed institutional libraries at 11 Connecticut corrections facilities and monitored conditions of confinement to ensure compliance with court decrees. Served as liaison between representatives of the legal community, general public, and institutions to resolve inmate issues. Assisted with confidential investigations. Managed 5 staff and oversaw 35 inmate law clerks.

| **Administrative Manager, continued** | **Connecticut Department of Corrections** |

- **Created a positive environment for change** by immediately addressing a challenging inmate-staffing situation, establishing control, and bringing in all new staff.
- **Reined in out-of-control inventory, saving $50,000 annually by eliminating duplicate materials and reducing shipping costs.** Sought staff input and gained their support, then identified problem areas,developed tracking spreadsheets, renegotiated vendor arrangements, streamlined material purchasing and shipping, and mitigated state's risk by ensuring identical library resources at all sites.
- **Saved $10,000 annually** by improving security to reduce office-supply shrinkage.
- **Efficiently managed state-approved annual budget in excess of $1 million.** Maintained tight controls and accurate reporting systems — never exceeded budget or required review by internal finance committee.
- **Developed proposals and secured grant funding for innovative inmate programs that benefited inmates, the state, and its citizens.**
  - Guide-Dog Training — Developed and co-authored grant proposal that brought this program to the Shelton Correctional Center. *Benefits:* Inmates learned anger control and behavior management; state residents gained well-trained guide animals.
  - Youth Offender Education Grant — Drove the effort to obtain grant funding to teach "employability" skills to inmates aged 15 to 22. *Benefits:* More than 100 youthful offenders learned skills to survive outside of the institutional setting, reducing likelihood of recidivism.

| **Executive Secretary, 1995–1997** | **Office of Governor John Rowland, Hartford, CT** |

Represented governor's office to constituents and served as liaison to the state's departments of Prisons, Welfare, Employee Training, and Worker's Compensation. Provided full scope of executive-support services including scheduling, document preparation, file management, travel planning, legislative monitoring, and light legal research. Also worked independently and proactively to analyze information, resolve problems, develop recommendations, and provide exceptional service to citizens of the state.

| **Brokerage Assistant, 1991–1995** | **Fidelity Investments, Hartford, CT** |

Transferred securities in accordance with the rules and regulations of the Securities and Exchange Commission. Responded within 3 days to all written correspondence and inquiries. Provided a high volume of support to shareholders, brokers, and clearing agents.

Professional Training

Branford Hall Career Institute, Branford, CT

Earned Paralegal Certification — 1996.

New Horizons Computer Learning Centers, 1998–Present

Adobe GoLive, Illustrator, PageMaker, Photoshop
MS Access, Excel, FrontPage, Outlook, PowerPoint, Project, Publisher, Word
CorelDRAW!, Macromedia DreamWeaver, QuarkXPress, QuickBooks Pro
Flash 5.0, HTML, JavaScript

FRANK G. THOMAS

988 Tennyson
Novi, MI 48170

838.559-0283
FrankT@coldrain.com

GENERAL MANAGER / PLANT MANAGER

Hands-on, results-oriented Operations Executive with 15+ years management experience at every level of plant operations, from machine operator to plant manager. Possesses a strong entrepreneurial background in addition to strong general management, P&L management, and operating experience in a manufacturing, assembly, and distribution operation. Combines expertise in organizational leadership with success in identifying and capitalizing upon market opportunities to drive revenue and profit growth.

- Strategic Planning
- Financial Reporting & Budgeting
- Corporate Administration
- Quality & Productivity Improvement
- Customer Service & Retention

- Purchasing & Supply Chain Management
- Human Resources & Staff Development
- Marketing & Business Development
- Cost Containment & Profit Growth
- Marketing & Business Development

CAREER HISTORY

CONSULTANT, 2001 - Present
FLEX AUTOMOTIVE, Plymouth, MI

Company acquired Thomas Plastics, Inc. (former employer) in 2001. Retained to guide smooth transition of one company to another. Directing closing of existing plant and moving its machinery from current location to new location. Overseeing training of personnel on machinery and assisting with implementation of ISO 14001.

PRESIDENT/FOUNDER, 1984 - 2001
THOMAS PLASTICS, INC., Royal Oak, MI
A tier 2 supplier for the automotive industry.

Launched entrepreneurial injection-molding manufacturing business starting with "0" and earning up to $3.2 million annually. Company occupied a 16,000 sq. ft. facility and employed 25 people. Developed all operational strategies to improve productivity, efficiency, quality, and delivery of plastic interior and exterior parts and cables. In the beginning, responsible for everything at the company to include, purchasing, marketing, sales, human resources, quality assurance, shipping and receiving, material/production control, and industrial relations. Handled all financials and created the entire operating infrastructure.

- Transitioned company from concept through start-up to full-scale operations. Created all operating, business, financial, sales, shipping, and customer relations programs, positioning company for strong market performance.
- Created a marketing program to build business to $3.2 million annually.
- Implemented innovative process improvements impacting all core business operations.

THOMAS PLASTICS, INC., continued......

- Spearheaded introduction of a series of continuous improvement initiatives that consistently strengthened productivity, product quality, and customer satisfaction.
- Developed purchasing procedures to accommodate volume and exploit discount opportunities.
- Trained employees in team building and problem solving as well as mold-making.
- Researched and purchased state-of-the-art equipment to increase business and productivity in a highly competitive market.
- Minimized defects of products by providing cross-training of employees on all machines; maintained quality and minimized downtime.
- Negotiated with material suppliers for best prices to hold down costs.
- Set up a shipping and receiving department to meet company and customer needs.

PLANT MANAGER, 1967 - 1984
FENTON MOLD, INC., Livonia, MI
Fast-track promotion throughout a series of increasingly responsible plant operations, supervisory, and management positions during 17 years with company. As Plant Manager, oversaw molding and mold-making, provided quotes for molds and parts, and purchased all needed tools and equipment. Supervised 35 employees.

- Traveled to client's site (Saginaw Steering) to troubleshoot a problem with the mold concerning heat expansion. Analyzed all aspects and implemented a solution acceptable to both sides.
- Launched the injection-molding phase of the business for company, increasing overall revenue 35%.
- Created seven alternator fan molds for Delco-Remy, developing them from start to finish.
- Trained apprentices to be mold-makers.

EDUCATION

HENRY FORD COLLEGE - *Tool & Die Apprenticeship*

CHARLES "RUSTY" CRONIN

4200 Jackson Avenue, Albuquerque, New Mexico 87101 crc22@arc.org ℘ 505.555.5555

WHAT I CAN OFFER **YOUR ORGANIZATION** AS YOUR NEXT PLANT OPERATIONS AND MAINTENANCE PROFESSIONAL

❏ Maximizing **productivity** ❏ **Controlling costs** ❏ **Motivating** employees
❏ **Leading by example** ❏ **Communicating** to get results ❏ Learning **new systems** fast and well

RECENT WORK HISTORY WITH EXAMPLES OF PROBLEMS SOLVED

❏ **Chemical Operator**, Ace Plastics Division, Morales, New Mexico, May 00 to Present
The Morales plant covers 500 acres of production space and operates around the clock.

Chosen as part of the team to evaluate and "debug" new software that would run our entire operation. With no experience in this program, little time on the job, and minimal training, found more than 20 potential "show stoppers" by working 70-hour weeks. *Payoffs:* Nearly all of my **recommendations accepted**. Helped **avoid $1.0M per day shutdowns**.

❏ **Utility Systems Operator**, Veterans' Administration Hospital, Los Santos, New Mexico, Feb 89 to May 00
The Los Santos facility is a 200-bed hospital.

Payoffs: Made time to **transform** overly confident, but under-trained, **worker into productive team member** — after five other people had given up on him.

Used experience to help **fix problems that** had **crippled** our power generation **for nearly 20 years**. Did my homework and presented our plan to management. *Payoffs:* We **avoided hundreds of thousands of dollars** in unnecessary replacement costs. Operating **costs fell and stayed low**.

❏ *Hired away by the Maintenance Coordinator to be* **Plant Operations Maintenance Mechanic**, Crestview Hospital, Montgomery, Arizona, 86 to Feb 89
Jackson Hospital's physical plant supported a 200-bed hospital, complete medical support facilities, and physicians' offices.

Found a new approach to **maximize** the considerable **ROI** on our legacy air conditioning system. The contractor said it couldn't be done, but management approved my plans without change. **Payoffs: Recouped $80K investment in 6 months** (and realized the savings from then on). **Saved 16 man-hours a year. Avoided huge** construction **costs**.

❑ **Maintenance Mechanic**, Trane Corporation, Clovs, New Mexico, 81 to 86
Trane is a leader in manufacturing air conditioning components for the transportation industry.

Teamed up with an engineer to analyze our production process. Found a way to **boost quality, reduce costs, and streamline production.** *Payoffs:* My system for removing contaminants from raw materials **generated new savings after only three months**.

EDUCATION AND PROFESSIONAL DEVELOPMENT

❑ "System Automation Software," Johnson Controls, one week, 97
❑ "Honeywell Automation Systems," Honeywell, two weeks, 97
❑ Certificate in Air Conditioning and Refrigeration, Sand Hill Technical College, Albuquerque, New Mexico, 88
❑ Additional coursework in welding, Sand Hill Technical College, Albuquerque, New Mexico, 78

COMPUTER SKILLS

❑ Proficient in proprietary **automated environmental and preventative maintenance software**
❑ Working knowledge of Word, Excel, and Outlook

PROFESSIONAL RECOGNITION

❑ One of four, and the only one of nine from my division, chosen from 60 eligibles as a **top performer of the year**, Veterans' Administration Hospital, Montgomery, Arizona, 97

SUSAN J. PRENTICE

178 Clarke Street
Cranby, CA 95677

Email: Sue_Prentice@bigpoool.com

Mobile: 213.998.0907
Residence: 917.390.3272

OPERATIONS MANAGER • PRODUCTION MANAGER • TRAFFIC MANAGER

Unique blend of business pragmatism and creativity drives print-media communication projects throughout a multifaceted career spanning operations, finance, and production management. Outstanding eye for detail; attuned to the synergies of team members, clients, and suppliers, and acknowledged for executing balanced judgment in delivering deadline-critical projects on time and within budget. An empathetic and communicative leader resolutely determined to maximize quality, share knowledge, find solutions, and promote a harmonious environment. Cited by managers for intuitive problem solving, big-picture vision, and client-concentric focus that is "*as natural as breathing.*"

Professional strengths include:

- Production: Film & Printing"
- Project Planning & Scheduling
- Financial Analysis
- Budget Development

- Supplier Relationship Management
- Account Management
- Project Planning & Management

- Troubleshooting & "Fire-Fighting"
- Print Management
- Operations Management

Technology skill set: Microsoft Word, Excel, FileMaker, Quark, PowerPoint, Email, and Internet. Mac os9 and Windows for IBM

SELECTED CONTRIBUTIONS – IN FOCUS

- **Restored ailing relationships with suppliers** dissatisfied with low priority payments for completed work. Identified consistent performers distinguished by quality and on-time delivery, negotiated preferred supplier status, and established mutually advantageous payment plans and trading agreements that served to re-establish goodwill.
- **Increased revenues** by scrutinizing billable hours, analyzing projects against quotations, and identifying opportunities to capture additional costs.
- **Profitably managed** print-communication projects ranging from $6,000 to $100,000+.
- Launched cross-referenced photographic-image filing system to replace outmoded, costly and time-consuming infrastructure. Sourced film houses offering superior archival and retrieval systems providing all high resolutions on CD. Newly streamlined system arrested historical **"project panic"** by designers and cut scanning costs significantly.
- Developed a film-output protocol incorporating formal signoffs for printing approval that ensured smoother project output and eradicated disputes by clients over artwork anomalies.
- Introduced "work-in-progress" procedures for traffic management encompassing staff, projects, and resources. Reversed ad-hoc approach to workflow management with a definitive work-mapping process that pinpointed project progress, identified project overlaps and need for freelancers, increased designer productivity, and boosted team morale.
- **Pioneered profitability analysis** for projects over $10K in response to frequent budget blowouts stemming from mid-project alterations. Investigated key projects, demonstrating several had been unprofitable, and won management's approval to standardize this process, delivering significantly increased revenues and greater team accountability.

EMPLOYMENT CHRONOLOGY

CULTURE CHANGE MEDIA / TRANSFORM AMERICA P/L   1994–Present
$5M company providing communications for industry superannuation funds and not-for-profit organizations.

Track record of rapid career advancement from reception and administrative support roles to complete financial management of this $5 million national company, its subsidiaries, and three autonomous business unit across California.

National Finance Manager .... (1999-Present)
Production/Project Manager .... (1997-1999)
Production Coordinator .... (1995-1997)
Receptionist/Administration .... (1994-1995)
Assistant to Sales Manager .... (1994)

Experience Amplified

National Finance Manager

<u>Reported to</u>: CEO. <u>Staff</u>: 4

Promoted through performance excellence as a Production Manager to manage company's assets, cash flows, budgets, and projections, nurture supplier relationships, spearhead production innovations nationwide, direct projects and technology upgrades, and manage own client base. Despite a prolonged period of expansion and growth, the company struggled financially through an infrastructure burdened with protracted client and supplier payment schedules, inadequate and unscrutinized reporting and auditing processes, and residual debts from a partnership split. **Action & Contributions:**

- Renegotiated payment settlements and terms to elevate cash flows for the company's unprofitable publishing subsidiary. **Recovered $65,000, representing 50% of outstanding receivables in just 8 months;** influenced bookstore retailers to pay on books sold without stock returns—a benchmark for the industry.
- Conducted detailed financial and operational audits, and produced a report of recommendations that highlighted the negative cash flow impact of an unpaid loan stemming from a partnership split. Intuited business partner's unease with technical jargon, and prepared presentations that communicated current financial position and future visions in non-finance terminology. Firmed arrangements with business partners, **negotiating a structured debt repayment plan that formalized reduction of outstanding loan.**
- Tirelessly developed financial data for acceptance by the IRA. Repayment plan yielded results with the business saved from threatened IRA-led closure.

Production Manager (1997-1999)

<u>Printing Budget</u>: $900,000. <u>Film & Scanning Budget</u>: $300,000. <u>Project Scope</u>: $5,000-$900,000.

<u>Reported to</u>: State Manager. <u>Staff</u>: 2.

Successfully juggled an ever-increasing workload while introducing process improvements designed to streamline operations, remove duplicated work tasks, and deliver standardized formats. Introduced process and systems protocols to reduce workplace stressors in a "culture of panic" and to ensure continuity of professional practice. **Action & Contributions:**

- Introduced and designed new quotation database that **slashed lengthy processing and research times,** and boosted the quality of information available for forecasting and understanding client purchasing habits.
- Negotiated exclusive 2-year web printing agreements, winning bulk-printing concessions.
- Introduced WIP procedures for smoother, stress-free studio management and workflow planning.

EDUCATION

Bachelor of Business Program, <u>University of California.</u> One year of coursework completed

12 modules completed towards **Certificate in Personnel Management**

JAMES W. MANILOW

12 Birchwood Avenue - Sabattus, Maine 04280
Telephone: (207) 375-5555 - Email: JWManilow@arc.net

CAREER PROFILE

MANAGER / SUPERVISOR / CUSTOMER SERVICE / SALES

➤ Varied business and industry background with an outstanding record of achievement.
➤ Outstanding customer service and sales experience.
➤ Proven leader in business and on the job; recipient of numerous merit and cash awards.
➤ Effective manager, supervisor, motivator, and trainer of staff.
➤ Experienced in product (materials) selection, price negotiations, and purchasing.
➤ Experienced in preparing and submitting proposals.
➤ Strong manufacturing background with an emphasis on production scheduling and materials planning.
➤ Accurate forecasting of raw materials (including chemicals) to complete projects.

WORK HISTORY

JOHNSON PLASTICS, Lewiston, ME   1999 - 2003

Division of Harrison Industries — A multi-million dollar corporation —
World leader in decorative laminates for the building industry — private and commercial.

Production Scheduler / Materials Planner / Purchaser (Materials Group)
Position Highlights

- Oversaw all scheduling and planning for use of raw materials in the manufacturing of high- and low-pressure decorative laminates; forecasted and planned for all the phenolic resin needed.
- Forecasted raw materials needed from other major companies.
- Planned daily work schedules for three shifts; utilized PeopleSoft and Microsoft software.
- Supervised up to 60 employees daily.

Accomplishments

- Introduced and headed a team which implemented a KanBan System, JIT system, and a Mid-Point Scheduling System. Brought the entire company efficiency percentage from 60% to 90% in only 3 weeks.
- Implemented a second JIT system to generate a true requirement report, providing the information necessary to maintain a more accurate inventory while decreasing inventory on hand by 25% and saving the company $100,000 in the first month.

GLOBAL TECHNOLOGIES, Hartford, CT   1987-1993 & 1993-1999

Division of United Engineering Corporation — a multi-million dollar leader in the aircraft industry making various parts for private and commercial aircraft.

Production Planner (1997-1999) - Engineering Assistant (1996-1997), Promoted
Production Control Scheduler (1990-1993), Promoted
Shop Floor Control / Project Coordinator (1987-1990), Promoted
Position Highlights

- Scheduled, planned, and expedited work for major accounts, engineering programs, and other day-to-day manufacturing projects while interacting with multiple departments, managers, and staff.

(Continued on Page Two)

GLOBAL TECHNOLOGIES (Continued) ...

- Met production schedules to insure proper NC machining through the process of networking in Numerical Controlled (NC) Machining area; followed the flow of material through manufacturing from ordering to delivering the part for shipment. Worked with a system known as a Board System.
- Scheduled and coordinated the flow of material for jet fuel controls. Reviewed and adjusted production schedules in the MacPac System in regards to availability of material, processing methods, engineering changes, and production problems.

Accomplishments

- Selected to assist in helping in a division of Global (which was seriously backlogged) to get it back on schedule. Received a cash award for overall success and outcome of this project.
- Received a merit award for solving a quality problem in the main fuel control housing, saving the company $50,000 annually.
- Received a merit award for heading a team planning and establishing the PW500 Program to help catch up on the production of 100 units (valued at $35,000 each); production was successful, put back on schedule, and completed on time. Received a promotion for efforts.
- Assisted Program Office in the Electronics Division (Fadec System - brains of the aircraft) by relocating for the company and heading a team to put schedule back on track to successfully complete 50+ units. Achieved goal in 2 months and received a cash award.

UNIVERSAL LIFT TRUCK PARTS & SERVICE, West Springfield, MA   1993-1997

Industrial Mechanic / Technical Parts

Position Highlights

- Started with repairing and maintaining industrial lifting equipment.
- Maintained a fleet of industrial lift trucks for various corporations throughout the Northeast.
- Purchased parts from various vendors throughout the country.
- Provided extensive customer service and on-the-road sales.

Accomplishments

- Was promoted 2 years after hire into the office to represent the company in dealing with all technical parts questions regarding lift trucks.

EDUCATION ─────────────────────────────────

Specialized Training: Ongoing

- APICS Trained (Completed All Courses) / Registered #1222222 (Current on Latest Technology)
- J.D. Edwards Planning System
- MACPAC Systems
- Planning and Scheduling
- Microsoft Excel, Word, and Mail
  - PeopleSoft Software
  - Team Leading and Motivation
  - Advanced Blueprint Reading
  - Certified Life Saving Techniques

College Courses:

- Business Math, Physiology I, Algebra I, and Critical Writing

Enrico Fermi High School, Enfield, CT   Diploma, 1982

ALLEN L. FLORENCE

890 Estuary Lane
Raleigh, North Carolina 27612
(919) 760-9022
aflorencebuilds@builderz.net

OBJECTIVE

To utilize multi-year, wide-ranging commercial construction management and project management experience in a position where performance excellence, leadership, and business development results will be valued.

SKILLS SUMMARY

* Project Manager/Facilitator	* General Manager
* Quality Control/Project Management	* Large Project Management Achievements
* Contracting/Negotiations	* Multi-Project Experience with Capital Equipment
* Land Purchases	* Construction Financing
* Large Sub-Contractor Management	* Manufacturing/Manufacturer Knowledge
* Quality Control/Safety Management	* Expense Budget Development Control
* Key Project Planning Liaison	* Purchasing Management/Materials Management
* Job Cost Analysis/Site Planning	* Personnel Hiring/Supervision/Retainment
* On-Time/Under Cost Results	* Equipment Purchasing/Management

LICENSURE

General Contractor's License – North Carolina, South Carolina, and Virginia

QUALIFICATIONS SUMMARY

- Professional, dedicated, and focused construction development professional with a proven record of success in assuming increasing levels of responsibility, including: financial package (total management of this process), project management, implementation of multi-unit and multi-purpose construction plans, subcontractor hiring and management (multi-locations), analysis of personnel and equipment needs, and final implementation.
- Unique combination of project management responsibilities with many commercial projects that included multi-project, multi-site, and highly complex buildings/installations.
- Additional skills include specialized ability to adapt to major construction project and priority changes, suggest changes, handle multiple and complex project assignments, administrative and cost management functions.
- Proven record of providing accurate job/manpower cost estimates and to anticipate administrative functions of both office and field personnel and their assignments.

SELECTED GENERAL MANAGEMENT RESPONSIBILITIES

* Multi-project and multi-million commercial construction project coordination, work sequencing, functional analysis and coordination of field work, material and equipment cost control through job analysis, document preparation, scheduling, planning, site coordination, building permit development/obtainment, base building design review, building and land development budgeting, hiring, training, termination.
* Highly flexible manager; will adjust schedule and direct construction to accommodate safety, inspection, and compliance/code reviews. Excellent turnover success and post project success. Outstanding skills in developing, documenting and coordinating effective project financial terms as well as sale/turnover processes.
* Interact constantly with architects, site engineers, and others throughout projects.
* Comprehensive understanding of general contractor and subcontractor roles; served in subcontract role on many past assignments; have awarded contracts after careful research and qualification process.
* Responsible for comprehensive: quality control, safety compliance, leasing and management, installation verification with approved submittals, cash projections, budgeting coordination and scheduling, change order processing.
* Strong oral and written communication skills with the ability to clearly communicate technical and detailed information to those supervised and other team/management members to ensure streamlined project progress.
* Excellent planning, organizing, and reviewing work of a team to ensure proper management of integrated costs and budgets and limited time frames. Excellent analytical skills in determining and creating management plans.

PROFESSIONAL EXPERIENCE

FALCON RIDGE CONSTRUCTION & COMMERCIAL DEVELOPMENT, Chapel Hill, NC
President, 1997 to 2002

     Major project successes included:

100,000-square-foot commercial buildings for Bank of America, CCB, and BB&T in North Carolina and South Carolina.	*Multiple restaurant construction and retail store upfits throughout North Carolina, including specific project work for Brinker International.*
Development/Construction/Management of assisted living multi-family units in North Carolina and South Carolina.	*Site Development/Site Planning for 700 townhouse units and four apartment complexes in Charlotte, Greensboro, Greenville, NC and Greenville, SC.*
Commercial Metal Buildings (build to suit)	*Upfit of Multi-Family Units*
Complete Financing Packages (for all projects); working closely with banks and private investors to ensure integrity of bank and non-bank deals.	*Developing New Business/Sales/Marketing with the banking community with four multi-million dollar contracts signed in the past two years.*
Personnel Coaching/Talent Development for Managers; helped six managers obtain GC licensure in the past four years.	*Complete Project Management/Oversight, including three build-to-suits for three national tenants in the last 18 months.*

* Responsible for developing multiple deals, finance packaging, including market survey, spreadsheet, balance sheet, cost analysis, and appraisal.
* Worked with several bankers to find out project criteria, requirements and standards; utilized this information to assemble team of bankers, investors, brokers, and subcontractors to build and complete a project in time and under budget. Process saved company time and money with yearly estimates over $2.9 million.
* Prepared estimates, negotiated contracts, purchased material and equipment.
* Selected additional skills: land purchasing, construction site assessment, investor relations and investor identification, fee negotiations with brokers and agents, attorney liaison, zoning law expertise, accounting firm liaison to develop partnerships, site and building plan development, ongoing work with engineers and architects on all minor and major projects.
* Developed, implemented and reviewed product proposals and product cost estimates.
* Analyzed and developed effective marketing plan; prepared and presented client proposals and ensured total client satisfaction throughout the sales, building, and follow-up processes.
* Oversaw budget, cost controls, cost accounting, and cash flow analysis issues; negotiated with subcontractors, vendors, and bankers regarding all material purchases and financial issues.
* Developed forecasts for building and business operation costs for proposed projects.
* Wrote job descriptions/hiring procedures, supervised, trained and evaluated employees; taught OSHA-based safety procedures and ensured those safety procedures were followed according to regulatory standards.

CRESCENT/COLEMAN VENTURES, Durham, NC
Superintendent; promoted from Project Leader within four months of employment, 1996 - 1997

* Supervised custom operations for multiple site development and construction jobs; assessed and managed 56 subcontractors and supervised site construction crews totaling over 323 people.
* Highlighted project successes included: 890 single family homes, 179 apartment units; served as troubleshooter and turnaround specialist on single family project in Fredericksburg, VA for the US government that has led to partial restructuring of Department of Health and Human Services protocol for these units across the US.
* Established and maintained effective time and task management methods for personnel and project scheduling.
* Ensured product quality control and maintained communications with customers from start to finish of the new home processes.
* Assessed duties included job/cost management, scheduling, purchasing, architectural drafting, troubleshooting.
* Implemented analysis of cost controls and made presentations to management.

EDUCATION
    WAKE TECHNICAL COMMUNITY COLLEGE, Raleigh, NC   *A.A.S. in Business Management, May 1996*

ARNOLD G. McNULTY

12 Belleview Drive
Arnold, Maryland 21090
Email: agm@netscape.net

Phone: 410-889-3726   Fax: 410-889-1776

CAREER PROFILE:

- Twelve-year professional and management career in Purchasing, Integrated Logistics, and Supply Chain Management, including eight years with Barnes & Howell worldwide.
- Strong general management, operating management, strategic planning/analysis, team building/leadership, process design and organizational leadership competencies.
- Structured, negotiated, and managed strategic alliances, joint ventures, and acquisitions with global partners.
- Delivered measurable performance gains in productivity, efficiency, economies of scale, quality, cost reduction, and profitability.
- Irish descent. Raised in Australia. Lived and worked in Australia, Asia, and the US.
- Member, Australian Institute of Purchasing & Supply Management (AIPSM).

PROFESSIONAL EXPERIENCE:

BARNES & HOWELL – USA (*$200-Million Tool & Equipment Manufacturer*)   1997 to Present

Director of Purchasing – Worldwide Accessories

Promoted, relocated to the US, and challenged to reengineer and globalize B&H's non-performing Worldwide Accessories purchasing organization. Authored three-year strategic plan, developed financial and performance measurement processes, established strategic alliances and partnerships, and recruited/trained new purchasing team. Full P&L responsibility for global purchasing function with six direct reports and 10 indirect reports in the US, Taiwan, and the UK. Management accountability for $150+ million in annual purchasing expenditures. Report directly to the President of Worldwide Accessories.

- Surpassed all performance objectives. Delivered a 100% improvement in DPO (days purchasing outstanding) and a 7% gain in productivity. Reduced lead times 70% and inbound quality defects 50%.
- Achieved and sustained 97% customer service levels.
- Structured and established B&D's first Far East manufacturing joint venture for the Division. Led two successful acquisition negotiations.
- Strengthened purchasing organization and built from nine to 16 professionals.

BARNES & HOWELL – HONG KONG   1995 to 1997
(*$350-Million Tool & Equipment Manufacturer*)

Director of Sourced Product – Worldwide Household Products

Recruited to join a 3-person senior management team responsible for all B&H purchases throughout the Far East. Held full P&L accountability for purchasing, engineering, quality, and supply chain management for the $115 million Household Products Division. Led a team of 29 (including seven management reports) and controlled a $120+ million annual purchasing budget. Reported directly to the Vice President of Operations.

Challenged to develop and source products in Asia to reduce reliance on US manufacturing, streamline processes, and lower annual costs for 23 B&H operations worldwide. Developed a solid strategic plan, redesigned organizational infrastructure, implemented measurable performance standards, and provided decisive operating leadership. Extensive communications with internal customer base worldwide.

- Delivered over $7 million in total cost savings and achieved 95% customer service levels for the first time in the organization's history.
- Reduced supplier base and associated costs while accelerating volume and increasing product quality.

SUPER-X OFFICE PRODUCTS – LONDON   1994 to 1995
(*Start-Up Office Products Retailer*)

International Sourcing Manager (1995)
Category Buyer (1994 to 1995)

Fast-paced purchasing management positions with high-growth start-up venture that grew to $150 million in annual sales within two years and is currently generating over $500 million. Recruited as one of three buyers to develop strategic buying plan, establish organizational infrastructure, design business processes, and establish profitable strategic relationships with key domestic suppliers. Built category to 19% of total store sales in less than two years (projections at only 14%).

Promoted and given full responsibility for establishing a global sourcing function across all major product categories. Established cross-functional business structure for integrated logistics, quality assurance, merchandise planning, warehousing, distribution, brokerage, and supporting human resources and information technology systems. Managed 150+ SKUs.

- Delivered strong financial results including a 15-20% gross margin increase on sourced categories.
- Streamlined the entire supply chain process and structured/negotiated contracts with 40 strategic suppliers/business partners worldwide.

BARNES & HOWELL – LONDON (*$170-Million Business*)   1990 to 1994
Purchasing Manager

Recruited as a member of B&H's new management team to transition the organization from direct manufacturing to outsourced product development and logistics management. Challenged to rebuild the purchasing organization to improve productivity and quality, reduce costs, decrease product lead time, and increase inventory turns. Led a staff of seven and managed a $60 million annual budget. Reported to Director of Operations.

- Closed manufacturing facility, sold excess equipment/assets, and launched the start-up of an outsourced purchasing and logistics organization receiving inventory from 14 countries across three continents.
- Achieved/surpassed all performance goals. Reduced costs of goods 15% and delivered productivity savings of 5-6% while significantly reducing lead times.
- Negotiated unique partnerships and alliances with 30+ suppliers worldwide. Created and managed supplier accreditation program to ensure world-class cost, quality, and product development performance.

REXFORD HOTELS – LONDON *(London's Largest Hotel & Resort Complex)*   1987 to 1990

Purchasing Manager – Capital Acquisitions (1988 to 1990)
Food & Beverage Buyer (1987 to 1988)

Full responsibility for sourcing and purchasing all capital equipment and assets valued in excess of $25,000. Managed relationships with 200+ vendors worldwide. Trained/directed one buyer.

EDUCATION:

Graduate Diploma – Purchasing & Materials Management, PPTI University, London, 1991

- **Wharton Graduate School of Business** – Financial Statements
- **Center for Creative Leadership** – Leadership Development Program
- Successful Selling Strategies (Skills Training & Development)
- Negotiating in Asia (Cultural Awareness)
- Six Sigma (Transactional Six Sigma Elements)

MARTIN STYVERSON, CRP

11-B Markham Boulevard, Crystal City, Virginia 22303

Phone 703.222.9089   mstyvercrp@realestate.com

CORPORATE RELOCATION PROFESSIONAL
17 Years' Experience Directing Relocation Operations, Services, & Programs

Member of Relocation Management Team that built an emerging Corporate Relocations venture from virtual start-up to over $300 million in annual property sales to more than 200 corporate clients. Combines outstanding sales, marketing, and business development expertise with equally strong performance in operations management, systems/process development, staffing, training, and team building. Dynamic, decisive, and confident.

Certified Relocation Professional (CRP) – 1999
Licensed Real Estate Sales Associate - 1983

PROFESSIONAL EXPERIENCE:

FIRST STATES REAL ESTATE, INC., Washington, DC   1983 to Present

Director of Relocation & Business Services (1992 to Present)
New Business Development Manager – Regional Brokers Network (1991 to 1992)
Client Relations Director (1988 to 1991)
Client Referrals Manager (1985 to 1988)
Client Referrals Supervisor (1984 to 1985)
Client Referrals Coordinator (1983 to 1984)
Real Estate Sales Associate (1983)

Fast-track advancement through a series of increasingly responsible management positions to current promotion as the #1 relocation professional in the organization. Fully responsible for the strategic planning, development and operating management of newly created Relocation & Business Services Department. Honored for consistently strong operating and financial performance with:

- *Five Star Circle of Excellence Award* – 2001
- *Best Incoming Referrals Department Award* – 1999
- *Creativity Award* – 1995

Scope of management responsibility is broad and includes marketing, budgeting ($1-million annual operating fund), the entire staffing and training function (18 associates), sales, property management, corporate customer management, and a host of organizational development initiatives. Career highlights include:

Sales Leadership & Revenue Growth. Built Relocation Division from virtual start-up with less than $2 million in annual sales volume to $350 million in 1999. Manage and market an average of 300 properties annually. Increased number of closed outgoing referrals from 50 to 250 over two years.

New Business Development. Pioneered new programs and services offerings to penetrate new markets, new industries, and new accounts. Built customer base from 50 to 500+ companies throughout a 9-state region. Partnered with local economic development agencies to encourage corporate relocations and strengthen local economics.

Broker Network Development. Orchestrated development of regional broker referral network in Washington, Virginia, and Maryland that grew from concept to one of the largest broker networks in the U.S.

FIRST STATES REAL ESTATE, INC. (*continued*):

Corporate Acquisition & Integration. Participated in the acquisition of a competitive real estate and relocation company in 1997. Facilitated a seamless integration of personnel, properties, customers, and business operations, and achieved/surpassed all performance goals (reporting time, days on market, costs). Won national award for "*Best Incoming Referrals Department*" after only 18 months.

Sales & Marketing Communications. Wrote, designed, and produced a portfolio of sales, marketing, advertising and promotional materials. Created materials for in-house circulation, newspaper and magazine advertising, new business development projects, and property sales.

Sales Training & Team Leadership. Recruited, trained, and led a team of up to 18 sales and customer service professionals supporting a team of 2,000 sales associates. Created a cooperative and non-competitive working environment, designed sales presentation tools, and managed with an emphasis on individual contribution.

Customer Service & Relationship Management. Built, staffed, and directed one of First State's top-ranked customer service teams. Wrote customer communications, designed customer service processes, and trained personnel in building, nurturing, and managing both individual and corporate selling relationships. Improved customer service satisfaction from 49% to 81% within 18 months.

Organizational Change & Revitalization. Managed through an extensive period of reorganization as the company redefined itself, repositioned its market focus, upgraded executive team, expanded, diversified, and virtually reinvented itself.

Budgeting & Financial Management. Developed and administered $1-million annual budget for operating costs and $1.6-million revenue budget. Prepared financial forecasts, analyses, and reports. Introduced PC-based financial systems into the organization.

Management Presentations & Public Speaking. Extensive public speaking and professional presentation experience. Guest presenter at the Relocation Directors Council's 2002 Roundtable Meeting. Strong oral and written communication skills.

Committee Leadership & Appointments:

- Relocation Directors Council – 1988 to Present
- Employee Relocation Council – 1997 to Present
- National Task Force on Relocation & Business Services – 1996 to Present
- Relocation Services Advisory Council – 1995 to 1996

EDUCATION & PROFESSIONAL DEVELOPMENT:

1999 Real Estate Leadership Conference
First State's International Business Conference
Starkson Mobility International Conference (Planning Committee for Year 2000 Conference)
Employee Relocation Council
Relocation Directors Council

Richard Kessel

Professional Profile

- Senior-level retail executive experienced in national chain and specialty store operations.
- Ensure strong store standards, optimal performance, and complete customer satisfaction.
- Named one of the company's ten most successful employees.

Chain-Wide Retail Management

Specialty Store Management

Merchandising & Operations

P & L Management

Fifteen-year record of increasing sales, profitability, and customer service while reducing costs and employee turnover. Administer multi-million-dollar operating budgets and achieve maximum profits in highly competitive environments. Creative and intrapreneurial, with a flair for merchandising, forecasting trends, and managing people.

Expert troubleshooter with keen ability to plan and implement reorganizations, new store openings, merchandising and operations strategies, systems conversions, and effective training programs. Driven by an enthusiastic pursuit of excellence, working with vigor and absolute professionalism. Recognized as an accessible team-builder skilled in motivating associates to exceed objectives.

Career Development

HICKORY FARMS, Washington, Colorado, and New York	**1993 to Present**
Vice President of Stores	1999 to present
District Sales Manager — Boulder, CO	1997 to 1999
Store Manager, Riverhead, NY	1995 to 1997
Store Manager, Seattle, WA	1993 to 1995

Hickory Farms is a renowned 80-year old, 100-store catalog and retail supplier of gourmet foods and gifts. Currently direct all business functions for 13 outlet stores and two regional stores in chain's Northwest Region of Washington, Oregon, and Northern California.

The Northwest Region, the oldest region in the company, produces annual volume of $12 million. Recruit, hire, train, and supervise all store managers and oversee a roster of 112 employees.

Performance milestones include:

Set up and opened 21 of the company's 100 stores, including the top four producers in the chain.

- Selected to open the company's first East Coast store in Riverhead, NY, the gateway to the Hamptons. Store's success spawned 40 high-profit stores now operating in the Eastern U.S.
- Led planning and implementation of nearly 50% of store openings in the Northwest Region, three openings in Northwest Region, and turnkey store set-up of the company's third regional store in upscale Colby Square.
- At every store start, worked as many hours as needed to manage and coordinate activities. Hired staff, trained store managers and sales associates, set up fixtures and merchandise, oversaw computer installations, followed up on local advertising, and scheduled soft and grand openings.

Promoted to Northwest Region District Sales Manager to boost sales when region was experiencing major growth challenges and a negative sales record following nearly a year without district management. Developed and implemented strategic and highly successful management initiatives.

- Produced more than $10 million in volume in FY 2000 (April 1999 to March 2000).
- Generated $1.8 million FY 2000 profitability, an increase of over 50% from FY 1999, with sales growing 6% over 1999.

Career Development, continued

Hickory Farms Performance Milestones, continued

**Areas
of Ability**

Store Set-ups
& Openings

Store Layout
& Displays

Planograms

Inventory
Control

Warehousing
& Distribution

Systems
Development

Strategic
Planning

Reorganiza-
tions

Training &
Development

Managed operations for the 27-store, 11-state Central Division based in Boulder, CO, as Vice President of Stores.

♦ Generated $9.6 million year-one sales; increased volume to $12.5 million in year-two sales.
♦ Finished FY 2001 ahead of plan in sales, gross margin, and operating volume, ranking first company-wide in sales margin and second in operating income.
♦ Prior to promotion, was named one of firm's 10 most successful employees (of 5,000 year-round and 7,000 seasonal staff) and was featured in the corporate quarterly magazine.

Set up, opened, and managed company's first East Coast and second largest store as Sales Manager of Riverhead, New York outlet.

♦ Beat first-year sales plan by 60.8% and total net projected profit by 90.6%
♦ Gained $1 million in sales for two years as manager, the only time the store has ever reached seven-figure sales volume.
♦ Simultaneously coordinated opening of three additional stores.

Set up and managed a 2,800-square-foot Christmas holiday store in Chicago.

♦ Prepared site, hired assistant manager / temp help, supervised daily operation, and dismantled store.
♦ Produced $365,000 in sales during store's six-week life span.
♦ Store generated the most profit of company's four holiday shops across the nation.

Opened and managed record-breaking Seattle, WA store while simultaneously planning, setting up, and opening four additional Hickory Farms stores.

♦ Led Seattle store to became #1 in comp sales with an 11% first year increase.

Participated in a number of Hickory Farms operations and systems initiatives.

♦ Reorganized over-expanded district to provide better management coverage; created new district for ten stores in Nevada, Southern California, Arizona, New Mexico, and Colorado.
♦ One of only two managers appointed to critical selection and testing of new P.O.S. system.
♦ Co-authored store manager training guide and a complete training manual for store openings.

OFFICE DEPOT	1990 to 1993
Portland and Vancouver, OR	

Store Merchandising Manager, Portland, OR	1993
Operations Manager, Portland, OR	1991 to 1992
Receiving Manager, Vancouver, OR	1990 to 1991

Maintained inventory levels of $1.2 million and developed/implemented planograms, displays, signing, and merchandising as Merchandising Manager of $9.8-million Portland office supply store. Recruited, hired, trained, and supervised a sales and merchandising staff of 11.

Managed freight scheduling/receiving for $6.7-million Vancouver store, the largest volume store in the district. Rapidly promoted to Operations Manager of $7-million Portland store, supervising 25 sales and merchandising employees, two managers, and two supervisors. Directly contributed to store's 25% increase in sales. Integral member of management transition team during and after buyout.

STEPHEN R. FISHER

617-825-9764 (Cell) ▪ srfisher@email.com ▪ 617-222-5456 (Home)

1387 Westminster Lane ▪ Boston ▪ Massachusetts ▪ 02116

RETAIL MANAGEMENT EXECUTIVE

Accomplished management executive with a documented record of turning around failing operations and executing initiatives that drive revenue and profit growth. Team-based leadership style; effective communicator.

PERFORMANCE OVERVIEW

Significantly improved financial viability.
Change-managed a region with profit earnings of -$1.5 million, driving a $7.1-million turn-around and achieving profit earnings of $6.6 million within the first year. Generated comparable sales of 9.1% within a down economy versus corporate average of 6.5%. Reduced customer complaints by 70% within the first year.

Recruited, trained, motivated, and managed top-performing management teams.
Identified underperforming managers, replacing 40% of management staff within the first year. Implemented training programs, first-ever critical operating standards (COS), and performance measurements. Improved management ratings by almost 50% within the first 18 months.

Repeatedly recognized for leadership initiative.
Named District Manager of the Year three times (1992, 1995, and 1997). Established a reputation for turning around tough markets, earning a promotion to Regional Operations Manager in one of the company's largest markets.

Launched cost-saving initiatives.
Planogrammed store stockrooms to reduce inventories, shrink, and supply orders, achieving current inventories of 5% under plan and shrink reduction of 3% over 2001 figures. Introduced a service assistant program to improve overall front-end productivity and reduce payroll hours, improving productivity levels by 1.2% and reducing payroll by $147,000.

Pioneered succession planning programs to ensure continuity of leadership.
Launched the region's first management candidate tracking program. Successfully developed approximately 10 people to District Manager or higher positions within 10 years.

PROFESSIONAL EXPERIENCE

WALGREENS CORPORATION, Deerfield, Illinois
(The nation's leading drug store chain generating more than $20+ million in annual sales)

Regional Operations Manager, Boston, Massachusetts – since 2000
Direct a 135-store region generating $6.6 million in EBIT and $660 million in annual sales volume. Manage 20 direct reports and over 4,600 indirect reports.

- Currently 150% over last year's earning plan in one of the nation's toughest markets.

District Manager, Atlanta, Georgia – 1994 to 2000
Promoted to lead a "super" district comprised of 42 stores (versus the average 27-store district), overseeing 50 direct reports and 1,350 indirect reports.

- Drove one-year revenues from $4 million to more than $7 million, earning recognition as "District Manager of the Year."
- Reduced shrink to 1.7% versus the company average of 2.9% within the first year, and consistently held one of the top 3 positions for lowest shrink for five consecutive years.

District Manager, Dallas, Texas – 1993 to 1994
Personally selected to turnaround and revitalize a failing market losing approximately $2 million a year. Managed 27 stores and a 900-person staff.

- Broke even the first year, positioning the district to return to profitability and earning a promotion to manage a "super" district.

District Manager, Tallahassee, Florida – 1991 to 1993
Brought in to restore the morale, financial viability, and operational profitability of a district with a history of underperformance.

- Led the district to profitability the first year, and generated $3 million in revenue within two years.

Regional Operations Manager, Miami, Florida – 1987 to 1990
Revitalized a stagnant market comprised of 100 stores and 3,000 employees. Enhanced store appearance and operations, reduced out-of-stocks, implemented inventory controls, and improved customer service levels.

- Doubled sales revenues within the first two years, doubling them again (to $9+ million) in year three. Drove comparable sales increases from 3.5% to 5.2% versus a 2.5% industry average.

District Manager – 1978 to 1987
Established a reputation for turning around failing markets (Tampa, Dallas, and Atlanta). Regularly promoted to higher volume territories.

EDUCATION & TRAINING

Winning Coach	Knock Your Socks Off Customer Service
Management Effectiveness	Dealing With Problem People
Managing Change	First Things First

Completed approximately 45 credit hours towards Associate's Degree
Austin Community College, Austin, Texas

Jeff Keller

1222 Huntingdon Ridge Lane
Atlanta, Georgia 30301   jkeller@arc.net   770.389-3909 (Cellular)
770.221-9836 (Home)

S T O R E

BENEFITS RITE-AID CAN ACCRUE BY ADDING ME TO YOUR TEAM

- The **vision** to turn problems into profits,
- The **leadership** to attract and retain the best employees — even under the worst conditions, and
- The **skill** to help teams keep customers coming back.

WORK HISTORY WITH EXAMPLES OF PERFORMANCE:

*More than 18 years of progressively responsible managerial positions with **Food Max**, one of the South's leading grocery chains, including these most recent assignments in Atlanta, Georgia:*

- *Promoted three times to* **Location Director** *at three locations*   Apr 91 – Present

  Given **full management responsibility** for stores of up to 45K ft² of selling space, **165 employees, 24/7 operations,** and annual sales of **$20M**.

- *Promoted to* **Co-Manager**   Nov 89 – Apr 91
- *Promoted to* **Assistant Manager**   Oct 87 – Nov 89
- *Promoted to* **Produce Manager**   Apr 87 – Oct 87

Turned around tough inventory and shrinkage problems others had tried — and failed — to fix for years. Matched the right person to the right job, then built everyone's support for tighter standards. *Benefits:* $10K a month **loss stopped in 30 days. Morale** and **productivity** are **up** — profits are too.

"Rescued" a part-time employee whose petty thefts were offsetting her hard work. Built her trust by promoting her to full-time department clerk — and held her to tough standards. *Benefits:* Thefts are gone. Her team does **a great job in 45 less manhours** a week. **Sales rose 5% in the first month.** Customers happier.

Fixed a problem the media were highlighting: out-of-date merchandise still in stock. Stopped very high turnover in stockers with no additional labor costs. *Benefits:* Corporate experts could only find one out-of-date item in the hundreds we carried — unlike the 20% in other stores. **Others leveraged their success** with our system.

Made our operation a model for managing a diverse workforce. Found our best two under-privileged, minority part-time baggers and encouraged them to grow with us. Rewarded their hard work publicly. *Benefits:* **Both now successful junior assistant managers,** a lesson not lost on other, hard-to-keep employees.

Analyzed and corrected an inventory trend that was losing the store I inherited $200K a year. Tied UPCs to shortfalls. Then increased controls over just a few critical products. *Benefits:* **$120K more to our bottom line** in the first year alone.

PROFESSIONAL DEVELOPMENT:

✚ Two years of college-level courses in **General Business** and **Management**, Cranston University,
Atlanta, Georgia   79 – 84
Fitted a full academic load into a 40-hour work week.

✚ "Handling the Full Line of Food Products Safely," ChemStar Corporation   01
✚ "Being a More Effective Manager," Tim Brodwell Training Company, two days, every year.   97 – 99

CERTIFICATIONS:

✚ Certified Professional Food Manager, Experior Assessments, Inc.
                                                                                    Aug 00

One of few to win this credential by passing the examination on the first try.

COMPUTER SKILLS:

✚ Expert in proprietary employee scheduling, HR, POS, inventory control and reconciliation software.
✚ Working knowledge of Word and Quicken.

AWARDS AND HONORS:

✚ "Creative Merchandising Award," Food Max. *Two-time winner.*

BETTE R. BAINES

757-892-5566
bettebaines@email.com

19856 Wyndham Drive
Norfolk, VA 23551

SALES PROFESSIONAL

Dynamic sales career delivering strong and sustainable revenue, market, and profit contributions. Excel at infiltrating hostile territory, building trust, and winning the sale. Proven ability to deal effectively with diverse and challenging situations. Keen presentation and communication skills. LPN.

Highlights:

Sales Skills … Ranked in the top 1% of the company for generating sales and for consistently maintaining percentage growth to plan. Solid track record closing sales to physician offices, hospitals, doctors, nurses, thought process leaders, case managers, and materials managers.

Relationship Management … Built and fostered the profitable relationships that quadrupled sales within 1.5 years.

Territory Development … Penetrated a hostile market, rebuilt the company reputation, and drove the number of direct referrals from 20% to 50%.

Product Knowledge … Developed the training material that contributed to significant company growth and established a solid reputation for product knowledge and service. Only female selected to participate in new product strategizing groups.

Medical Expertise … Licensed Practical Nurse with broad-based medical knowledge.

PROFESSIONAL EXPERIENCE

HEALTH OPTIONS, INC., Norfolk, Virginia – since 1998
(*Comprehensive solutions for diabetes, high-risk pregnancies, and respiratory disorders*)
Provider Operations Account Executive

- Only sales representative in the southeastern United States to attain President's Club status in 2001. Achieved 116% of plan despite company-wide profitability decreases.
- Ranked in the top 5 out of 75 sales reps nationwide for generating sales and maintaining percent to plan.
- Infiltrated the office of a 47-doctor group and established a long-term relationship of trust that resulted in standards of care consulting and direct referrals from two managing partners.
- More than doubled the number of "B" accounts.

PRESSURE RELIEF SYSTEMS, Norfolk, Virginia - 1994 to 1998
(*Distributor of RIK Fluid Mattresses*)
RIK Fluid Mattress Specialist

- Turned around a failing territory, quadrupling annual sales revenue within one year and increasing the number of units from 3 to 40.
- Outperformed the competition and captured the largest specialty bed account within a 15-county area.

- Selected for reputation among peers to serve on the steering committee charged with developing growth strategies and revitalizing employee compensation packages to improve retention.
- Recognized as Sales Professional of the Year after first year of hire. Nominated for Distributor of the Quarter numerous times.

NATIONWIDE HEALTHCARE, Richmond, Virginia – 1990 to 1994
(Sale of oxygen and durable medical equipment)
Sales Representative

- Turned around the company's reputation and earned the trust of key decision-makers, driving direct referrals from 20% to 50%.
- Developed a patient checklist to assist physicians in educating patients in the use of equipment that led to a 75% decrease in after-hours service calls.
- Authored policies, procedures, and customer orientation package that resulted in receiving Joint Commission Accreditation.

FAVORITE NURSES, UNDERHILL AND RESCARE, Raleigh, North Carolina – 1986 to 1990
Contract Nurse

EDUCATION / TRAINING

Numerous educational seminars including …
    Problem Pregnancies
    Pre-Term Labor
    Hyperemisis
    Diabetes in Pregnancy
    Wound Care
    Joint Commission Standards & Quality Improvement

In-house sales seminars including …
    Sales School 101 and 102
    Sales Management

LICENSES / CERTIFICATIONS

Licensed Practical Nurse, Raleigh Vocational Technical Institute
Pharmacology Certification, National Practical Nursing Education & Standards

PROFESSIONAL AFFILIATIONS

Member - Healthy Start Coalition of Norfolk

REGINALD A. RAYMOND

regray@ix.netcom.com

12463 McNamee Lane
Pierson, Florida 33479

Home: 914-382-9372
Office: 914-990-1005

B2B SALES & MARKETING PROFESSIONAL – VICE PRESIDENT & DIRECTOR
Advanced Financial Products, Services, & Resources

Top-Revenue Producer & Business Manager with 10+ year career building profitable new markets throughout the US. Well-known and well-respected among national broker network for exceptional training and leadership skills.

* Marketing & Business Strategy
* Competitive Market Positioning
* Client Relationship Management
* Public Speaking & Presentations

* Partnerships & Strategic Alliances
* Multimedia Sales & Marketing Tools
* Sales Training, Teaming, & Leadership
* Sales Forecasting, Budgeting, & Reporting

PC Proficient with MS Word, MS Excel, MS Access, MS Outlook, MS FrontPage, WordPerfect, and Windows.

PROFESSIONAL EXPERIENCE:

Vice President – Business Development   2000 to Present
Creative Financial Resources, Tampa, Florida

High-profile management position leading all sales, marketing, and business development programs for this commercial factoring and finance company with $40 million in annual sales and nationwide market presence. Challenged to create and drive forward a number of new corporate initiatives to expand broker network, increase customer base, accelerate revenue growth, and deliver double-digit profit growth.

Personally develop and manage key customer and broker relationships, including presentations, negotiations, and sales closings. In addition, forge innovative strategic alliances and marketing partnerships. Senior advisor to staff and executive management team on marketing strategy, sales, and customer management.

- ***Achieved/surpassed all revenue and growth objectives.*** Brought several hundred new brokers into Creative's network and forged strategic alliances with other financial institutions (e.g., Allied Capital, Oxbow Credit) to expand market reach and penetration.
- ***Led the start-up and development of the company's first-ever branch office***, projected to generate over $4 million in first year sales.
- ***Built a highly successful broker training program*** to enhance broker sales and marketing skills within specialty financial niche markets. Managed scheduling, budgeting, marketing communications and presentation of all training programs nationwide.
- ***Upgraded and enhanced corporate marketing and advertising programs*** to create a recognizable brand. Consulted with outside design firm to create new materials, upgrade website content and look, and build a consistent theme. Launched email broadcast program as part of marketing effort.
- Redesigned and simplified administrative, documentation, and reporting functions.

Vice President & General Manager   1998 to 2000
RXT Financial Group, Tampa, Florida

Member of 3-person management team launching a new commercial factoring/financial services venture. Planned and directed the entire sales and marketing function in addition to full operating, HR, budgeting, reporting, administrative, and P&L management responsibility.

Vice President & General Manager (*continued*):

Defined marketing strategy and market objectives, prospected for new accounts, cultivated relationships throughout existing broker network, and sourced new partnership opportunities. Consulted with prospective clients to evaluate financial needs, negotiate terms and conditions, and close final transactions. Managed existing client relationships and leveraged cross-selling opportunities.

- ***Built business from start-up to 1000+ brokers nationwide and sales of over $60 million annually.*** Achieved virtually immediate profitability with nationwide market presence.
- ***Partnered with Global Financial News*** to create a nationwide broker training program that reached 200+ new brokers each month. Initiative was the single greatest contributor to rapid, profitable growth.
- ***Co-authored multimedia portfolio*** of print, electronic, and video training, "The Complete Financial Kit."
- ***Initiated innovative marketing and business development initiatives***, including appearing on nationally broadcast infomercial.
- Worked with corporate principals to negotiate and close company financing and credit insurance policies.

Director of Marketing
Capital Financial Services Group, Miami, Florida
1995 to 1998

Directed nationwide sales, marketing, partnership, trade show, and business development programs for $50-million financial services company. Concurrently, managed major broker recruitment and training initiative.

- ***Negotiated partnership with the American Financial Association*** and created a 1000-person nationwide broker network generating $20+ million in annual sales.
- ***Conceived, designed and produced*** all marketing, advertising, sales and presentation materials.

Co-Owner
Tiburon Communications, Islamorada, Florida
1988 to 1995

Fast-paced management position building this small telecommunications interconnect and installation company. Independently managed all sales, marketing, and business development efforts targeted to commercial and industrial accounts throughout the South Florida market. Directed daily business operations, purchasing and vendor relationships, staffing and business planning/expansion initiatives.

- ***Doubled sales revenues*** (100%+ growth), successfully penetrated the local municipal and government markets, and positioned Tiburon Communications as a growing telecom venture.
- ***Conceived, designed, and implemented a service and equipment contract program*** to generate recurrent revenue stream and solidify long-term customer relationships.

Stock Broker
Arnold Smith Associates, Boca Raton, Florida
1986 to 1988

Sold/marketed a portfolio of investment products to retail clients throughout the U.S. Honored as *"Broker of the Month"* on several occasions for outstanding performance in new business development, client relationship management, and revenue growth. Passed NASD Series 7 examination for securities license.

EDUCATION:

FLORIDA ATLANTIC UNIVERSITY / NOVA SOUTHEASTERN UNIVERSITY
Business Studies in Marketing, Economics, & Accounting (1982 to 1992)

NIAGARA COUNTY COMMUNITY COLLEGE
AS Degree in Communications & Media Arts (1979)

ANNABELLA VALERIANA

931 Ballerina Court
Van Nuys, California 91405

818 994-4215
avaleriana@earthlink.net

SALES AND MARKETING
International Business Development

Strategic Market Planning / Competitive Market Positioning / Multi-Channel Distribution
Sales Training and Team Leadership / New Product Launch / New Market Development

Dynamic, hands-on sales and marketing management career across broad industries, markets, and accounts. Achieved strong and sustainable revenue, market, and profit contributions through expertise in business development, organizational development, and performance management. Keen presentation, contract negotiation, communication, and multicultural skills (Europe, Middle East, South America). Worldwide traveler with excellent knowledge of histories, economies, and business trends in countries around the globe. Computer literate.

Equally strong qualifications in financial planning/analysis, manufacturing, and distribution operations, management, purchasing, human resources, training and development, administration, quality and change management. Excellent team building, team leadership, and interpersonal relations skills.

Work well under pressure without losing control and with all levels of management in a professional, diplomatic, and tactful manner. Develop client and vendor loyalty above and beyond the customer service relationship. Provide energetic and decisive leadership; able to merge disparate technologies and personnel into a cohesive team-centered unit.

PROFESSIONAL EXPERIENCE

EUROPEAN MARKET MANAGER   1993 – 1998
Boone Aircraft • Visalia, CA

Recruited and promoted to European Market Manager. *Challenged to plan and orchestrate an aggressive turnaround and rejuvenation of the European sales operation. Scope of responsibility included all sales, marketing, business development, and customer management/retention operations throughout Western Europe. Started to develop the Middle East and the South American markets.*

< Spearheaded division reengineering: interviewed, hired, trained, motivated, and terminated staff. Wrote performance reviews. Created evaluation process and model to identify top performers. Transitioned crew and built new cross-functional team to further drive revenue growth. Expanded communications structure between headquarters and worldwide sales organizations to respond to specific marketing, advertising, regulatory, and promotional needs. Led a team of 8.

< Provided strong organizational leadership and active participation in key account sales and business development. Resulted in a significant gain in employee morale, productivity, and sales performance. Designed and implemented an international product support matrix process to standardize and expedite product launches.

< Identified and capitalized upon market opportunities to introduce new products and reposition existing product lines. Managed a complex "turnaround" initiative to meet U.S. market demand and established a strong competitive position. Negotiated and obtained multi-million-dollar contracts. Sourced vendors to expand supplier base and reduce acquisition costs. Interfaced with international and domestic shipping carriers.

Accomplishments:

- Served as a consultant to the President of Boone Aircraft.
- Increased annual revenues by 50% within three years through aggressive and well-targeted business development program. Consistently exceed quotas.
- Introduced several adjunct programs and services (e.g., trade show sales, professional roundtables) to strengthen customer relationships and drive earnings growth.
- Developed and maintained personal and business networks within the sales and marketing arenas.

Awards:
Numerous Improvement Certificates

SALES / PURCHASING REPRESENTATIVE   1990 – 1992
Tarry Aircraft • Glendale, CA

Fast-track promotion from Purchasing to Sales Representative. Selected by international department to maintain domestic and European sales and purchasing accounts.

Acted as direct liaison to all department heads throughout the organization to identify and obtain their specific product requirements at best price/best quality. Personally handled large-dollar purchasing negotiations and major vendor relationships. Secured large OEM contracts through outstanding customer service and contract options, JIT service, and investment in client inventory.

PURCHASING SUPERVISOR   Carson, Inc. • Burbank, CA   Prior to 1990

NON-RELATED EXPERIENCE

Realtor, Coldwell Banker, Newhall, CA   1998 – Present

EDUCATION and CONTINUAL TRAINING

California Real Estate License
Certificate of Completion, Assertive Communications Skills for Women. Boone Aircraft, Visalia, CA
Graduate, Hoover High School, Glendale, CA

KIMBERLY ANN FOX

609-382-5590
kimfox@email.net
2832 Sunset Way., Atlantic City, NJ 08404

SALES EXECUTIVE
Global Technical Sales … Training & Development … Contract Negotiation & Execution

Results-oriented sales professional with a diverse technical background and solid record of accomplishments. Strong analytical and problem-solving skills with a focus on creating mutually beneficial solutions. Skilled at communicating with people at all levels of responsibility, conveying technical information, establishing rapport, and building long-term relationships. Documented track record of successfully closing complex corporate sales. Areas of strength include …

Customer Relationship Management	Competitive Product Positioning
Sales Cycle Management	Account Development & Management
Strategic Market Planning	High Impact Presentations

PRODUCT KNOWLEDGE

Internet Applications & System Architecture: ASP, ERP, HTML
WAP Applications
Microsoft Windows Applications: Word, Excel, PowerPoint
Customer Relationship Management Software (CRM): ACT, Sales Logix
Financial Systems: Oracle, SAP
ERP, Supply Chain Management, Systems Integration, and e-Business Solutions.

NOTABLE CAREER HIGHLIGHTS

Sales

- Exploded into the technology sales arena with average annual sales revenues in excess of $300 million, achieving recognition as the *top national sales person for 2.5 years within the first 3 years of hire.*
- Personally selected to open the highly competitive northeast region. *Consistently outperformed the competition by increasing market share by more than 60%.*
- Challenged to open two additional markets, *capturing 55% of the market share in Pittsburgh and 30% of the market share in Cleveland, with combined annual sales revenues exceeding $235 million.*
- *Chosen by senior management for presentation skills, leadership ability, and technology expertise* to represent the organization as a speaker at the NBTA trade show.

Leadership

- Led the organization's first-ever attempt to forge a mutually beneficial relationship between management and union representatives. Established informational seminars dealing with lost-time issues and performed safety and efficiency reviews. *Reduced lost time an average of 18% at 20 locations, saving more than $3 million annually.*
- *Selected from among the top 1% of peers as the Sales Manager's Primary Candidate.* Chosen by the Vice President of Airline Operations as *one of only three other women* for inclusion in the General Manager's Hiring Pool.
- Spearheaded the campaign to solicit cost-savings ideas from employees in order to facilitate capital equipment funding. Generated ideas that *saved over $350 million*, permitted self-funding of a 757 aircraft, and led to a second campaign 5 years later.

Training & Development

- Developed and led cross training of field service, reservation, M&E, and flight service management personnel, *improving service to customers and reducing overall staffing requirements and costs*.
- Conducted "Putting People First" *customer service training*.
- Facilitated "Part of the Solution" *employee motivational focus groups*.

PROFESSIONAL EXPERIENCE

NORTHEAST TECHNOLOGIES *(IT services company)*, Albany, New York
Vice President of Sales – since 2001
  Recruited to handle C-level sales of enterprise resource planning, supply chain management, relationship management, systems integration and e-business consulting, implementation, integration, upgrade, and sourcing services.

- Facilitated an efficient team concept by establishing open lines of communication between the sales, marketing, and delivery teams that resulted in a streamlined sales cycle and created the largest sales funnel in company history.
- Established the organization's first-ever sales planning and analysis tools to accurately forecast and benchmark sales, and a contact management database for sales tracking.
- Identified, created, qualified, and actively worked a personal sales funnel of $20 million in relation to a yearly sales goal of $4 million. Built the corporate RFP process and submitted the company's first-ever $7.9-million RFP to a Fortune 500 company.

ONLINE TRAVEL SOLUTIONS *(Application integration systems provider)* Boston, Massachusetts
Sales Director / Mid-West Sales & Service – 1997 to 2001
  Charged with closing complex, high-risk, and sensitive technology sales to Fortune 500 clients. Acted as peer mentor and facilitated trade shows, meetings, and conferences.

  - Representative Fortune 500 clients include EDS, A.H. Belo, Mary Kay, Texas Instruments, PepsiCo./Frito Lay, Perot Systems, Alcatel, Alltel, Halliburton, the Associates, Alliance Data Systems, and Tokyo Electron America.

DELTA AIRLINES, Atlanta, Georgia
Regional Lost Time Manager, Central Region-Employee Development & Services – 1995 to 1997
  Built strategic and mutually beneficial relationships between management and union representatives. Developed curriculum and facilitated training.

Senior Analyst / Field Performance Analyst – 1994 to 1995
  Directed field stations in establishing service quality objectives to support continuous improvement.

Senior Analyst / Field Business Planning; Financial Analyst/IdeAAs in Action – 1990 to 1994
Analyst / Finance; Supervisor / Flight Data Analysis; Sales Analyst – 1986 to 1990

EDUCATION

Associate of Arts in Business – Albany Community College, Albany, New York

SEMINARS / TRAINING

Miller-Heiman	Conceptual Selling; Strategic Selling; Large Account Management
Decker Communications	Presentation Skills

JASON OGDEN

811 Rambling Woods - Plymouth, MI 48333
333.555.9300

SALES MANAGEMENT PROFESSIONAL

Highly motivated sales professional with almost 20 years' of proven success in automotive sales. Possesses dynamic people skills and a solid reputation for maintaining above-average profit contributions with uncompromising regard for customer retention and first-class service quality. Proven ability to select, train, and motivate sales staff to achieve ambitious goals. Strategic planner skilled at both short- and long-range goal setting. Strong ability to accomplish objectives by focusing on essential activities. Effective communicator with excellent relationship-building skills. Excellent closing skills.

SALES EXPERIENCE

FORD-LINCOLN MERCURY, Dearborn, MI
GENERAL SALES MANAGER   2001 - Present

Oversee all new and used car sales, in addition to the financing of sales. Direct a sales staff of 30 and control an $800,000 advertising budget. Handle day-to-day operations, in addition to planning and executing sales and marketing plans.

- Increased sales 5%, adding $700,000 to profits in one year in a highly competitive and slumping economy.
- Master Certified as a Lincoln Mercury manager.

VARSITY FORD / LINCOLN MERCURY, Southfield, MI
GENERAL SALES MANAGER / NEW CAR MANAGER   1997 - 2000
USED CAR MANAGER   1994 - 1997
USED CAR ASSISTANT MANAGER   1986 - 1994
USED CAR SALES   1983 - 1986

Fast-track promotion through a series of increasingly responsible positions. As General Sales Manager, directed all aspects of the new and used car business. Forecast and set sales goals, recruited and trained employees, oversaw financing, administered the advertising budget, and appraised all vehicles for new car trades. Extensive knowledge in wholesale and purchase of used vehicles.

- First month as Used Car Manager, sold and delivered 125 vehicles, when company goal was 75.
- Each member on the sales staff of five made over $100,000/year - year after year - due to excellent sales efforts.
- Store became #1 in the country in new car sales for five years running. Three months out of one year, sold over 500 new cars each month - no other dealership in the country has ever done that.
- Selected, hired, trained, coached, and managed highly motivated individuals and gave them the tools and training necessary to succeed. Communicated a focus of customer service and communication to sales staff.
- Promoted positive ongoing customer relationships and served as a problem-solver and resource to customers.
- Set up and launched a new used-car facility that exceeded all sales goals its first year.

EDUCATION

Coursework in *Business*, UNIVERSITY OF WINDSOR, Windsor, Ont.
ASSUMPTION COLLEGE HIGH SCHOOL, Windsor, Ont.

ADDITIONAL INFORMATION

- At age 18, while still in high school, bought an Arcade with $5,000 saved from after-school jobs, and added a Coney Island to the Arcade. Sold company for $50,000 after just one year.
- Was a member of the National Canadian Wrestling Team for 6 years and the Canadian Olympic Wrestling Team for 1 year.
- Opened a very successful business in Venezuela, manufacturing cinder blocks contracted to the government for construction of the Guery Dam.

Dennis C. Harriman

7557 Indian Trail Court, Skillman, NJ 08558
(609) 466-1696 • dennisharri@coldrain.com

Executive Sales / Sales Management / General Management

Career Profile

- Dynamic sales, sales management, and sales/marketing consulting career with consumer products/services companies. Expert in capturing market opportunities, managing top sales regions, increasing market share, and positioning new product launches. Mass merchandisers, big-box retailers, military and premium industries.

- Blend a participative management style with vision, tenacity, and team leadership. Anticipate trends and create business-building client relationships that surpass objectives. Produce results through controlling profits (from cost to sell to retail), sales team motivation and savvy use of competitive market/product knowledge.

- Productive team player with strong vision of company goals. Hardworking, reliable leader able to train and motivate sales staff to produce with a high ROI value.

Areas of Expertise

- ✓ Revenue, Profit & Market Share Growth
- ✓ New Market & Business Development
- ✓ National and Key Account Management
- ✓ Client Relationship Management
- ✓ Competitive Market Positioning
- ✓ Consultative Sales
- ✓ New Product Launches
- ✓ Team Building & Training
- ✓ Sales Cycle Management
- ✓ Distributor/Channel Sales

Career History

MAX MARKETING INC., Princeton Junction, NJ   1997 to present
President
Sales and marketing consulting firm serving entrepreneurial companies (B2B and B2C). Focus on competitive market positioning, brand development, sales and customer service training, solutions selling, and vertical market development.

CLIENTS INCLUDE:
Specialty Physicians Group, LLC (Clinton, NJ)
- Broadened patient base for multi-specialty medical facility by instituting innovative outreach programs for corporate and community groups. Launched PR campaign targeting legal profession. Increased new patient visits and revenues to $780,000.

Industrial Production, Inc. (Edison, NJ)
- Facilitated merger of Garrett Ball Bearing's NYC Metro sales force into Industrial Production. Established realistic sales objectives, and improved presentation and closing skills, leading to 7% increase in sales for first year (in a declining market).

Vending Supplies National, Inc. (Woodbridge, NJ)
- Designed and delivered new front-end sales, back-end customer service, and time management training to invigorate lagging sales. Sparked 9% sales increase within 90 days, leading to overall sales growth of 11% for the first year.

Time Pieces International (New York, NY)
- Successfully positioned company for profitable sale. Launched strategic and tactical plans that increased target market account participation to 2,000 stores nationally, reduced landed cost of goods, and saved in-house personnel costs.

PROFESSIONAL EXPERIENCE

Career History
Continued

THE MARKETING ALLIANCE, New York, NY   1996 to 1997
Vice President of Sales
Full P&L responsibility for national sales, marketing and promotions, and new business development for premium watch company. Managed 12 direct reports in nationwide territory. Oversaw and controlled $300,000 annual expense budget.

- Created customized sales and marketing promotions and annual ad schedules for clients, driving market segmentation quotas and $55 million in annual sales.

- Key player in account expansion and revenue increases of more than 10% within the first 10 months. Reviewed, monitored, and improved SKUs by account.

ROLODEX, INC., New York, NY   1992 to 1995
National Sales Manager
Recruited to invigorate key watch division, directing a team of seven regional sales managers, 50 outside sales reps and a network of manufacturers' reps. Utilized participative management style with sales staff to grow national and key accounts.

- Spearheaded the development of national account department, realigned existing regions, trained and developed productive regional managers and sales teams, and introduced expanded styles and selections to gain competitive market share.
- Increased year-over-year sales by 7%, maximizing profits and national market share against strong competition in a niche market. Developed distributor and channel sales to $150 million annually.

CENTRAL WATCH COMPANY OF AMERICA, New York, NY   1987 to 1992
Director of Sales
Strengthened regional key accounts, built account base, and developed mass merchandiser channel sales to 2,000+ stores. Captured $10 million in key rollout for K-Mart. Introduced competitive price points, driving profits and market share growth.

MERIX TIMEPIECES, INC., Franklin Park, NJ   1982 to 1986
Director of Sales
Led product launch of new brand (Timex), achieving $80 million in sales within two years. Recruited, trained, and motivated sales team (managers and reps) to roll out brand nationwide. Consulted on product development to hit special price points.

Education

A.A., Management and Marketing, Trenton State College, Trenton, NJ
Ongoing Professional Development: Sales, Marketing, and Executive Development

Professional Associations

American Society for Training and Development - ASTD
Communications and Marketing Association - CAMA

Martin W. Jackson
sales professional

3100 Jameson Drive
Knoxville, TN 37901
☏ 865.329-3872 — mwj58@bellwest.net

WHAT I CAN OFFER YOUR ORGANIZATION AS YOUR NEWEST SALES PROFESSIONAL

- ◯ Pre-selling
- ◯ Leveraging our strengths against our competitors' weak areas
- ◯ Cutting cost of sales
- ◯ Capturing and keeping customers at every level
- ◯ Generating follow-on sales
- ◯ Exploiting new markets

RECENT WORK HISTORY WITH CONTRIBUTIONS TO OUR PROFITABILITY

◯ Nov 01 – Present **Marketing Representative**, MaxSell, Knoxville, TN
MaxSell is a national leader in restoring homes and offices damaged by fire and water. Annual sales for my location approach $1.5M.

Built a solidly supported recommendation to reduce the age of our accounts receivable and **sell a new service** — after just five days on the job. *Results:* Management looking at my **proposal to save $150K annually**.

◯ Nov 00 – May 01 *Hired away to be* **Store Manager**, The 19th Hole, Knoxville, TN
The 19th Hole was a brand new anchor store in a shopping mall. Sales in the first 6 months quickly rose to $125K.

Transformed an empty shell of a building into a fully operating retail outlet in 17 calendar days. Did it all, from buying and installing fixtures, to building solid vendor relationships, to hiring our employees, to placing $250K in inventory. **Results:** Made the very tight deadline just before the **season's busiest shopping day**.

Positioned us well against a much larger competitor by reading everything I could find in their promotional material and "mystery shopping" their local outlet. *Results:* Undercut their price points, made our hours longer than theirs, and focused on customer service. Sales projections right on track.

Used a golf simulator to generate revenue fast. When the owner invited a favored customer to our store, I used the simulator to help our visitor improve his game. **Results:** He gave us **a major sale on the spot and sent more customers our way**. He was **our best "advertisement" and I didn't spend an extra dime to get it**.

◯ Jan 99 – Sep 00 Co-owner, CleanSweep, L.L.C., Knoxville, TN
This contractor provided contract cleaning services.

○ May 92 – Nov 98　　　　National Vehicle Accident Manager *promoted to* National Vehicle **Sales Manager** (holding both jobs simultaneously), Child Prodigy Centers, Knoxville, TN
Child Prodigy was the largest provider of day care in the nation.

Employed effective listening to exploit an opportunity that appeared unexpectedly on the golf course. Made an "offhand" suggestion to a CEO and a CFO that let us offer services to their company and save them money at the same time. **Results: Generated nearly $500K** for us.

Turned around a low producing account I inherited. Went the extra miles — literally — to learn how we could offer more. Sold this customer on my special plan that put more money in both our pockets. **Results: Added $150K** a year to our sales.

Recaptured a customer who was so difficult my boss had "fired" him. Used friendly persistence and price incentives to close a small but confidence-building deal. Then leveraged his trust in me. **Results: Sales from this account increased 400 percent** in just eight months.

PROFESSIONAL DEVELOPMENT

○ Effective Communication, Wilson Learning, 95
○ Integrating Working Styles, Wilson Learning, 94
○ "Effective Speaking," "Developing Human Resources," Dale Carnegie, 86

COMPUTER SKILLS

○ Expert in proprietary inventory and customer contact database suite
○ Capable in Word
○ Familiar with Lotus 1-2-3, PowerPoint, and Internet searching skills

JEREMY F. SOLOMON

23 Lowell Road
Rochester, New York 19098

Phone: 292-909-3763   Email: jfsfabricator@lucent.com   Cell: 898-382-3827

SALES & MARKETING EXECUTIVE

Fifteen years experience planning and directing field sales programs targeted to diverse technology and industrial equipment users. Top revenue and profit producer with a consistent record of over-quota sales performance within intensely competitive markets. Natural communicator with strong organizational, leadership, negotiation, and motivational skills. Expertise includes:

- Strategic Sales Planning & Leadership
- Key Account Development & Management
- New Product & Technology Introduction
- Networking & Relationship Development
- Public Speaking & Sales Training/Presentations

- Multi-Channel Sales Distribution
- Partnerships & Strategic Alliances
- Competitive Market Positioning
- Operations & Production Management
- Team Building & Leadership

Entrepreneurial spirit fueled by drive, intensity and a proven ability to produce profitable sales revenues. Keen problem-solving and decision-making skills.
Dynamic and creative presentation style.

PROFESSIONAL EXPERIENCE:

GARDNER MACHINE CORPORATION, Rochester, New York   1987 to 2003

PRESIDENT/DIRECTOR OF SALES & MARKETING

Launched start-up venture distributing industrial equipment and technology to key accounts throughout Virginia, Maryland, and Washington, D.C. Challenged to build a strong market presence in a historically "non-manufacturing" region. Independently managed the entire sales development function, from identifying qualified prospects to developing account relationships, negotiating and closing large-dollar sales transactions, and retaining client relationships against encroaching competition.

- Transitioned new venture from concept into one of the region's "Top 10" distributors with $2+ million in annual sales. Closed a total of $7 million over three years.
- Negotiated distribution agreements to represent the products, services, and technologies of top manufacturers worldwide.
- Partnered with distributors nationwide to expand product offerings and capture/retain new key account relationships.
- Designed and led motivational sales training programs for corporate clients throughout the region.

SOLOMON MACHINE CORPORATION, Corning, New York   1980 to 1987

VICE PRESIDENT – IMPORT DIVISION
GENERAL MANAGER – MANUFACTURING DIVISION

Member of family-owned corporation specializing in the manufacture of private-label products and the marketing/distribution of industrial machinery and technology nationwide. As a member of the senior management team, actively involved in strategic planning, new ventures, corporate finance, contracts, and administration.

Sales, Marketing, & Business Development Achievements:

- Instrumental in the company's strong financial performance with annual sales growth from $8 million to $22 million and profit improvements from 18% to 32%.
- Pioneered the company's launch into the international import business through a strategic partnership with a large U.K. manufacturer. Laid the foundation for what grew into a $3.5-million business channel.
- Established and directed a nationwide network of independent distributors to expand sales channels and market penetration. Built from start-up to over $5 million in annual sales.
- Nurtured a critical account relationship with Petrie Industries (global industrial products manufacturer) and positioned Solomon as their #1 distributor worldwide (at peak, selling 50% of their entire worldwide production).
- Designed, wrote, and produced a series of direct mail and telemarketing campaigns to further increase market penetration.

Operating & General Management Achievements:

- Reengineered core manufacturing processes, implemented improved production scheduling and control systems, introduced employee training and state-certified apprenticeship programs, and improved daily production yields by 25%. Directed a staff of up to 35.
- Introduced an aggressive cost reduction program that generated $1+ million in savings.
- Increased "time to sell" through simplification and computerization of sales reporting processes.
- Appointed to the Marketing Communications Committee of the Association for Fabrication Technology (formerly, North American Machinery Association). Member of judging panel for annual marketing communications contest.

UNITED STATES COAST GUARD   1976 to 1980

Photojournalist / Editor

EDUCATION:

B.S. Candidate, Denver College, Denver, Colorado (1971 to 1975)
Graduate, Defense Information School, Monterey, California (1977)

HAILEY F. SOWERS

410.884.0876
hfs@arc.net

EXCEPTIONALLY SUCCESSFUL SALES AGENT
PHARMACEUTICAL SALES

◆ Primary Care	◆ OB/GYN	◆ Urologists
◆ Neurologists	◆ Cardiologists	◆ Vascular Surgeons
◆ Excellent Communications	◆ Liaison	◆ Word & Excel
◆ Business Plan Development	◆ PowerPoint Presentations	◆ Sales Proposals
◆ *'Complete Projects in Record Time'*	◆ *'Make Things Happen'*	◆ *'Well Received'*

REWARDING CAREER HIGHLIGHTS

** Recipient of the *Premier Sales Award*, representing the top 3% of the sales force, 2000 to 2001

** Recipient of the *Incentive Award* — 1999, 2000, 2001 and *the Drive for Performance Sales Promotion Award* — 2000 ... based on total increase in therapeutic class and product market share of 37%

PROFESSIONAL EMPLOYMENT

Senior Sales Specialist, Pharmaceutical Sales, Drugs, Inc., Richmond, Virginia　　　1996 — Present

* Call on a variety of physicians, interact as a cooperative and contributing team member with peers and management, and gain access to targeted customers through effective daily planning and the coordination of educational programs in an expedient effort to drive product sales. Acted as the Product Manager, leading the district in sales initiatives. Monitor the full sales lifecycle and ensure follow-up.

Excel as a Sales Specialist and consistently exceed goals in a high competitive market:
- Successfully devise and implement strategic territory business plans to achieve high sales objectives within established time requirements. Quickly promoted to the Management Track Program as Senior Sales Specialist within first year of employment.
- Received annual sales appraisals of "Exceeds Expectations" — representing the highest rating.
- Personally selected to participate in "Fireside Chat Sessions" with the CEO.
- Aid the District Manager in interviewing and hiring new candidates. Mentor new employees.
- Instrumental in obtaining product formulary approval in the hospital and managed-care arena. Work closely on numerous managed-care projects and with pharmacies to promote products.

Sales Associate, Legg Mason, Richmond, Virginia　　　1994 — 1996

* Managed sales and marketing programs, business development, and account relationships, conferring with the CFO. Sold financial services including mortgages, stocks, and insurance.

- Expertly identified business opportunities, analyzed/forecasted market trends, and defined sales goals in support of a $78M asset base.
- Interfaced with clients to analyze needs and investment goals. Created and presented proposals.

PROFESSIONAL ADVANCEMENT

Tom Hopkins International Sales Training　　　　　　　　Zig Ziglar Professional Development
Dale Carnegie Sales Training Program　　　　　　　　　Series 63 & Licensed

AARON BERNSON, CSEP

31605 W. Howager Avenue
Val Verde, California 91381

661 299-3557
Facsimile: 661 299-3566
E-mail: pesto@worldnet.net

EVENT AND PROJECT MANAGER / CONSULTANT

Building Corporate Value and Increasing Corporate Earnings
Conventions, Conferences, Trade Shows, Product Launches, Galas, Festivals, Political Campaigns

---

Visionary, dynamic, extremely detail-oriented **Certified Special Events Professional** who possesses a unique sense of innovation and resourcefulness with proven integrity and expertise in devising original solutions to complex problems. Hardworking and dependable with a strong work ethic. Expert at fitting a theme into overall company objectives with celebratory flair. Understanding of cultural diversity and art. Thorough knowledge of corporate culture and government protocols both internationally and domestically.

Expertise in identifying and capitalizing upon market opportunity to introduce new products, reposition existing product lines, and drive sustained revenue, market, and earnings growth. Provide the strategic and tactical actions that deliver millions of dollars in revenue gains and cost savings through organizational development and workforce optimization. Well-versed in establishing group direction, encapsulating and presenting client issues in larger industrial/economic contexts. Conduct thorough research through site inspection to reveal gaps and hidden obstacles to prevent hindrances and to ensure smooth flow of operation. Qualifications include:

Event Research & Design	Needs Assessment	Pyrotechnics	Helicopters
Event Partnering	Administration	Lasers	Lighting Effects
Event Contract Negotiation	Safety and Security	Air Flames	Soundscaping
Event Marketing	S.W.O.T./Gap Analysis	Air Tubes	Fog/Smoke
Event Risk Management	Regulatory Compliance	Flying	Fragrance

- < Combination of technical expertise, organizational talent, analytical, and research skills.
- < Outstanding communication and interpersonal skills. Interact with all levels of management and administration.
- < Sourced international network.
- < Computer literate (Microsoft Word, Excel, PowerPoint, Publisher).
- < Basic communication with Spanish-speaking crews.

Experience applicable to diverse industries, markets, and opportunities.

CAREER HIGHLIGHTS

Results-oriented high achiever able to engineer major increases in sales, get relevant partners aligned, and capture new business opportunities.

Key strengths are **devising creative solutions** to overcome obstacles, adapt to changing circumstances, and achieve business goals. Provide positive, highly visible organizational presence. Constantly generate new ideas. Refocus brand strategy to meet changing consumer demographics and buying preferences. Communicate well with business professionals, build strong business partnerships, easily establish rapport, and gain client confidence. Extremely sociable and articulate.

Scope of responsibility is diverse and includes preparing RFPs and bid packages, as well as the complete project management cycle from initial design and estimating through planning, scheduling, and site supervision. Execute sponsorship development, strategic planning, budgeting, and management of all administrative and business affairs. Direct event planning, preproduction, off-site coordination, and site logistics. Establish proactive working relationships with major broadcast media to favorably manage press communications. Design and produce engaging and compelling marketing collateral. Create a proactive employee communications campaign to link management expectations with employee incentives and performance goals. Implement and manage productive marketing programs for tangibles and intangibles.

Guide conference planning and special event programs with full responsibility for logistics, menus, guest speakers, agendas, facilities, and legal, ethical, and risk management affairs while ensuring project is always within budget and on schedule. Partner with community leaders in support of high-profile community affairs, revitalization, and funding activities. Lead special event team responsible for implementing all logistics including travel, lodging, local transportation, security, credentials, meals, and event agenda. Coordinate project scheduling to minimize impact upon daily business and operations of both site and sponsoring organization.

Administer six-figure budgets and maintain fiscal responsibility ensuring money is allocated at proper times. Handle invitations, reservations, registrations, seating, and obtain underwriting for gifts, awards, and memorabilia. Obtain necessary permits. Coordinate events for 10 to 100,000 people. Execute appropriate contracts. Adhere to regulatory compliances such as ADA, OSHA, Social Responsibility Act, and municipal fire regulations.

RECENT PROFESSIONAL EXPERIENCE

PRODUCTION ASSISTANT - House of Jazz, Tampa, FL   July 2002
Orchestrated pharmaceutical product launch for major international pharmaceutical company by producing five name acts. Coordinated all riders associated with those groups. Coordinated media scheduling in cooperation with new product roll-out team to accelerate new launch and distribution.

PRODUCTION ASSISTANT - Ritz Carlton, Marina del Rey, CA   July 2002
Produced Hall of Fame Show for American Heart Association.

PRODUCTION CONSULTANT AND NARRATOR   April 2000
International Special Events Society (ISES) Western Regional Meeting
Technical Director for day-long conference. Handled production schedule. Conducted technical rehearsal.

ENTERTAINMENT COORDINATOR - The Millennium Celebration   December 1999
Produced all entertainment for this private show.

EVENT MANAGER - Event Solutions Expo, San Jose, CA   October 1998
Recruited to manage 24 contractors to create the opening night B.A.S.H.

MARKETING DIRECTOR   April 1998
First-ever Event Exposition & Exhibition produced by the Greater Los Angeles Chapter of the International Special Events Society; 50+ exhibitors; 250+ attendees in 4 hours.

ACHIEVEMENTS

Corporate/Government

< Formation and implementation of ongoing public service campaign resulting in the City of Reno saving thousands of dollars.
< Recruited by the Governor of Nevada to chair the Board of Examiners for health inspectors.
< Increased advertising and editorial space more than 50% and circulation, 60%, within a four-issue period.
< Expanded circulation from 500 to 3,000+ as editor of *The Big Picture*, newsletter of the Santa Clarita Valley Film & Entertainment Bureau.
< Achieved highest rating and greatest market share as radio air talent.

Private

< Reduced advertising costs by more than 50% as visibility tripled, contracts increased by 150%, and revenue increased by more than 40% for an entertainment supplier.
< Nationally syndicated talk show producer.

AFFILIATIONS

< Member, Membership and Certification Committees, International Special Events Society
< Life Member, National Eagle Scout Association

HONORS AND AWARDS

< 1 of 95 out of 3,000 ISES **Certified Special Events Professionals**
< **Finalist,** 1999 ISES *Esprit* Awards, category of Best ISES Team Effort for a Nonprofit or Fundraising Event
< Nominee for Best ISES Theme Effort by Sacramento Chapter, 1999
< **Top 10** in recruiting for international direct sales network
< Named **Optimist of the Year,** Optimist Club of Encino

DONALD GRIFFITH

621 Ocean Street
Auburn, Maine 04210, USA

Telephone: (207) 555-5555

Email: dgriffith@telnet.com

CAREER PROFILE

International Communication Systems Analyst / Programmer / Engineer with many years of training and proven experience in varied areas with an emphasis on state-of-the-art telecommunication systems. Knowledgeable in international telecommunication requirements for interconnecting and networking large systems in remote areas requiring much unique interaction and interface with existing providers.

- Ability to analyze the total needs for companies of all sizes; recommend and implement timely and cost-effective changes and/or enhancements.
- Ongoing and recent technical certifications (coupled with knowledge of state-of-the-art equipment) assure the highest possible standards in service, design, and engineering.
- Maintain an excellent rapport with many company clients, suppliers, and staff through more efficient and cost-effective communications.
- Skilled at integrating, upgrading, maintaining, and replacing (in some cases) entire existing telephone and computer networks to achieve goals.
- Extensive knowledge of the industry, technology, equipment, and related vendors allows for effective (timely) research into equipment and services to meet these goals.
- Consistently assure the company is provided with up-to-date technical knowledge and implementation of the technology.

QUALIFICATIONS

- **Associates Degree in Telecommunications**
    - Trinity University, USA
- **Certified Design Consultant and Network Architect**
    - Siemens Training Center, USA & Germany
- **Certified I&M PBX Technician** (Multiple Software & PBX Levels)
    - Mitel Certified Training Centers, USA
- **Certified SX50, SX200, SX200D**
    - Business Applications, Hospitality Applications, ACD Call Center Applications, T-1 Applications, and VX Voice Mail System.

OTHER TRAINING

University of Maine, Augusta - Computer Science
- Programming IBM Basic, Cobol, Pascal
- Business Administration and Office Management
- Technical Writing
- Advanced Mathematics

Mid-State College, Auburn, ME
- International Travel, Tourism, and Hospitality

DANA CRANBORNE

739 Gramercy Street, New York, NY 10023

212-455-7310

danacranborne@attbi.com

Telecommunications / Technology Industry Executive

Business Strategist / Turnaround Specialist
Start-Up, High-Growth, & Multinational Companies

Strategic, innovative, and hands-on leader in the launch, expansion, revitalization, and revenue generation of start-up and established telecommunications ventures worldwide. Top record of performance in creating shareholder value, devising business strategy, executing turnaround assignments, managing technical operations, driving business development, and leading strategic business initiatives to successful completion. Effective team builder able to create entrepreneurial, high-performing organizations. Technical expert in telecommunications systems, networks, and technologies.

▸ P&L Management	▸ Start-up, Turnaround, & Revitalization
▸ Executive Sales & Business Development	▸ US & Global Operations Management
▸ Revenue & Sales Growth	▸ Leading-Edge Technology Introduction

Experience & Achievements

EXECUTIVE VICE PRESIDENT   **Star Exchange, New York, NY**   2000–Present

Hired as Executive Director of Operations and, within 3 months, promoted to top leadership role and challenged to invigorate faltering initiative to introduce Star Exchange into the US market — devising market-penetration strategies, building and leading all facets of the organization, and directing technical installation to support business growth.

Business Strategy & Growth
- ▸ Grew revenue from zero to nearly $30MM, three times $10MM target.
- ▸ Launched 4 unique telecom exchanges in the marketplace, all fully e-commerce enabled.
- ▸ Created a $10MM asset and negotiated its profitable sale without affecting strategic growth areas.
- ▸ Established entrepreneurial culture and built high-performing business teams.
- ▸ Positioned firm for sale, creating exit strategy that delivered shareholder value and returned substantial assets to parent company.

Business Development
- ▸ Took the lead in successfully rolling out innovative services to the high-tech industry, as company spokesperson, trade-show and event presenter, and media source.
- ▸ Captured 65 Tier 1 telecom providers as exchange partners, exceeding goal of 50 by 30%.

Operations Leadership
- ▸ Secured favorable New York headquarters location at sizable savings over existing lease.
- ▸ Negotiated equipment purchases with Cisco, Lucent, and other highly rated providers.

VP GLOBAL OPERATIONS   Voice & Data, Inc., New York, NY   1997–2000

Member of executive team that defined and executed strategy to transition angel-funded international callback-software company into international voice & data carrier and eventually into full-blown exchange service provider. Managed 15-member operations team.

Business Strategy & Business Development

- ▶ Turned around financial performance through aggressive revenue-generating initiatives; set strategic direction and laid foundation for successful growth.
- ▶ Drove technical expansion and integration to capitalize on emerging market opportunities and create revenue streams; delivered $20MM annual revenue that enabled strategic business transformation to exchange service.
- ▶ Launched a carrier-services operation that grew from zero to over 50 million minutes monthly; directed operations and spearheaded sales and business development to accelerate growth.

Technical & Operations Leadership

- ▶ Successfully built and implemented a global voice/data frame-relay network with 15 global locations; built a centralized network-operations center to monitor the network.
- ▶ Negotiated, executed, and led installation of a new state-of-the-art switching platform.
- ▶ Led team of engineers in creating a web-based telecommunications trading floor.
- ▶ Completed AT&T SS7/C7 certification processes that enabled growth in new markets.
- ▶ Negotiated and implemented more than 20 direct international routes.

MANAGER OF OPERATIONS   Global Communications, New York, NY   1993–1997

Spearheaded installation of major New York-based switching facility that was instrumental to successful expansion of US/Latin American telecom provider. Selected electronics and switching components; oversaw contractors, technicians, and suppliers; and built a carrier operation that routed 75 million minutes monthly. Managed networks for the entire company.

- ▶ Created technical platform that enabled rapid growth from zero to $50MM revenue in the New York market. Strength of this market was a direct contributor to downstream success: IPO, growth through M&A activity, and eventual sale to a Tier 1 carrier.

TECHNICAL TEAM LEADER   Cable & Wireless, New York, NY   1988–1993

Led team in installation, operation, and significant growth of international switching facility.

- ▶ Earned 3 top awards for technical expertise.

Education & Professional Affiliations

Certificate in Computer Maintenance, SUNY at Onondaga	1987
Member, Telecom Advisory Board *(industry advisory and lobbying group)*	2001–Present
Board Member, WorldConnect Services *(international telecommunications company)*	2001–Present

JOSH WHIDBY

12 Anchorage Avenue
Simpson, Texas 77893
Phone 772-909-3727   joshwhidby@ix.netcom.com

BROADCAST INDUSTRY EXECUTIVE
Building Top-Performing Radio & Television Broadcast Stations Within Intensely Competitive Markets

Dynamic leadership career developing and managing top-ranked network affiliates. Combines expert strategic planning, marketing and business development expertise with a solid commitment to employee development, customer development and market retention. Keen negotiation, decision-making, and problem-solving skills.

PROFESSIONAL EXPERIENCE:

TEXAS-MEXICO BROADCAST COMPANY, Houston, Texas   1991 to Present
Vice President (1997 to Present)   **General Manager** (1991 to 1997)

Senior Executive with full strategic planning, marketing, business development, operations, production, engineering/technology, human resources, and P&L responsibility for five TV stations, two radio stations, and a direct mail company housed within one facility. Lead a staff of 160 through 12 management reports.

KRFD-TV (ABC Affiliate)	**KEBN-TV** (FOX Affiliate for Yuma/El Centro Market)
KLDM-TV (FOX Affiliate)	**KXKD-FM** (Radio Station)
KPWD-TV (Telemundo Affiliate)	**KRMD-AM** (Radio Station)
KPWK-TV (WB Affiliate)	**Texas-Ten Direct Marketing** (direct mail company)

Conceived, developed and launched strategic plan in 1992/3 to forge an aggressive expansion initiative. Greatest challenge was to drive profitable growth while controlling costs, leveraging staff competencies, providing a common vision, and creating an energetic, motivated, and customer-driven organization.

- **Revenue & Profit Growth**. Increased sales revenues from $4 million in 1991 to $17 million in 2002. Grew operating income from $770,000 to $4.3 million. Built production sales to $400,000+ annually from virtual start-up. Achieved/surpassed all revenue and income objectives.

- **Asset Value**. Dramatically increased the value of KRFD-TV from $6 million to $19 million over four years. Currently valued at $40+ million (divested in 1995).

- **Market Ratings**. Transitioned Hispanic KXKD-FM from a virtual unknown into one of the top 2/3 radio stations in the market (23 rated stations). Consistently ranked #1 in the 18-34, 18-49, and 25-54 demographic ratings.

- **Acquisition Leadership**. Planned and directed complex negotiations for the acquisition of two radio stations in 1997. Structured and negotiated 10-year network franchising deal with Telemundo, requiring no up-front costs to Texas-Mexico.

- **Industry Innovation**. Planned, structured, and executed one of the first radio-to-television Local Market Agreements (LMA) in the US.

- **Customer Service**. Pioneered innovative customer (advertisers, viewers, and listeners) development, service, loyalty, and retention programs to foster team-wide commitment to customer satisfaction. Introduced TQM initiatives to further strengthen customer service and all other in-house operations.

- **Corporate Sponsorships & Community Outreach**. Positioned Texas-Mexico Broadcast as high-profile corporate citizens and sponsor of hundreds of community, health care, and educational events.

THE REED GROUP, Dallas, Texas   1990 to 1991
Senior Account Executive

Joined regional advertising agency to orchestrate their expansion into the Dallas market. Over 11 months, established a firm market presence, captured prominent local accounts, and positioned Reed for long-term growth/expansion.

- Within first two weeks, negotiated and closed a $600,000+ account.

KRNV-TV, Dallas, Texas   1987 to 1989
Sales Manager

Led sales department through two years of accelerated growth and expansion. Recruited, trained, and directed sales team of seven. Consistently set new sales records on a monthly basis.

- Drove sales from $1.6 million to $3 million within just two years.

KPPR Radio, Irving, Texas   1995 to 1997
Operations Manager (1996 to 1997)
Sales Manager (1995 to 1996)
Sales Representative (1995)

Fast-track promotion through a series of increasingly responsible sales and operations management positions with one of the top broadcast stations in the market. Ranked as the #1 sales producer within three months of hire while assuming additional responsibility for promotions, marketing, and operations.

- Led the station through a period of rapid change, reorganization, and growth. Transitioned from #4 in the market with 6.8 share to #1 with 21.9 share. Achieved a better than 7 share competitive lead.

Early Professional Experience (1972 to 1995). Began radio career as an on-air broadcaster. Subsequently advanced through positions in sales, promotions, marketing, production, and operations.

PROFESSIONAL & CIVIC AFFILIATIONS:

Board of Directors, Texas Broadcast Association (1994 to Present)
Chairman, United Way of Metro Texas (1996/97 & 1997/98). *Raised a record $1.4 million in final year.*
Board Appointment, Texas Transit Authority. *Managing $9-million renovation.*
Chairman, Governing Board, William Morrison Hospital (1997 to Present). *Managing $13-million expansion.*
Board of Directors, William Morrison Hospital (1994 to 1997)

PUBLICATIONS:

- "Negotiating Your First Local Market Agreement (LMA)," *Electronic Broadcasting*, 2000
- "A Broadcast Balancing Act," *Media Age*, 1999
- "The Day We Played And Won," *Racquetball News Magazine*, 1994

Dustin Frasier

2894 North 400 South
Huntington, Indiana 46167

877-887-4294
E-mail: fdfrasier@econet.com

Senior Management   –   Strategic Planning

Commercial Projects   -   Business Development   -   Market Expansion

My professional career reflects over 15 years of marketing, strategic planning, and business expansion in the highly competitive and diligently regulated industries of commercial construction, corporate development, and international transportation. Possess a demonstrated record of success in attracting large revenue-generating organizations to communities through financial incentives and partnerships between business and government institutions.

Leadership responsibilities have included, but are not limited to, multinational operations, fund development, legal and regulatory compliance, capital management, quality assurance, facility utilization/expansion. Directed up to 220 personnel and a $300M annual budget.

Academic Credentials

Pursued a **Master of Science** degree in Transportation Management and Business Affairs from Ball State University. Graduate studies supported by a **Bachelor of Arts Degree** in Political Science & Economics from the University of Illinois.

Have enhanced professional and academic credentials with additional training in business management, marketing, sales, consumer service and quality, mergers and acquisitions, project supervision, risk management, cost containment, fundraising, underwriting, union/non-union negotiations, and various computer business applications.

Professional Objective

My skills and experience would enable me to serve your organization in a variety leadership positions. Main roles would include establishment of tactical and organizational plans, research of major business objectives, fund development, financing strategies, and coordination of corporate expansion projects. These abilities could be maximized as **Vice President of Business Development, Director of Fund Development, or Senior Operations Strategist.** Given the opportunity to represent myself to you in person, I am confident you will find me to be a worthy candidate.

Selected Accomplishments

- Redesigned route schedules to improve customer satisfaction, increased daily shipping capabilities, and generated 20% additional income for drivers.
- Served as key liaison between corporate office and government regulatory agencies in $16M litigation case, resulting in payment of only $300K.
- Coordinated with government officials to support Planning & Development Department, bringing $62M in grant-based funding, $1.5B in private-industry funding, and 7,500 wage-paying jobs over the past 10 years.
- Implemented data management systems to provide real-time tracking of all freight containers for domestic and international logistics operations.
- Skillfully negotiated contracts between government, private sector, and community organizations to provide services and programs throughout the region.

Director of Planning and Development
International Port Commission

1992-present
Ft. Myers, Florida

- Developed strategic and business plans for capital development in the Indiana port systems.
- Drafted tax credits for legislative grants to attract new business and provide credits for facility expansion.
- Administered $62M grant funds to three separate Indiana ports.
- Functioned as critical link between Port Commission, Indiana State General Assembly, Department of Environmental Affairs, US Army Corp of Engineers, and Economic Development Council.

Director of Strategic and Long Range Planning
Port Authority of Portland and Long Beach

1985-1992
North West Regional

- Developed master plan for maritime development in Port Newark and Elizabeth terminals.
- Evaluated Brownfield sites for rail-delivery improvements and terminal facility expansions.
- Led feasibility studies to expand Red Robin, Bowman's Lodge, and Croft terminals.
- Designed capital development program for all maritime terminals.
- Performed detailed process analysis for process design, workflow efficiency, facility utilization, risk prevention, and risk/cost factors to determine expansion objectives.

Lt. Colonel/Director of Transportation and Logistics
United State Army

1968-1985
Washington, DC

- Responsible for routing, timing, sequences, equipment, materials, and logistics of all tactical maneuvering, with minimal advance notice.
- Developed proactive prevention and contingency plans with oversight of 220 personnel, hundreds of vehicles, and $3M operating budget.
- Directed personnel and equipment transport in the Republic of Vietnam.
- Served as Port Operations Manager in Thailand.
- Designed and implemented logistics program that reduced shipping fees by $10M/year.

References Available Upon Establishment of Mutual Interest

Jackson Linder

101 Oakview Drive
Camby, Indiana 46113

247-891-6754
E-mail: jacklinder@lycol.com

Operations / Process Management / Consumer Relations

My professional career reflects over 20 years of operations supervision and team leadership for large utility service provider. Possess a demonstrated record of success in increasing efficiency, enhancing performance, and generating significant consumer approval ratings. State-wide leadership included, but was not limited to policy development, systems design and implementation, regulatory compliance, capital equipment overhaul, distribution, and trouble-shooting strategies for a territory with over 300 service personnel. Expertise includes hydraulic, electrical, mechanical, and thermodynamic processes.

Credentials and Objective:

Pursued an undergraduate degree from Indiana Purdue University in **Electrical Engineering Technologies.** Academic insights were supported by seven years training as an Electrician and Electronics Technician with the United States Coast Guard. Have enhanced these credentials with additional training in the areas of process design, policy design and implementation, management performance enhancements, electrical engineering, union and non-union staff supervision, regulatory compliance, and multiple computer-based business applications.

These skills and experiences would enable me to serve your organization in a variety of leadership capacities. I believe the abilities could be maximized as **Director of Operations, Senior Project Coordinator, Plant Manager, or Manager of Consumer Services.** Given the opportunity to represent myself to you in person, I am confident you will find me to be a worthy candidate.

Selected Accomplishments:

- Spearheaded program to bring entire operations system online and into the PC age.
- Developed automation parameters to monitor service, safety, and regulatory compliance for a regional organization with one operating center, 3 power plants, 2,000 personnel and annual revenues of $450M.
- Served as liaison between corporate center and outside vendors to insure purchase availability and sales support of emergency back-up power.
- Functioned as 'point of contact troubleshooter' for regional power grid service, maintenance, and staffing.
- Skillfully managed union and non-union personnel; developed training protocols to increase ownership of the corporate goals and objectives, reducing turnover and increasing production efficiency.
- Electrical and mechanical expertise includes: water treatment, coal handling, boiler operation, turbine operation, generator regulation, power transmission, supervisory control, data acquisition, and radio communications.

Career History:

INDIANA POWER AND LIGHT	Nationwide
Operations Systems Coordinator	1990-2002
Load Dispatcher	1986-1990
Relay, Communications, and Control Specialist	1975-1986
Power Plant Electrician	1972-1975

References Available Upon Establishment of Mutual Interest

GREGORY WEATHERSTONE
webmaster@weatherstone.com

222 Grande Pointe Road
Roxford, Ohio 47638
513-909-3987

OBJECTIVE: Webmaster / Electronic Communications Coordinator

TECHNICAL QUALIFICATIONS:

- Well-qualified Webmaster & Electronic Communications Coordinator with three years' experence working with state-of-the-art Web, Internet, and Windows technologies.
- Led creative and technical design, development, and delivery of the CA MEC website.
- Proficient with HTML, MS Office, FrontPage 2000, and all Windows programs.
- Outstanding communication, organizational, and project management skills.

TECHNOLOGY EXPERIENCE:

Webmaster / Electronic Communication Coordinator   1999 to Present
Crispin Airlines Master Executive Council, Toledo, Ohio

- Orchestrated design, development, and launch of CA MEC website (www.caafa.org). Managed project from concept through the entire development process to full-scale global implementation and all subsequent website upgrades and enhancements.
- Created and launched the first-ever CA MEC Worldwide Webcast (viewed by 20,000+ members live and archived).
- Developed and currently publish electronic newsletter "E-Biz" with 4,000 subscribers worldwide.
- Designed and currently maintain the online Discussion Board with 1,300 registered users.
- Write articles and submit photographs for publication in quarterly newsletter, "Union Update."
- Consult/advise 20 Local Council Presidents on a variety of communication issues (e.g., member communications, crisis communications, industry information, national union affairs).

Communication & Education Chairperson   1999
United AFA Local Council 139, Gretna, Virginia

- Managed newsletter design and content for local distribution to 200+ council members.
- Consulted with Local Council President on communication issues impacting local members.

EMPLOYMENT EXPERIENCE:

Flight Attendant – Crispin Airlines   1995 to Present
Paramedic – Tampa Regional Medical Center   1993 to 1994
Customer Relations Host – Walt Disney World Attractions   1990 to 1993

EDUCATION: .

Website/Webmaster Training, CompuMaster, Gretna, Virginia   2001
Coursework: HTML Coding & Tables, Metatags, FrontPage 2000, WYSIWYG, Website Promotion

A.A.S. Degree in Communications, Parkerston Community College, Orlando, Florida   1988
Coursework: Organizational Communication Technology, Communication Strategies

Appendix A
Contributing Resume Writers

Following is a list of the professional members of the Career Masters Institute who have earned their Credentialed Career Master (CCM) designation and contributed resumes to this publication. You will note that these individuals have earned a number of other certifications and credentials. For your reference, the most common are referenced below:

CCM - Credentialed Career Master
CCMC - Certified Career Management Professional
CECC - Certified Electronic Career Coach
CEIP - Certified Employment Interview Professional
CIPC - Certified International Personnel Consultant
CPC - Certified Personnel Consultant
CPRW - Certified Professional Resume Writer
CRW - Certified Resume Writer
CSS - Certified Staffing Specialist
IJCTC or JCTC - International Job & Career Transition Coach
LPC - Licensed Professional Counselor
NBCC - National Board Certified Counselor
NCC - National Certified Counselor
NCCC - National Certified Career Counselor
NCRW - National Certified Resume Writer
PCC - Professional Certified Coach

Diane Burns, CCMC, CCM, CPRW, CEIP
Career Marketing Techniques
5219 Thunder Hill Road, Columbia, MD 21045
410-884-0213
dianecprw@aol.com
www.polishedresumes.com

George Dutch, Ph.D., JCTC, CCM
George Dutch Career Consulting, Inc.
Ste 750 - 130 Slater Street, Ottawa, Ontario, Canada K1P 6E2
800-798-2696
george.dutch@sympatico.ca
www.georgedutch.com

Joyce Fortier, MBA, CPRW, JCTC, CCM, CCMC
Create Your Career
23871 W. Lebost
Novi, MI 48375
248-478-5662
careerist@aol.com
www.careerist.com

Susan Guarneri, MS, CCM, NCC, NCCC, LPC, CCMC, CPRW, CEIP, IJCTC
Guarneri Associates/Resumagic
1101 Lawrence Road
Lawrenceville, NJ 08648
609-771-1669
Resumagic@aol.com
www.careermagicoach.com

Gayle Howard, CPRW, CRW, CCM
Top Margin Resumes Online
PO Box 74, Chirnside Park
Melbourne, 3116, Australia
011-61-3-9726-6694
getinterviews@topmargin.com
www.topmargin.com

Myriam-Rose Kohn, CPRW, JCTC, CCM, CEIP, CCMC
JEDA Enterprises
27201 Tourney Road, Suite 201M
Valencia, CA 91355
661-253-0801
myriam-rose@jedaenterprises.com
www.jedaenterprises.com

Cindy Kraft, CCMC, CCM, CPRW, JCTC
Executive Essentials
PO Box 336
Valrico, FL 33595
813-655-0658
careermaster@exec-essentials.com
www.exec-essentials.com

Louise Kursmark, CPRW, JCTC, CCM, CEIP, MRW
Best Impression Career Services, Inc.
9847 Catalpa Woods Court
Cincinnati, OH 45242
513-792-0030
LK@yourbestimpression.com

Ric Lanham, MDiv, M.A., MRE, CCM, CECC
R.L. Stevens & Associates, Inc.
8888 Keystone Crossing #950
Indianapolis, IN 46240

888-806-7313
rlanham@rlstevens.com
www.interviewing.com

Rolande LaPointe, CPC, CIPC, CPRW, IJCTC, CCM, CSS, CRW
RO-LAN Associates, Inc.
725 Sabattus Street
Lewiston, ME 04240
207-784-1010
RLapointe@aol.com

Meg Montford, CCC, CCM, CPRW
Abilities Enhanced
PO Box 9667
Kansas City, MO 64134
816-767-1196
meg@abilitiesenhanced.com
www.abilitiesenhanced.com

John O'Connor, MFA, CRW, CPRW, CCM, CECC
CareerPro Resumes & Career Management
3301 Womans Club Drive #125
Raleigh, NC 27612
919-787-2400
john@careerproresumes.com
www.careerproresumes.com

Don Orlando, MBA, CPRW, JCTC, CCM, CCMC
The McLean Group
640 South McDonough Street
Montgomery, AL 36104
334-264-2020
yourcareercoach@aol.com

Jennifer Rydell, CPRW, CCM, NCRW
Simplify Your Life Career Services
6327-C SW Capitol Hwy, PMB 243
Portland, OR 97239
503-977-1955
jennifer@simplifyyourliferesumes.com
www.simplifyyourliferesumes.com

Deborah Wile Dib, CCM, NCRW, CPRW, CEIP, JCTC, CCMC
Advantage Resumes of New York
77 Buffalo Avenue
Medford, NY 11763
631-475-8513
deborah.dib@advantageresumes.com
www.advantageresumes.com

Appendix B
Resume Preparation Activities

Crafting a winning resume begins with preparation. Start by identifying your core skills, knowledge, and achievements, and then link them to your current career objectives. Take out four sheets of paper and complete these four activities:

1. My Skills and Knowledge

Make a complete list of the things that you do well. This list should include both professional functions (e.g., sales, product design, joint venture negotiations, technology implementation, strategic planning, budgeting) as well as more "general" skills (e.g., organization, project management, interpersonal relations, team building/leadership, efficiency improvement, oral and written communications, problem solving, decision making).

2. My Career Achievements

Make a comprehensive list of the notable achievements, successes, project highlights, honors, and awards of your career, with a focus on the past 10 years of employment. Whenever possible, use numbers or percentages to quantify results and substantiate your performance.

3. My Career Objectives

List the industries and positions in which you are interested in career opportunities.

4. Link Your Skills and Achievements With Your Objectives

Using your responses to Activity #3 (My Career Objectives), select skills and accomplishments from your responses to Activity #1 and Activity #2 that relate to your objective(s). In doing so, you're making a connection between what you have to offer and what type of position you are interested in. For example, if your objective is a position in Technology Sales & Marketing Management, the fact that you have strong plastic products assembly skills is probably not relevant and therefore not necessary to include. However, the fact that you have excellent negotiation and account management skills is critical and should be at the forefront of your resume. The strategy is to select items from #1 and #2 that support #3. Use the format guide below:

OBJECTIVE #1: _____

   Related Skills: _____

                    _____

                    _____

                    _____

   Related Accomplishments:

                    _____

                    _____

                    _____

                    _____

OBJECTIVE #2: _____

   Related Skills: _____

                    _____

                    _____

   Related Accomplishments:

                    _____

                    _____

                    _____

                    _____

The information above will now serve as the foundation for your resume. You have clearly outlined the specific skills, qualifications, experiences, and accomplishments that you offer that tie directly to the position(s) you are seeking. When you begin to write your resume (particularly your Objective, Career Summary, and Professional Experience), remember these are the most important things to highlight in order to communicate that you have the "right stuff."

Keep in Touch . . .
On the Web!

www.impactpublications.com

www.ishoparoundtheworld.com

www.hoteltravelshop.com

www.mycruiseshop.com

www.contentfortravel.com

www.winningthejob.com

www.veteransworld.com

www.contentforcareers.com